Absolutely Every [*]

BED & BREAKFAST

*Almost

COLORADO

EDITED BY CARL HANSON

SASQUATCH BOOKS
SEATTLE

Printed in the United States of America.
Distributed in Canada by Raincoast Books Ltd.
03 02 01 00 99   5 4 3 2 1

Cover design: Jane Jeszeck
Cover illustration: CORBIS/Wolfgang Kaehler
Interior design: Alan Bernhard
Composition: Alan Bernhard
Editor: Carl Hanson
Copy editors: Diane Sepanski, Christine Clifton-Thornton

ISSN 1522-5496
ISBN 1-57061-187-4

Sasquatch Books
615 Second Avenue
Seattle, Washington 98104
(206) 467-4300
books@SasquatchBooks.com
http://www.SasquatchBooks.com

CONTENTS

ABSOLUTEY EVERY BED & BREAKFAST SERIES

Welcome to *Absolutely Every° Bed & Breakfast: Colorado (°Almost)*, a comprehensive guide to virtually every bed and breakfast establishment in Colorado. We've done the work for you: Everything you need to know in choosing a bed and breakfast is included on these pages, from architectural style to atmosphere, from price range to breakfast variety. Listings are in alphabetical order by town, so locating the perfect stay at your destination is a snap, and the simple format makes comparing accommodations as easy as turning the page. So whether you're looking for an elegant Victorian experience, a majestic castle getaway, or a down-home ranch adventure, *Absolutely Every° Bed & Breakfast: Colorado (°Almost)* will help you find it.

In addition to Colorado, the *Absolutely Every* series covers Arizona, New Mexico, northern California, southern California, Oregon, Texas, and Washington; look for the latest edition of each in your local bookstore. Each guide in the series lists small- and medium-sized inns, hotels, and host homes that include breakfast in the price of the room. The lists of B&B establishments are compiled from a variety of sources, including directories, chambers of commerce, tourism bureaus, and the World Wide Web. After gathering a complete list, the editors send each innkeeper a survey, asking for basic lodging information as well as those special details that set them apart. The completed surveys are then examined and fact-checked for accuracy before inclusion in the book. The °*Almost* in the series title reflects the fact that a small number of innkeepers may choose not to be listed, may neglect to respond to the survey and follow-up phone calls, or are not listed because of negative reports received by the editors.

The editors rely on the honesty of the innkeepers in completing the surveys and on feedback from readers to keep the *Absolutely Every Bed & Breakfast* series accurate and up-to-date. (*Note:* While innkeepers are responsible for providing survey information, none are financially connected to the series, nor do they pay any fees to be included in the book.) Please write to us about your experience at any of the bed and breakfasts listed in the series; we'd love to hear from you. A guest comment form is included at the back of this book.

Enjoy your bed and breakfast experience!

—The editors, *Absolutely Every Bed & Breakfast*

HOW TO USE THIS BOOK

Absolutely Every Bed & Breakfast: Colorado is organized alphabetically by town and by establishment name, and includes an index. The concise, at-a-glance format of the complete bed and breakfast listings covers fifteen categories of information to help you select just the right bed and breakfast accommodation for your needs. This edition offers you a choice of establishments in cities, towns, and outlying areas.

THE BED & BREAKFAST LISTINGS

Note that although specifics of each establishment have been confirmed by the editors, details such as amenities, decor, and breakfast menus have been provided by the innkeepers. Listings in this guide are subject to change; call to confirm all aspects of your stay, including price, availability, and restrictions, before you go. Some bed and breakfast listings offer only selected information due to lack of response or by request of the innkeeper; complete listings include the following information.

Establishment name
Address: Note that street addresses often vary from actual mailing addresses; confirm the mailing address before sending a reservation payment.
Telephone numbers: Includes any toll-free or fax numbers.
Innkeepers Languages: Languages spoken other than English.
Location: Directions from the nearest town, highway, or landmark.
Open: Notice of any seasonal or other closures.
Description: Overview of architecture, furnishings, landscaping, etc.
Rooms: Number of rooms with private bathrooms vs. shared baths; availability of suites and/or additional guesthouses; and the innkeeper's favorite room.
Rates: Range of room prices, which vary based on private or shared bathroom, season, and individual room amenities. Also noted here are any minimum stay requirements and cancellation policies (usually two weeks' notice is required for a full refund).

Breakfast: Description of breakfast served (full, continental, continental plus, or stocked kitchen).

Credit cards: Indicates which, if any, credit cards are accepted. Note that credit cards may be listed for reservation confirmation purposes only; be prepared to pay by check or cash.

Amenities: Details any special amenities that are included.

Restrictions: Lists any restrictions regarding smoking, children, and pets. Also listed here are any resident pets or livestock.

Awards: Any significant hospitality or historic preservation awards received.

Reviewed: Publications in which the B&B has been reviewed.

Rated: Indicates whether the B&B has been rated by institutions such as the American Automobile Association (AAA), American Bed & Breakfast Association (ABBA), or the Mobil Travel Association.

Member: Indicates membership in any professional hospitality associations or organizations.

Kudos/Comments: Comments from guests who have stayed in the establishment.

ALAMOSA

Located in the center of the San Luis Valley—one of Colorado's most productive agricultural areas—Alamosa is the gateway to Great Sand Dunes National Monument and home to Adams State College. Dune trekking and exploring the trails of the Sangre de Cristos are the main attractions here, but don't overlook the Alamosa-Monte Vista National Wildlife Refuge and the spectacular Crane Festival in March. Take time to browse the Rio Grande Art Market, and check out the Sunshine Festival in June and the Gallery & Artists Home Tour in November. From Denver, 200 miles southwest via I-25 and Highway 160, 28 miles from the New Mexico border.

COTTONWOOD INN & GALLERY— A BED & BREAKFAST INN

123 San Juan Avenue, Alamosa, CO 81101   719-589-3882
Julie Mordecai, Resident Owner   800-955-2623
Spanish spoken   FAX 719-589-6437
EMAIL julie@cottonwoodinn.com   WEBSITE *www.cottonwoodinn.com*

LOCATION	Alamosa is in south-central Colorado at the junction of Highways 285, 160, and 17, thirty minutes southwest of the Great Sand Dunes. The inn is three blocks north of Main Street on the corner of Second and San Juan.
OPEN	All year
DESCRIPTION	A 1908 two-story Craftsman and a 1929 two-story neo-colonial Four Square apartment fourplex, both filled with antiques and artwork.
NO. OF ROOMS	Seven rooms with private bathrooms. Two rooms share two bathrooms. Julie Mordecai's favorite room is the Rosa Room.
RATES	March through October, rates range from $78-95. Off-season rates are $52-79 for a double. Additional children are $10 and adults are $15. There is a minimum stay during summer weekends and special weekends. Cancellation requires one weeks' notice during the off-season and two weeks during the summer with a $15 per night fee.
CREDIT CARDS	American Express, Discover, MasterCard, Visa
BREAKFAST	Full breakfast is prepared with local and homegrown produce and herbs whenever possible and is served in the dining room. Tea and cookies are served in the afternoon. Dietary restrictions will be met. Dinners are available for large groups.
AMENITIES	Robes in shared baths; TVs in suites; telephones in all rooms; Neutrogena bath products; fresh cookies, sodas, and mineral water; hot beverage area; golf, scenic railway, hot springs, and horseback riding packages; in-house massage.

Cottonwood Inn & Gallery—A Bed & Breakfast Inn, Alamosa

RESTRICTIONS	No smoking. Pets allowed in two rooms—a pet deposit is required.
REVIEWED	*The Colorado Guide, Fodor's Colorado, Frommer's Colorado, America's Wonderful Little Hotels, Recommended Country Inns, Lonely Planet Guide to Colorado*
MEMBER	Bed & Breakfast Inns of Colorado, Colorado Hotel & Lodging Association, Tourist Houses of America

ALLENSPARK

A gemlike setting in Roosevelt National Forest at the southeast corner of Rocky Mountain National Park, this little hamlet is 16 miles south of Estes Park on Scenic Highway 7. The Longs Peak Scottish Festival in September is a major event.

ALLENSPARK LODGE AND CRYSTAL SPRINGS CABINS

184 Main, Allenspark, CO 80510   303-747-2552
Bill & Juanita Martin, Resident Owners   FAX 303-747-2552 *(call first)*
WEBSITE *www.coloradodirectory.com/alansparklodge*

LOCATION   Downtown Allenspark.

OPEN	All year
DESCRIPTION	A 1933 three-story classic log lodge with eclectic furnishings.
NO. OF ROOMS	Five rooms with private bathrooms and eight rooms share three bathrooms. The best room is the Hideaway.
RATES	Year-round rates are $90-105 for a single or a double with a private bathroom and $60-75 for a room with a shared bathroom. The entire lodge rents for $850-1200. There is no minimum stay in the lodge and a 15-day cancellation policy with a $25 fee.
CREDIT CARDS	American Express, Discover, MasterCard, Visa
BREAKFAST	Full breakfast is served in the dining room and includes selections of teas and juices; coffee; hot and cold cereal; fresh-baked muffins, coffeecake, or nutbread; a small fruit basket; and various jams and breads for toasting. During busier times the lodge offers soups and sandwiches, nacho plates, etc. Lunch and dinner are also available.
AMENITIES	Complimentary coffee, cookies, and teas; hot tub; Ping-Pong; pool table; a library; picnic tables; grills; games. Seminars and retreat groups can be accommodated (maximum 70 people).
RESTRICTIONS	No smoking, no pets, children over 14 are welcome in the lodge. The resident cats, who aren't allowed downstairs, are Esmeralda and Katie Ann Calico.
REVIEWED	*Frommer's Colorado*
MEMBER	Colorado Association of Campgrounds, Cabins and Lodges
RATED	Mobil 2 Stars

SUNSHINE MOUNTAIN INN

18078 Colorado Highway 7, Allenspark, CO 80510　　　303-747-2840
Marge Hoglin, Resident Owner

ANTONITO

A scant five miles from the New Mexico border in southcentral Colorado, Antonito offers access to the narrow-gauge Cumbres & Toltec Scenic Railroad, Platora Reservoir, and Great Sand Dunes National Monument.

CONEJOS RIVER GUEST RANCH

25390 Highway 17, Antonito, CO 81120   *719-376-2464*
Ms. Shorty Fry, Ranch Foreman
Some Spanish spoken
WEBSITE *www.conejosranch.com*

LOCATION	Thirteen miles west of Antonito on Highway 17 between mile markers 25 and 26.
OPEN	Mid-May to January 2
DESCRIPTION	A renovated 1893 ranch house with western ranch decor and wraparound deck, set along the banks of the Conejos River in the Rio Grande Forest.
NO. OF ROOMS	Eight rooms with private bathrooms. Best view: the Riverview Room. Most romantic: the Loft Room.
RATES	Seasonal rates are $79-95 for a single or double and $85 for a suite or guesthouse. There is a minimum stay of two nights and cancellation requires 72 hours' notice with a $15 fee.
CREDIT CARDS	MasterCard, Visa
BREAKFAST	Full breakfast, served in the dining room, includes beverages and a choice of four hot meals or a light breakfast of oatmeal, muffin, and toast. Dinner and box lunches are available with advance notice.
AMENITIES	Lawn games, volleyball, children's playground, hiking, private fishing on property, fireplace in common den, deck facing river, campfires on weekends, horse boarding and rentals, meeting and retreat facilities, catering, cookout facilities, and handicapped access to several rooms.
RESTRICTIONS	None. Resident pets include one quarterhorse named Rambo; a burro named Sadie; two mixed-breed dogs, Rex and Ginger; a black-faced sheep named Elvira; and two standard poodles, Sheba and Sam.
MEMBER	Bed & Breakfast Innkeepers of Colorado
AWARDS	Bed & Breakfast Innkeepers of Colorado Award of Excellence

ARVADA
(DENVER)

Just 15 miles northwest of downtown Denver, this thriving community offers first-rate cultural events of its own through the Arvada Center for the Arts and Humanities.

ON GOLDEN POND BED & BREAKFAST

7831 Eldridge Street, Arvada, CO 80005   *303-424-2296*
Kathy & John Kula, Resident Owners   *800-682-0193*
German spoken   *FAX 303-431-6580*
WEBSITE *www.bbonline.com/co/ongoldenpond/*

LOCATION	From I-70 take exit 266 (Ward Road) north to 72nd Street, go left to Alkire, then right to 78th, and left on Eldridge.
OPEN	All year
DESCRIPTION	A 1977 two-story contemporary country inn with eclectic furnishings on 10 acres with a pond.
NO. OF ROOMS	Five rooms with private bathrooms. Kathy suggests the Peacock as her best room.
RATES	Year-round rates are $60-130 for a single or double, $100-130 for a suite, and the entire inn rents for $500. There is a minimum stay during holidays and a seven-day cancellation policy.
CREDIT CARDS	American Express, Diners Club, Discover, MasterCard, Visa
BREAKFAST	Full breakfast, served in the dining room, includes bread puddings with fruit or German potato eggnests, homemade streusel with fruit in season, cinnamon bread, and apple pancakes.
AMENITIES	Robes, refrigerators, cold pop, air conditioning, one room with handicapped access, swimming pool and hot tub, afternoon "kaffeeklatsch," all rooms feature balconies or private patios.
RESTRICTIONS	No smoking. The resident critters are an outside dog, Mocki; two barn cats, Max and Moritz; two goats, Loui and Lenny; and five peacocks.
MEMBER	Bed & Breakfast Innkeepers of Colorado
AWARDS	*Westword* magazine's 1997 Best Getaway
KUDOS/COMMENTS	"Eclectic with grand hosts." (1994)

A Touch of Heaven/
Talmar Bed & Breakfast

16720 West 63rd Place, Golden, CO 80403   *303-279-4133*

Aspen
(Carbondale)

Yesterday's silver-mining boom town is today's swank, world-class resort town, with alpine skiing on a four-mountain complex. Ski-season events include the Winterskol in January and the World Cup Giant Slalom in March. When the snow melts, summer comes alive with the acclaimed Aspen Music Festival, the Food and Wine Classic in June, and the Beer Festival in July. Other nice things to do: hiking around the Maroon Bells, fishing the Gold Medal Roaring Fork River, visiting nearby Ashcroft and the sled-dog rides at Krabloonik's Kennels, aspen-viewing in the fall, and, of course, celebrity-watching all year. As for shopping, bring a dumptruck full of money and at least a measure of perspective. From Denver, 200 miles west via I-70 and Highway 82—or try a summer-only, white-knuckle shortcut over Independence Pass.

Alpine Lodge

1240 East Cooper, Aspen, CO 81611   *970-925-7351*
Jim & Christina Martin, Resident Owners   *FAX 970-925-5796*
Spanish, French, and German spoken

LOCATION	First place on the right after city limit sign when arriving from Independence Pass and last place on the left when coming from town.
OPEN	All year
DESCRIPTION	An 1890 two-story Bavarian lodge and four cottages with Victorian and rustic furnishings.
NO. OF ROOMS	Four rooms with private bathrooms; three rooms share two bathrooms; and four cabins with private bathrooms. Christina recommends room 3.
RATES	Winter rates are $100-105 for a single or double with a private bathroom, $88 for a single or double with a shared bathroom, and $118 for a cottage. Off-season rates are $50-68 for a single or double with a private bathroom, $35-49 for a single or double with a shared bathroom, and $68-78 for a cottage. There is a minimum

stay during Christmas and a 30-day cancellation policy subject to a $25 fee.

CREDIT CARDS	American Express, Discover, MasterCard, Visa
BREAKFAST	Continental plus is served in the dining room and includes fresh-baked muffins, yogurt, fresh fruit, cereal, coffee, tea, and juice. Dinner is available during the winter season only.
AMENITIES	Outdoor hot tub, down comforters, fresh flowers in all rooms, teddy bears, TV in lobby, and airport pick-up.
RESTRICTIONS	No smoking, children welcome. Bear is the "official lodge dog and takes his job seriously."
REVIEWED	*The Colorado Guide, Colorado Handbook, Let's Go USA*

ASPEN MOUNTAIN LODGE

311 West Main Street, Aspen, CO 81611   970-925-7650
Jeff Senne, Resident Manager   800-362-7736
FAX 970-925-5744

OPEN	All year
DESCRIPTION	A three-story lodge. Large central fireplace. Dining area on the second floor.
NO. OF ROOMS	Thirty-eight rooms with private bathrooms.
RATES	Summer rates are $129-200 for a single or double and winter rates are $89-299.
CREDIT CARDS	American Express, MasterCard, Visa
BREAKFAST	Continental breakfast is served in the dining room.
RESTRICTIONS	No smoking, no pets

BEAUMONT INN

1301 East Cooper, Aspen, CO 81611   970-925-7081
Bill Bockham, Resident Owner   800-344-3853
Spanish and some French spoken   FAX 970-925-1610
EMAIL *beaumont@sopris.net*   WEBSITE *www.thebeaumont.com*

LOCATION	East end of town at the base of Independence Pass.
OPEN	All year except May
DESCRIPTION	A contemporary country inn with European country furnishings.

NO. OF ROOMS	Thirty rooms with private bathrooms.
RATES	Winter has three rate schedules for a single or double: low season, $140-210; regular season, $215-285; and holiday season, $285-355. Summer has two schedules: low season, $100-195; and regular season, $150-225. There is a minimum stay during holidays. Ask about a reservation/cancellation policy.
CREDIT CARDS	American Express, Diners Club, MasterCard, Visa
BREAKFAST	Continental plus is served in the dining room. Special meals are available by arrangement only.
AMENITIES	Summer: mountain bike rentals, hammock, and heated pool in garden area. Winter: complimentary hot drinks, desserts and appetizers, hot tub. Year-round: laundry facilities, ample parking, and airport transport.
RESTRICTIONS	No smoking in common areas, smoking rooms available. There is a $10 fee for pets. The cat, Smudge, likes to visit rooms and the dog, Geze, is "friendly but shy."
REVIEWED	*America's Wonderful Little Hotels & Inns*
RATED	Mobil 3 Stars

HEARTHSTONE HOUSE

134 East Hyman, Aspen, CO 81611

970-925-7632
888-925-7632
FAX 970-920-4450

HOTEL DURANT

122 East Durant, Aspen, CO 81611
Rhonda Ardis, Resident Manager
EMAIL *durant@rof.net*
WEBSITE *www.aspenguide.com/durant*

970-925-8500
877-438-7268
FAX 970-925-8789

LOCATION	On the corner of Durant Avenue and Aspen Street.
OPEN	All year
DESCRIPTION	A contemporary French country inn.
NO. OF ROOMS	Twenty-one rooms with private bathrooms.
RATES	Seasonal rates are broken into five categories that range from $69-299 for a single or double. There are minimum stay requirements and cancellation requires 30 days' notice.

CREDIT CARDS	MasterCard, Visa
BREAKFAST	Continental plus is served in the lobby.
AMENITIES	Hot tub, new deck, cable TV and phones in rooms, après-ski, and most rooms have microwaves.
RESTRICTIONS	No smoking, no pets, children are welcome.

HOTEL LENADO

200 South Aspen Street, Aspen, CO 81611   *970-925-6246*
Daniel Delano, Frank Peters, Jayne Poss, Resident Owners   *800-321-3457*
Spanish spoken   *FAX 970-925-3840*
EMAIL hotlsard@rof.net   *WEBSITE www.com/sardylenado*

LOCATION	From Glenwood, turn right at the first light in town. The hotel is one block toward Aspen Mountain on the left.
OPEN	All year
DESCRIPTION	A 1984 two-story contemporary lodge with elegant rustic interior and country furnishings.
NO. OF ROOMS	Nineteen rooms with private bathrooms. Try room 18.
RATES	Summer rates (June through September) range from $175-265. Winter rates (January through March) are $245-355 for a single or double. Low-season rates (May, October, and November) are $90-130. Holiday rates (December 21 through January 3) are $345-455.

Hotel Lenado, Aspen

There is a minimum stay on weekends; reservations require a 50% deposit due 30 days prior to arrival; and cancellation requires 30 days' notice.

CREDIT CARDS	American Express, Diners Club, MasterCard, Visa
BREAKFAST	Full breakfast includes a variety of egg dishes, waffles, blueberry pancakes, and beverages. There is also a light bar menu available all day.
AMENITIES	Robes, hot tub, library, concierge services, bellman/houseman, conference room, TV screening room, TV and phones in all rooms, Markham's Bar.
RESTRICTIONS	Limited smoking, no pets
REVIEWED	*The Colorado Guide, Best Places to Stay in the Rockies, Recommended Country Inns Rocky Mountain Region, America's Wonderful Little Hotels & Inns*
RATED	Mobil 3 Stars

INDEPENDENCE SQUARE BED & BREAKFAST

404 South Galena Street, Aspen, CO 81611 970-920-2313
EMAIL *reservations@friasproperties.com* 800-633-0336
WEBSITE *www.friasproperties.com* FAX 970-920-2020

LOCATION	Center of Aspen on the mall.
OPEN	November 22 through April 14, and June 1 through September 30
DESCRIPTION	Victorian B&B hotel with French country furnishings.
NO. OF ROOMS	Twenty-eight rooms with private bathrooms.
RATES	June 1 through September 30, rates are $95-230. Winter rates (November 22 to April 14) range from $95-360. Ask about specials and minimum stays. There is a reservation/cancellation policy.
CREDIT CARDS	American Express, MasterCard, Visa
BREAKFAST	Continental plus buffet is served in the library.
AMENITIES	Rooftop Jacuzzi and sun deck; complimentary use of the Aspen Club health and racquet facilities; TV, phone, wet bar, and refrigerator in the rooms; individual ski lockers; airport transportation; and air conditioning.
RESTRICTIONS	Limited smoking, no pets, children OK.
REVIEWED	*America's Wonderful Little Hotels & Inns*
MEMBER	Colorado Hotel and Lodging Association

INNSBRUCK INN

233 West Main, Aspen, CO 81611   970-925-2980
Heinz Corrdes, Resident Owner   FAX 970-925-6960

LOCATION	Downtown Aspen.
OPEN	All year
DESCRIPTION	Large inn.
NO. OF ROOMS	Thirty rooms with private bathrooms.
RATES	Year-round rates are $69-199.
CREDIT CARDS	American Express, MasterCard, Visa
BREAKFAST	Continental breakfast is served in the dining room.
RESTRICTIONS	No smoking, no pets, children are welcome.

MOLLY GIBSON LODGE

101 West Main Street, Aspen, CO 81611   970-925-2580
Dave Tash, Resident Manager   800-356-6559
EMAIL molly@rof.net   FAX 970-925-2582
WEBSITE www.mollygibson.com

LOCATION	Three blocks from downtown Aspen, on free ski shuttle route.
OPEN	All year
DESCRIPTION	Two renovated ski lodges.
NO. OF ROOMS	Forty rooms, ten suites, seven apartments.
RATES	During the low season, rates are $89-259; during the high season, rates are $165-365.
CREDIT CARDS	American Express, Discover, MasterCard, Visa
BREAKFAST	Full breakfast is served in the dining room.
AMENITIES	Free shuttle pick-up, swimming pool, two Jacuzzis.
RESTRICTIONS	No smoking in rooms, no pets, children are welcome.

MOUNTAIN HOUSE LODGE

905 East Hopkins, Aspen, CO 81611   970-920-2550
P. J. Sullivan & Syd Devine, Resident Owners FAX 970-920-3440/ext.532

LOCATION	One block off Highway 82, on the corner of Hopkins and West End Street.
OPEN	All year
DESCRIPTION	A 1987 two-story western lodge with "light" southwestern furnishings.
NO. OF ROOMS	Twenty-four rooms with private bathrooms. P. J. suggests the Aspen Suite.
RATES	There are six rate schedules for the year and the range is considerable, from $50-275. Please call for details. There is a minimum stay and 45-day cancellation policy and a substantial cancellation fee.
CREDIT CARDS	American Express, Diners Club, Discover, MasterCard, Visa
BREAKFAST	Full buffet breakfast is served in the dining room in winter and "generous" continental is served in the summer.
AMENITIES	Hot tub, phone, cable TV, refrigerators, on-site parking, indoor ski lockers, lounge with fireplace, and laundry.
RESTRICTIONS	No smoking, no pets

SARDY HOUSE

128 East Main Street, Aspen, CO 81611   970-920-2525
Daniel Delano, Frank Peters, Jayne Poss, Resident Owners 800-321-3457
Spanish spoken   FAX 970-920-3840
EMAIL *hotlsard@rof.net*   WEBSITE *www.aspen.com/sardylanedo*

LOCATION	When coming from Glenwood Springs, the inn is located at the first stoplight in town on the left-hand side.
OPEN	All year
DESCRIPTION	A restored 1892 two-story Queen Anne Victorian inn with Victorian furnishings.
NO. OF ROOMS	Twenty rooms with private bathrooms. Jayne Poss recommends the Atkinson Suite.
RATES	There are eight seasons at this inn. The cheapest room is $95 (in the heart of "mud season"), and the most expensive room is $750 (at Christmas time). Minimum stays vary; call for details. Cancellation requires 30 days' notice.

CREDIT CARDS	American Express, Diners Club, MasterCard, Visa
BREAKFAST	Full breakfast, with specials each morning, is served in the dining room. Room service is also available, and dinner is served in the restaurant.
AMENITIES	Robes, hot tub, outdoor heated pool, sauna, concierge service, bellman/houseman, conference room, TV in all rooms, suites have VCR and stereo, full-service dining room, and Jack's Bar.
RESTRICTIONS	Limited smoking, no pets
REVIEWED	*Official Guide to American Historic Inns, The Colorado Guide, America's Wonderful Little Hotels & Inns, Best Places to Stay in the Rockies, Recommended Country Inns Rocky Mountain Region*
MEMBER	Distinctive Inns of Colorado
RATED	Mobil 4 Stars
KUDOS/COMMENTS	"Friendly, polite hosts, truly interested in their guests, historic landmark with modern amenities, special ambiance." (1997)

SNOW QUEEN VICTORIAN BED & BREAKFAST

124 East Cooper Avenue, Aspen, CO 81611　　　　　970-925-8455
Norma Dolle & Larry Ledingham, Resident Owners　FAX 970-925-7391
Some Spanish, German spoken
EMAIL sqlodge@rof.net　　　WEBSITE *www.destinationaspen.com/snowqueen*

LOCATION	Greater downtown Aspen on the corner of Cooper and Center Streets.
OPEN	All year except April 15 to approximately May 25
DESCRIPTION	An 1890 Victorian inn with Victorian furnishings.
NO. OF ROOMS	Six rooms with private bathrooms. Norma recommends the Best Friend Room.
RATES	Summer rates are $78-110 for a double. Winter rates are $75-168 for a double. Christmas rates are slightly higher. There is a 30-day cancellation policy and a $20 handling charge.
CREDIT CARDS	MasterCard, Visa
BREAKFAST	Continental plus is served in the kitchen area. May change to full breakfast.
AMENITIES	TV in most rooms and in the parlor, phones in most rooms, outdoor hot tub, wine parties.
RESTRICTIONS	No smoking, no pets, the resident cat is Maya. Children are welcome.

ULLR LODGE BED & BREAKFAST

520 West Main Street, Aspen, CO 81611   970-925-7696
Anthony Percival, Resident Owner   FAX 970-920-4339
Dutch spoken
EMAIL ullr@rof.net   WEBSITE www.aspen.com/ullr

LOCATION	On the corner of Fifth and Main Streets on the residential west end of Aspen.
OPEN	All year
DESCRIPTION	A small, privately owned (for 18 years) 1968 two-story Swiss chalet.
NO. OF ROOMS	Fourteen rooms with private bathrooms.
RATES	Winter season (December through March) rates are $85-125 for a double and $120-270 for a suite. Off-season rates are $45 for a double and $65-90 for a suite. Rates will fluctuate somewhat during the ski and summer seasons. There is a five-night minimum stay in the winter and a 45-day cancellation policy. Summer cancellation is 14 days.
CREDIT CARDS	American Express, Diners Club, MasterCard, Visa
BREAKFAST	Full breakfast in the winter and continental in the summer.
AMENITIES	TV, phones, game room, indoor and outdoor whirlpool, swimming pool in the summer.
RESTRICTIONS	Limited smoking and no pets. "We encourage a quiet atmosphere."
RATED	AAA 2 Diamonds

BAILEY

On the South Platte River in the Pike National Forest, this is prime trout fishing country. Visit McGraw Historical Park for a trip back in time. Only 35 miles southwest of Denver on Highway 285.

GLEN-ISLE RESORT

PO Box 128, Bailey, CO 80421   303-838-5461
Gordon & Barbara Tripp, Resident Owners

LOCATION	One-and-three-quarters miles west of Bailey on Highway 285.
OPEN	Cabins all year, the B&B from June 4 through September 5
DESCRIPTION	A 1900 slab-and-shingle lodge and cabins furnished with antiques, located on 160 acres, and listed on the National and State Historic Registers.

NO. OF ROOMS	Fourteen rooms share seven bathrooms. The best room is room J.
RATES	Year-round rate is $55 for a double with a shared bathroom. There is no minimum stay and a 30-day cancellation policy.
CREDIT CARDS	No
BREAKFAST	Full breakfast, served in the dining room, includes pancakes, French toast, bacon and sausage, fruit, and beverages. Special chuckwagon dinners are available.
AMENITIES	Fireplaces in cabins, children's playground, Ping-Pong, billiards, shuffleboard, sing-alongs, square dancing, horseshoes, movies, bingo games, library, trout fishing, horseback riding, and meeting facilities.
RESTRICTIONS	None. The resident critters include two cats, three dogs, one llama, and two horses.

BASALT

Once a booming railroad town (the Chamber of Commerce is housed in a red caboose), this choice spot is located halfway between Glenwood Springs and Aspen/Snowmass on the Gold Medal waters of the Frying Pan and Roaring Fork Rivers, down the road from 1000-acre Ruedi Reservoir. Basalt is handy to some of the best skiing in Colorado. In July, the Mountain Festival is pure fun. From Denver, 160 miles west via I-70 and Highway 82.

ALTAMIRA RANCH BED & BREAKFAST

23484 Highway 82, Basalt, CO 81621   970-927-3309
Martha Waterman, Resident Owner
WEBSITE *www.cimarron.net/usa/co/altamira.html*

LOCATION	One mile south of the Basalt exit off Highway 82.
OPEN	All year
DESCRIPTION	A 1906 ranch house on a working ranch rebuilt in the style of Frank Lloyd Wright, with antique and contemporary furnishings.
NO. OF ROOMS	Two rooms with a shared bathroom.
RATES	The year-round rate is $75 for a double with a shared bathroom. There is a three-night minimum stay on July 4th and Christmas and a one-week cancellation policy.
CREDIT CARDS	No
BREAKFAST	Full breakfast is served in the dining room and includes a choice of entrée, homemade pastries, and fruit. Special dietary needs can be met.

AMENITIES	Antiques shop and stocked fishing pond.
RESTRICTIONS	No smoking, no pets, children over six are welcome. The resident golden retriever is called Ginger Snap.
MEMBER	Bed & Breakfast Innkeepers of Colorado

SHENANDOAH INN

0600 Frying Pan Road, Basalt, CO 81621   970-927-4991
Bob & Terri Zeits, Resident Owners   FAX 970-927-4990
French and Spanish spoken
EMAIL *shenando@sopris.net*   WEBSITE *www.shenandoahinn.com*

LOCATION	From greater downtown Basalt, go 0.3 mile up Midland Avenue to the inn.
OPEN	All year
DESCRIPTION	A 1964 two-story country inn with "country/southwest/eclectic" furnishings located on the Frying Pan River.
NO. OF ROOMS	Four rooms with private bathrooms. One cabin with private bathroom.
RATES	High-season (February, March, June through September) rates are $98-115 for a double. Off-season rates are $88-105 for a double. The cabin is $165. There is a minimum stay on weekends and holidays and cancellation requires 14 days' notice, 30 days for holidays.
CREDIT CARDS	American Express, MasterCard, Visa
BREAKFAST	Full gourmet breakfast is served in the dining room and includes five courses with specialty coffees and teas, freshly squeezed juice, homemade breads and preserves, a hot entrée, fresh fruit, and beverages.
AMENITIES	Fresh flowers, turndown service, hot tub on riverfront deck, robes, TV/VCR in library, fireplace in living room, catering, and large dining room for meetings and retreats.
RESTRICTIONS	No smoking, no pets, children over 12 are welcome.
REVIEWED	*American Mornings Cookbook, Pure Gold Colorado Treasures Cookbook, Inn for the Night*
MEMBER	Bed & Breakfast Innkeepers of Colorado

Bellvue

This small community is a great jumping-off spot for exploring the Cache la Poudre-North Park Byway and the wild and scenic Cache la Poudre River (which is also known as the "trout route," so bring your fly rod). Twenty miles west of Fort Collins via Highway 14.

Mountain Meadow Bed & Breakfast

13341 Rist Canyon Road, Bellvue, CO 80512   970-482-3769

The Raindrop Bed & Breakfast

6901 McMurry, Bellvue, CO 80512   970-493-0799
Tara Parr, Resident Owner   888-793-4136
EMAIL raindrop@frii.com   WEBSITE www.bbonline.com

LOCATION	Call for directions.
OPEN	All year
DESCRIPTION	A 1978 passive solar host home with eclectic furnishings, modern art, fine crafts, and many plants.
NO. OF ROOMS	One room with a private bathroom and two rooms share one bathroom.
RATES	Year-round rates range from $75-125 for a single or double with a private or shared bathroom. There is no minimum stay and a one-night deposit is appreciated.
CREDIT CARDS	No
BREAKFAST	Full breakfast is served just about anywhere and includes eggs, fruit, homegrown vegetables, and beverages. Special meals are available.
AMENITIES	Outdoor hot tub, large greenhouse, massage therapy room, fresh flowers, facilities for small group retreats or training.
RESTRICTIONS	No smoking, no pets. There are two resident Labs and a crowd of chickens and turkeys.

Scorched Tree B&B, Bellvue

SCORCHED TREE B&B

31601 Poudre Canyon Highway, Bellvue, CO 80512   970-881-2817
Brenda Wray & Roland Treiber, Resident Owners
Spanish spoken

LOCATION	On Highway 14 (Poudre Canyon) exactly 31.6 miles from the intersection of Highway 287 and Highway 14 on the Cache La Poudre River.
OPEN	All year
DESCRIPTION	A 1925 northwestern Indian-style log host home with rustic Indian furnishings on the Cache La Poudre River.
NO. OF ROOMS	Two rooms with private bathrooms. The best room: Saddle Blanket.
RATES	Year-round rates are $99-125 for a single or double. There is no minimum stay; cancellation requires two week's notice.
CREDIT CARDS	Discover, MasterCard, Visa
BREAKFAST	Full breakfast, served in the dining room, includes fresh trout from "our" river, stuffed French toast, frittatas, eggs Benedict, and fresh fruit. Breakfast is "a full meal to last until dinner," says Brenda. Four- and five-course gourmet dinners with wine are available by reservation for $75-95 per couple.
AMENITIES	Fresh flowers, hot tub, board games, video library, wine and hors d'oeuvres, microbrews, in-house chef, picnic lunches, robes, hair dryers, CD player, outfitting for hunting and fly-fishing available.

No smoking, no pets, children over 10 are welcome if both rooms are rented. The resident cat is called Retta. Camille is the poodle, but she's no "froufrou dog," says Roland. "She's an excellent hunting dog."

BERTHOUD

A small, peaceful farming village halfway between Boulder and Fort Collins. Head out to Carter Lake for fishing, water skiing, or sailing.

BERTHOUD BED & BREAKFAST

---

444 First Street, Berthoud, CO 80513   *970-532-4566*
Janet & Gary Foster, Resident Owners   *FAX 970-532-4566 (call first)*
EMAIL pt17baby@aol.com   *WEBSITE www.bedbrkfst.com*

LOCATION	From I-25, take exit 250 and go exactly five miles on Highway 56. The B&B is on the left.
OPEN	All year
DESCRIPTION	A three-story Victorian with each room decorated according to a different theme, e.g., French, Oriental, tropical.
NO. OF ROOMS	Seven rooms with private bathrooms. Janet suggests the Egyptian Room.
RATES	Year-round rates are $78-135. There is no minimum stay and cancellation requires five days' notice.
CREDIT CARDS	American Express, Diners Club, Discover, MasterCard, Visa
BREAKFAST	Full breakfast is served in the dining room or on the south lawn in the spring. Dinner is also available.
AMENITIES	Hot tub in the flower and vegetable garden, parking on site, afternoon tea, local phone calls and fax available, Victorian-style meeting room, shuttle to and from the airport, Stearman PT17 airplane rides available.
RESTRICTIONS	No smoking. Children are welcome. The dogs are Orville, Oscar, and Yeti; the llamas are Sebastian and Niki. There are also three sheep.
REVIEWED	*Official Guide to American Historic Inns, Plane Bargains, Mountain Flyer*
MEMBER	Bed & Breakfast Innkeepers of Colorado
RATED	Mobil 5 Stars

BEULAH

A delightful little town in the scenic Beulah Valley, on the eastern edge of the Wet Mountains and San Isabel National Forest. Beulah is worth a detour. Twenty-five miles southwest of Pueblo via I-25 and Highway 72.

DANIEL'S BED AND BREAKFAST

8927 Grand Avenue, Beulah, CO 81023   *719-485-3426*
Daniel L. Garcia Sr., Resident Owner

LOCATION	Half a mile from the center of Beulah at the end of Highway 78.
OPEN	All year
DESCRIPTION	A single-level, rustic country home built at the turn of the century.
NO. OF ROOMS	Four bedrooms, one with a private bathroom.
RATES	Year-round rates are $75 for a single or double with a private bathroom and $55-65 for a single or double with a shared bathroom.
BREAKFAST	Full healthy breakfast is served in the dining room.
AMENITIES	Reception hall available for retreats and weddings, patio in the back.
RESTRICTIONS	No smoking, pets OK, children are welcome.

KK RANCH & CARRIAGE MUSEUM

8987 Mountain Park Road, Beulah, CO 81023   *719-485-3250*
Katherine Keating, Resident Owner

LOCATION	Take Highway 78 west from Pueblo 20 miles to Beulah Valley. At the first fork in the road keep left and continue past three roads, then at the fourth intersection take a hard right onto Mountain Park Road (just off South Pine Drive).
OPEN	All year
DESCRIPTION	Authentic 1870 homestead ranch house with an interior that includes antiques, fireplaces, and wood-burning stoves. The homestead and carriage museum are situated on 67 wooded acres with streams, adjacent to a 600-acre mountain park.
NO. OF ROOMS	Three rooms share one bathroom. Katherine Keating favors the room with the fireplace.

RATES	Year-round rates are $40 for a single or double with a shared bathroom. The deposit is $25. Cancellation requires 48 hours' notice.
CREDIT CARDS	No. Personal checks are OK.
BREAKFAST	Continental breakfast is served in the kitchen, which looks out over mountains and pasture. Breakfast includes hot breads or rolls, cereal, fruit or juice, and coffee. Kitchen privileges can be arrranged.
AMENITIES	Barns and corrals are available, but the owner does not rent horses.
RESTRICTIONS	No smoking, children of all ages are welcome, horses welcome. Children under 12 stay free in parents' room. Resident dogs, cats, horses, donkeys, and mules.
REVIEWED	*The Colorado Guide, Great American Guest House Book*

RAVEN'S ROOST BED & BREAKFAST

6174 Pennsylvania Avenue, Beulah, CO 81023   719-485-3227
Darla Ewing, Resident Owner

LOCATION	Call for directions.
OPEN	April through October
DESCRIPTION	Large pine-covered two-story inn with grand Adirondack porch located on 20 forested acres.
NO. OF ROOMS	Three rooms with private bathrooms, seven rooms share two bathrooms. There is also a fourteen-room bunk house.
RATES	Rates are $65-85. Call for details.
CREDIT CARDS	American Express, MasterCard, Visa
BREAKFAST	Full healthy breakfast is served in the dining room and special meals are also available.
AMENITIES	Heated swimming pool.
RESTRICTIONS	No smoking inside, pets allowed. Children under five are allowed on a first-come, first-served basis.

BLACK HAWK

This Victorian mountain town and National Historic District was the site of Colorado's richest gold strike. Now it's possible to strike it rich (or go bust trying) in the town's many casinos. Explore the historic museums or take a mine and house tour. Black Hawk is handy to Golden Gate State Park, and the Central City Opera is only one mile from town. It's a pretty drive getting here—29 miles west of Denver on Highway 6 and 119.

AFTER SUPPER B&B

PO Box 398, Black Hawk, CO 80422   303-582-5787
Dixie & Bill Lovingier, Resident Owners

CHASE MANSION BED & BREAKFAST

201 Chase Gulch, Black Hawk, CO 80422   303-582-0112
Debra Start, Resident Owner   FAX 303-582-0112 *(call first)*
French spoken

LOCATION	Drive one block north of the second light on Highway 119 and turn left at Chase.
OPEN	All year
DESCRIPTION	An 1879 Victorian mansard with "Victorian clutter" furnishings.
NO. OF ROOMS	One room with a private bathroom and three rooms share one bathroom. Check out the Victorious Room.
RATES	May through September and holidays, rates are $75-110. Low-season rates are $50-85. Cancellation requires 24 hours' notice with a $20 fee.
CREDIT CARDS	MasterCard, Visa
BREAKFAST	Continental breakfast is served in the dining room.
AMENITIES	Social director on premises; wedding and special party arrangements; videos; books; games; refrigerator and kitchen use.
RESTRICTIONS	None

THE SHAMROCK INN

351 Gregory Street, Black Hawk, CO 80422   303-582-5513
Susan Knecht, Resident Owner

LOCATION	West on Highway 6, or I-70 to Highway 119. Upon entering Black Hawk city limits, take a left at the second light (Bullwackers Casino on corner). Go three blocks to the yellow house on the right.
OPEN	All year
DESCRIPTION	An 1880 two-story Victorian inn with some antique furnishings. Listed on the National and State Historic Registers.
NO. OF ROOMS	Three rooms with private bathrooms. Room B has a clawfoot tub.
RATES	Seasonal rates are $65-75 for a single or double with a private bathroom. No minimum stay requirements. Cancellation requires 24 hours' notice.
CREDIT CARDS	Discover, MasterCard, Visa
BREAKFAST	Guests serve themselves a full breakfast including homemade pastries, fruit, biscuits and homemade sausage gravy, beverages, oatmeal, and cold cereals.
AMENITIES	Porch and balcony overlook "main drag" of downtown Black Hawk, 30 casinos within walking or (free) shuttle distance, cable TV in rooms, private entrances.
RESTRICTIONS	Children over 12 are welcome, smoking OK, and pets OK with manager's approval. Lakota, a husky/Lab mix, is the resident dog.
REVIEWED	*The Colorado Guide*
MEMBER	Gilpin County Chamber of Commerce

BOULDER

This beautiful, small town is home to the University of Colorado, the National Center for Atmospheric Research, Celestial Seasonings (tea and tours available), the Bolder Boulder 10K, and an 8000-acre system of mountain parks and greenbelts. Boulder is an excellent place to linger on the way from Denver to Estes Park and Rocky Mountain National Park. Shop and dine on the Pearl Street (pedestrian) Mall.

THE ALPS BOULDER CANYON INN

38619 Boulder Canyon Drive, Boulder, CO 80302   303-444-5445
John & Jeannine Vanderhart, Resident Owners   800-414-2577
EMAIL *alpsinn@aol.com*   FAX 303-444-5522
WEBSITE *www.bedandbreakfastinns.org/alps*

LOCATION	In Boulder Canyon, 1.8 miles west of downtown.
OPEN	All year
DESCRIPTION	An 1870-1906 Adirondack Camp country inn with English country furnishings.
NO. OF ROOMS	Twelve rooms with private bathrooms. The best room in the house is the Wallstreet Room.
RATES	Year-round rates are $115-250 for a single or double. The entire B&B may be reserved for $2100 per night. There is a minimum stay during holidays, football weekends, and Colorado University graduation. One night's deposit due at reservation. Cancellation requires seven days' notice.
CREDIT CARDS	American Express, Carte Blanche, Diners Club, Discover, JCB, MasterCard, Visa
BREAKFAST	Full breakfast, served in the dining room, includes a varied selection of hot entrées such as stuffed French toast with apple cider syrup or eggs Florentine; fresh fruit; homemade granola and yogurt; muffins or coffeecake; bagels or breakfast breads; and freshly squeezed orange juice. Special meals are available for picnics and catering.
AMENITIES	Six rooms with double Jacuzzi tubs; all rooms with antique fireplaces and showers; TV, radio, phones, down comforters and pillows in most rooms; robes; complimentary afternoon refreshments; meeting facilities for up to 30; gardens; wedding facilities for up to 125 guests.
RESTRICTIONS	No smoking, no pets, children over 12 are welcome. The resident Gordon setter is Maggie, and the resident cats are Sid and S. K. "Please don't feed the animals—they are talented beggars."
REVIEWED	*Frommer's, Recommended Country Inns of the Rocky Mountain Region*
MEMBER	Colorado Hotel and Lodging Association, Professional Association of Innkeepers International, Boulder Hotel and Motel Association, Distinctive Inns of Colorado, Colorado Restaurant Association
RATED	AAA 3 Diamonds, Mobil 3 Stars
AWARDS	Best Inn in Colorado 1995, *Westword* magazine.
KUDOS/COMMENTS	"... a dream come true, beautiful setting, spacious rooms with double Jacuzzi and fireplace!" (1994)

THE BOULDER VICTORIA HISTORIC INN

1305 Pine Street, Boulder, CO 80302   *303-938-1300*
Matthew Dyroff & Jeffrey White, Resident Owners   *FAX 303-938-1435*

LOCATION	Downtown on the northeast corner of Pine and 13th, two blocks from the Pearl Street Mall.
OPEN	All year
DESCRIPTION	This elegantly restored 1889 two-story Victorian inn has period antique furnishings and is listed on the State Historic Register.
NO. OF ROOMS	Seven rooms with private bathrooms. The best room in the house is the White-Dyroff suite.
RATES	May through October, rates are $109-189 for a single or double and suites are $159-189. November through April, rates are $109 for a single or double and suites are $159. There is a two-night minimum stay on weekends and cancellation requires seven days' notice.
CREDIT CARDS	American Express, MasterCard, Visa
BREAKFAST	Continental plus is served in the dining room or guestrooms and includes homemade granola and muesli, fruitbreads, muffins, yogurt, bagels, croissants, and fresh fruit.
AMENITIES	Fresh and dried roses in the rooms; robes; TV; phones; steam showers; down comforters; rooms with private entrance or balcony; afternoon tea with scones, cookies, and port; special event and meeting space.
RESTRICTIONS	No smoking, no pets, children over 12 are welcome.
REVIEWED	*America's Wonderful Little Hotels & Inns; Recommended Country Inns Rocky Mountain Region; Frommer's Denver, Boulder and Colorado Springs; The Colorado Guide*
MEMBER	Distinctive Inns of Colorado, Professional Association of Innkeepers International
RATED	AAA 3 Diamonds
AWARDS	Historic Preservation Award 1991, Historic Boulder; Landscape Award, Commercial Division 1994, City of Boulder
KUDOS/COMMENTS	"An exquisite Victorian mansion, very professional, attentive young staff; guest oriented. Though the breakfast is continental plus, it was superb with wonderful presentation; a great location." (1997)

BRIAR ROSE BED & BREAKFAST

2151 Arapahoe Avenue, Boulder, CO 80302   303-442-3007
Margaret & Bob Weisenbach, Resident Owners   FAX 303-786-8440
French and Spanish spoken
EMAIL *BRBBX@aol.com*   WEBSITE *www.globalmall.com/brose*

LOCATION	Coming into town on Highway 36, turn left at the second light (Arapahoe Avenue), then go west about 0.5 mile to 22nd Street. The inn is on the corner.
OPEN	All year
DESCRIPTION	An 1890 two-story red-brick English Country inn and carriage house, with "light" Victorian furnishings surrounded by shaded lawn and gardens.
NO. OF ROOMS	Nine rooms with private bathrooms. Margaret suggests the Anniversary Room.
RATES	May through December, rates are $104-159 for a single or double. Off season rates are $79-139. There is a minimum stay during major University of Colorado events and cancellation requires 48 hours' notice.
CREDIT CARDS	American Express, Diners Club, MasterCard, Visa
BREAKFAST	Continental plus is served in the dining room or on the sun porch and includes fresh fruit compote, yogurt with berries, croissants and fresh-baked breads, homemade jams and granola, and "waffles and crepes when the spirit moves us." Lunch is available for groups on extended stays.
AMENITIES	TV and telephones in rooms, down comforters, fresh flowers, robes, tea trays, and homemade cookies.
RESTRICTIONS	No smoking, no pets
REVIEWED	*Non-Smokers Guide to Bed & Breakfasts; America's Wonderful Little Hotels & Inns; Country Inns and Back Roads; Frommer's Denver, Boulder & Colorado Springs; Recommended Country Inns Rocky Mountain Region*
MEMBER	Distinctive Inns of Colorado, Bed & Breakfast Innkeepers of Colorado, Professional Association of Innkeepers International, Boulder Hotel and Motel Association, Colorado Hotel and Lodging Association
RATED	AAA 3 Diamonds, Mobil 3 Stars
KUDOS/COMMENTS	"Warm and comfortable." "Convenient, spotless, excellent food and service, friendly innkeepers who make you feel right at home." "Cozy, restored Victorian with great hosts; good food and a warm atmosphere." (1997)

BROOMFIELD GUEST HOUSE

9009 West Jeffco Airport Avenue, Broomfield, CO 80021   *303-469-3900*
Betty Aldrich, Innkeeper   *880-233-5633*
WEBSITE www.guest-house.com   *FAX 303-438-1457*

LOCATION	Three-quarters of a mile south of the Broomfield exit off Highway 36.
OPEN	All year
DESCRIPTION	A 1988 two-story traditional guest house with views of the Rocky Mountains and Denver skyline and decorated with Thomasville furnishings.
NO. OF ROOMS	Sixteen rooms with private bathrooms. Betty suggests the Fraser Room.
RATES	Year-round rates are $94-150 for a single or double and $109-149 for a suite. There is no minimum stay and cancellation requires 48 hours' notice.
CREDIT CARDS	American Express, Diners Club, MasterCard, Visa
BREAKFAST	Full breakfast is served in the dining room or on the patio and includes homemade baked goods, fruit, homemade granola, a hot dish, bagels and cream cheese, yogurt, four kinds of dry cereal, and assorted breads. Wednesday is waffle morning.
AMENITIES	Homemade cookies; soda; pretzels and popcorn; refrigerator, microwave, fireplace, air conditioning, and phone with modem jack and voice messaging in each room; one room is handicapped accessible; three rooms have Jacuzzi tubs for two.
RESTRICTIONS	No smoking, no pets
MEMBER	Colorado Bed & Breakfast Association

COBURN HOUSE

2040 16th Street, Boulder, CO 80302   *303-545-5200*
Derek Wood & Wendy Smith, Resident Managers   *800-858-5811*
Some Spanish spoken   *FAX 303-440-6740*
EMAIL coburn@nilenet.com   *WEBSITE www.nilenet.com/~coburn*

LOCATION	From Denver, take Highway 36 west into Boulder. Turn left on Canyon and go to 16th Street. Turn right; the hotel is half a block beyond Pearl Street on the right.
OPEN	All year
DESCRIPTION	A 1994 two-story (plus garden level) eco-hotel with elegant western decor.

NO. OF ROOMS	Twelve rooms with private bathrooms. Try rooms 11 and 12.
RATES	Year-round rates are $144-167 for a single or double. There is no minimum stay and cancellation requires 48 hours' notice.
CREDIT CARDS	American Express, Discover, MasterCard, Visa
BREAKFAST	Continental plus, served in the dining room, includes fresh-baked breads, muffins, granola, waffles, pancakes, quiches, stratas, organic coffees and teas, and seasonal fruit.
AMENITIES	Individually controlled air conditioning and heat, four rooms with Jacuzzi tubs, seven rooms with fireplaces, four rooms with king-size beds, three rooms with balconies, three rooms with French doors, 100% cotton linens, meeting facilities, fax and copier.
RESTRICTIONS	No smoking, no pets, children over 14 are welcome.
REVIEWED	*The Insiders' Guide to Boulder & Rocky Mountain National Park*
MEMBER	"Green" Hotels Association, Boulder Hotel & Motel Association

EARL HOUSE HISTORIC INN

2429 Broadway Street, Boulder, CO 80304   *303-938-1400*

GUNBARREL GUEST HOUSE

6901 Lookout Road, Boulder, CO 80301   *303-530-1513*
Carolann Evans, Resident Owner   *800-530-1513*
EMAIL *ldyhawk@earthlink.net*   *FAX 303-530-4573*
WEBSITE *www.guest-house.com*

LOCATION	Seven miles northeast of downtown Boulder off Highway 119 and 63rd Street.
OPEN	All year
DESCRIPTION	A 1986 contemporary country inn featuring European-style lodging, with rooms situated around a central courtyard/patio.
NO. OF ROOMS	Thirteen rooms with private bathrooms. Try the Evergreen Suite.
RATES	Year-round rates are $94-144 for a single or double. Cancellation requires 48 hours' notice.
CREDIT CARDS	American Express, Diners Club, MasterCard, Visa
BREAKFAST	Continental plus, served in the dining room, includes coffee, tea, juice, cereals, homemade granola, coffeecakes, muffins, cream cheese, and fruit. Specialized catering is available.
AMENITIES	Fireplaces and kitchenettes in every room, Jacuzzi in the

Evergreen Suite, conference room and boardroom, handicapped access, phones and TV in every room, fax, on-site parking.

RESTRICTIONS	No smoking except on patios, no pets, children over 12 are welcome (please ask about exceptions).
MEMBER	Professional Association of Innkeepers International

INN ON MAPLETON HILL

1001 Spruce Street, Boulder, CO 80304   *303-449-6528*
Ray & Judy Schultze, Resident Owners   *800-276-6528*
EMAIL maphillinn@aol.com   *FAX 303-415-0470*
WEBSITE www.bbonline.com/co/mapleton

LOCATION	In downtown Boulder at 10th and Spruce Streets, just one block north of the Pearl Street Mall.
OPEN	All year
DESCRIPTION	A restored 1899 three-story brick Edwardian vernacular inn with turn-of-the-century decor.
NO. OF ROOMS	Five rooms with private bathrooms and two rooms share one bathroom. Try the Cottonwood Suite.
RATES	May through October 31, rates are $107-145 for a single or double with a private bathroom, $93-98 for a single or double with a shared bathroom, and $145 and up for a suite. November through April, rates are $96-130 for a single or double with a private bathroom, $83-88 for a single or double with a shared bathroom, and $130 and up for a suite. There is no minimum stay and cancellation requires five days' notice.
CREDIT CARDS	American Express, MasterCard, Visa
BREAKFAST	Continental plus is served in the dining room and includes fresh-baked bread or bagels, homemade granola, a choice of cereals, seasonal fruit salad, yogurt, home-baked "goodie of the day," orange juice, milk, tea, and custom-blended coffee.
AMENITIES	Fireplace in Great Room (and in some guestrooms); veranda, library, and study; late afternoon refreshments; meeting space; fax; phones in every room; air conditioning.
RESTRICTIONS	No smoking, no pets, children over 12 are welcome. Basil is the resident dog.
REVIEWED	*Fodor's The Rockies; Insider's Guide to Boulder & Rocky Mountain National Park; America's Favorite Inns, B&Bs and Small Hotels*
MEMBER	Boulder Hotel & Motel Association, Bed & Breakfast Innkeepers of Colorado, Professional Association of Innkeepers International

Inn on Mapleton Hill, Boulder

RATED	AAA 2 Diamonds
AWARDS	Historic Boulder, 1992 Historic Preservation Award

PEARL STREET INN

1820 Pearl Street, Boulder, CO 80302   303-444-5584
Kate Beeman, Innkeeper   888-810-1302
Some Spanish spoken   FAX 303-444-6494
WEBSITE *www.pearlstreetinn.com*

LOCATION	Center of Boulder, three blocks east of the Pearl Street Mall.
OPEN	All year
DESCRIPTION	An 1895 two-story Victorian with a 1985 addition featuring contemporary Victorian furnishings and a central courtyard.
NO. OF ROOMS	Eight rooms with private bathrooms.
RATES	Winter rates are $95-135 for a single or double, weekend rates are

$115-145. May through September, rates are $119-164 for a single or double on weekends, $115-145 during the week. There is no minimum stay and cancellation requires one weeks' notice during the summer—48 hours in the winter.

CREDIT CARDS	American Express, Diners Club, MasterCard, Visa
BREAKFAST	Full gourmet breakfast, served in the dining room, guestrooms, or courtyard, is cooked to order and includes three choices.
AMENITIES	Fresh flowers, cable TV, phone with voicemail, and fireplaces in all rooms; conference and banquet rooms; full bar; turndown and concierge service; complimentary wine and cheese; reserved parking; handicapped access.
RESTRICTIONS	No smoking, no pets, all children are welcome.
REVIEWED	*America's Wonderful Little Hotels & Inns; Frommer's Denver, Boulder and Colorado Springs; Recommended Country Inns Rocky Mountain Region*
MEMBER	Colorado Hotel and Lodging Association, Colorado Travel & Tourism Association

THE SANDY POINT INN

6485 Twin Lakes Road, Boulder, CO 80301
Juanita Miller, Resident Owner

303-530-2939
800-322-2939
FAX 303-530-9101

KUDOS/COMMENTS   "Great place to go with a family. Nice staff, would be great for business travelers also." (1996)

BRECKENRIDGE
(SUMMIT COUNTY)

A beautifully restored, 130-year-old gold rush town and National Historic District, Breckenridge is the biggest of the four major ski areas in the recreational mecca of Summit County. This three-mountain resort is a treasure trove of terrific, year-round events. Ullrfest in January honors the Norwegian god of snow ... and drinking. Watch for frequent wood carving and snow sculpting competitions in fall and winter. The summer hums with Bach and Beethoven and Jazz Festivals, and don't miss the Film Festival in September. From Denver, 70 miles west on I-70.

ABBOTT PLACE INN

205 South French Street, Breckenridge, CO 80424　　970-453-6489
Lynn & Carl Cavalluzzi, Resident Owners　　888-794-7750
　　FAX 970-453-1842

ALLAIRE TIMBERS INN

9511 South Main Street, Breckenridge, CO 80424　　970-453-7530
Jack & Kathy Gumph, Resident Owners　　800-624-4904
EMAIL *allairetimbers@worldnet.att.net*　　FAX 970-453-8699
WEBSITE *www.allairetimbers.com*

LOCATION	From Denver, take I-70 west to Frisco (exit 203). Take Highway 9 south to Breckenridge. We are 0.2 mile past the Conoco gas station on the right.
OPEN	All year
DESCRIPTION	A 1991 two-story contemporary log-and-stone inn with southwestern, contemporary, and rustic interior.
NO. OF ROOMS	Ten rooms with private bathrooms. Kathy Gumph likes the Summit Suite.
RATES	Year-round rates are $130-200 for a single or double and $210-310 for suites. There is a minimum stay during Christmas and ski season.
CREDIT CARDS	American Express, Discover, MasterCard, Visa
BREAKFAST	Full breakfast is served in the dining room and includes a buffet sidebar of coffees, teas, juices, homemade granola, cereals, fresh fruit, yogurt, and home-baked breads and breakfast cakes, plus a hot entrée served at your table.

AMENITIES	Robes, fleece socks, TVs, phones, and clock radios in every room; early morning coffee service; main outdoor hot tub; wheelchair access and hearing impaired facilities; afternoon happy hour and evening desserts; stone fireplace in Great Room; private hot tub and fireplace in suites.
RESTRICTIONS	No smoking, no pets (resident Airedale is named Josie), and children over 13 are welcome. There is a maximum of two guests per room at all times.
REVIEWED	*America's Wonderful Little Hotels & Inns, Recommended Country Inns of the Rocky Mountain Region, Distinctive Inns of Colorado, The Colorado Guide, Best Places to Stay in the Rockies, Frommer's Rocky Mountain B&B Guide*
MEMBER	Distinctive Inns of Colorado, Independent Innkeepers Association, Professional Association of Innkeepers International, Bed & Breakfast Inns of Colorado
RATED	AAA 3 Diamonds, ABBA 3 Crowns, Mobil 3 Stars
AWARDS	1995 and 1996 national finalist in the Jones Dairy Farm B&B Chefs Competition; 1993 Top 10 New Inns in America, by Inn Marketing Review; 1995 national winner in ABBA's Bed & Breakfast Chefs Competition.
KUDOS/COMMENTS	"An excellent example of what innkeeping is all about." "The ultimate in hospitality, decor, and service." "What a hot-tub view!" (1994) "Spectacular views, scrumptious breakfast, great location, quiet, relaxing, wonderful hospitality!" (1999)

THE EVANS HOUSE BED & BREAKFAST

102 South French Street, Breckenridge, CO 80424   970-453-5509
Pete & Georgette Contos, Resident Owners
French and Greek spoken
EMAIL *evans@imageline.com*   WEBSITE *www.colorado-bnb.com/evanshse*

LOCATION	Two blocks east of the Main Street and Lincoln stoplight on French Street in the Historic District.
OPEN	All year (but call in May and October)
DESCRIPTION	An 1886 two-story Victorian with the decor of the era and individually decorated rooms, listed on the National and State Historic Registers.
NO. OF ROOMS	Five rooms with private bathrooms. The Colorado Room is the most popular.
RATES	November through March, rates are $100-114 for a single or double, and a suite is $140. April through September, rates are $63-77 for a single or double, and $90 for a suite. There is a minimum

stay during holidays. Cancellation requires 30 days' notice with a
$25 per person fee. No refunds unless rebooked.

CREDIT CARDS	American Express, Diners Club, Discover, MasterCard, Visa
BREAKFAST	Full breakfast, served in the dining room (or the suite), includes crepes, Belgian waffles, apple cinnamon French toast, and a variety of popular egg dishes. Special breakfasts can be arranged.
AMENITIES	Fresh flowers in the rooms, robes, hot tub in historic shed with stained-glass windows, cable TV and phones in rooms, library and piano in common room, ski and bike storage, free ski shuttle at front door, on-site parking, Jacuzzi tub, microwave and fridge, private entrance, and afternoon refreshments.
RESTRICTIONS	No smoking, no pets
REVIEWED	*America's Wonderful Little Hotels & Inns, Recommended Country Inns Rocky Mountain Region*
MEMBER	Bed & Breakfast Innkeepers of Colorado, Professional Association of Innkeepers International, Summit County Bed & Breakfast Association, Breckenridge Bed & Breakfast Association
RATED	AAA 2 Diamonds, ABBA 2 Crowns, Mobil 2 Stars
AWARDS	Outstanding Hospitality award from the Bed & Breakfast Innkeepers of Colorado
KUDOS/COMMENTS	"Small but friendly, historic, great hosts." (1996)

FIRESIDE INN

114 North French Street, Breckenridge, CO 80424   *970-453-6456*
Mike & Mary Keeling, Resident Owners   *FAX 970-453-9577*
Fluent Spanish spoken   WEBSITE *www.firesideinn.com*
EMAIL *info@firesideinn.com*

LOCATION	One block north of the stoplight in the center of town (Ski Hill Road), then east two blocks to the blue house with a picket fence on the corner of French and Wellington.
OPEN	All year except May 1 until the Friday prior to Memorial Day
DESCRIPTION	An 1879/1979 converted miners' cabin listed on both the National and State Historic Registers. The furnishings are Victorian.
NO. OF ROOMS	Four rooms with private bathrooms and five rooms share three bathrooms. Try the Brandywine Suite.
RATES	Winter rates, January through March, are $85-105 for a single or double with a private bathroom, $120 for a suite, and the guesthouse rents for $1,000 a week. Low-season rates, May through December, are $60-80 for a single or double with a private

bathroom, $85 for a suite, and $500 per week for the guesthouse. There is a minimum stay during ski season and cancellation requires 30 days' notice and a fee of $25 per person.

CREDIT CARDS	American Express, Discover, MasterCard, Visa
BREAKFAST	Full breakfast is served in the dining room. "Award-winning" French toast is available daily.
AMENITIES	Hot tub, TV/VCR in private rooms, discount lift tickets and rentals, fireplace in parlor, guest refrigerators, ski and bicycle storage, extensive local knowledge of mountain bike trails.
RESTRICTIONS	No smoking, no pets
REVIEWED	*Recommended Country Inns Rocky Mountain Region, Mountain Biking in Summit County, Hiking the Colorado Trail*
MEMBER	Breckenridge Bed & Breakfast Association, Summit County Bed & Breakfast Association, Colorado Hotel and Lodging Association

HIGH COUNTRY LODGE

5064 Ski Hill Road, Peak 7, Breckenridge, CO 80424   *970-453-9843*
Donald Lake, Owner   *800-497-0097*
EMAIL *hcl@colorado.net*   *FAX 970-453-7595*
WEBSITE *www.colorado.net/hcl*

LOCATION	Five minutes from downtown at the base of Peak 7.
OPEN	All year
DESCRIPTION	A recently remodeled 1969 Lindal cedar A-frame vacation lodge on 10 acres with views of the Continental Divide.
NO. OF ROOMS	Eight rooms with private bathrooms and four rooms share four bathrooms. Try room 204.
RATES	Low-season rates are $72-105 for a double with a private bathroom. Ski-season rates are $98-152. Christmas holiday rates are $112-175. There is a three-night minimum stay during holidays.
CREDIT CARDS	Discover, MasterCard, Visa
BREAKFAST	Full breakfast, served in the dining room, includes crepes, pancakes, muffins, and beverages.
AMENITIES	Afternoon snacks, ten-seater Jacuzzi, exercise room, game room, three fireplaces, can sleep up to 36. Wedding and honeymoon packages available.
RESTRICTIONS	No smoking, no pets
MEMBER	Bed & Breakfast Innkeepers of Colorado

HUMMINGBIRD HOUSE BED & BREAKFAST

217 Hummingbird Drive, Breckenridge, CO 80424   970-453-6957
Bob & Betty Flint, Resident Owners

LOCATION	From I-70, take exit 203 and travel 10 miles to Breckenridge. Drive through town, turn on Boreas Pass Road ("T" intersection at the Conoco station), go 1.5 miles to Hummingbird Road, go straight about 50 feet, and the B&B is the two-story brown cedar-sided house on the left.
OPEN	All year
DESCRIPTION	A 1980 two-story host home with early American antiques.
NO. OF ROOMS	Two rooms with private bathrooms. Pick the Green Room.
RATES	Winter rates, December 16 through March 31, are $75-85 (includes tax) for a single or double. Low-season rates, April 1 through December 15, are $45-55 for a single or double. There is a two-night minimum stay during ski season, and cancellations made less than five days prior to stay incur a $15 charge.
CREDIT CARDS	No
BREAKFAST	Full breakfast served in the dining room includes (on alternating days) an egg dish, breakfast meats, French toast, and waffles. There is always fresh fruit and homemade pastries.
AMENITIES	Common room has TV/VCR, books, stereo, and wood-burning stove. The hot tub is on the deck. The wet bar has a refrigerator, microwave, and coffeemaker.
RESTRICTIONS	No smoking, no pets. A crib is available and all children are welcome.

HUNT PLACER INN

275 Ski Hill Road, Breckenridge, CO 80424   970-453-7573
Carl & Gwen Ray, Innkeepers   800-472-1430
German spoken   FAX 970-453-2335
EMAIL hpi@colorado.net   WEBSITE *www.breck.net/lodging/huntplacer/*

LOCATION	Turn onto Ski Hill Road from Main Street (Highway 9) at the third stoplight. The inn is two-and-a-half blocks up on the left.
OPEN	All year
DESCRIPTION	A 1994 three-story Bavarian mountain chalet with wood and stucco interior. The decor in each room varies, from British Empire to Old West to Country Cottage.
NO. OF ROOMS	Eight bedrooms with private bathrooms. Try the Britannia Room.

RATES	November through March, rates are $125-180 for a single or double and $180-235 for a suite. April through October, rates are $119 for a single or double and $129-159 for a suite. There is a two-night minimum stay during weekends—four to five nights during ski season. Cancellation requires 14 to 30 days' notice.
CREDIT CARDS	American Express, Diners Club, Discover, MasterCard, Visa
BREAKFAST	Full, three-course breakfast is served on English china with crystal and silver in the dining room. Entrées vary daily.
AMENITIES	Private balconies, afternoon tea and refreshments, coffee all day, concierge service, fireplaces in common areas and some rooms, meeting facilities, handicapped access with elevator, hiking trail begins on site.
RESTRICTIONS	No smoking, no pets, children over 10 are welcome. Tasha is the resident pooch. She is curious but very timid when approached.
REVIEWED	*Recommended Country Inns Rocky Mountain Region; Colorado Guide; America's Wonderful Little Hotels & Inns; The Complete Guide to Bed & Breakfasts, Inns & Guesthouses; Romantic Inns of America*
MEMBER	Bed & Breakfasts of Breckenridge, Bed & Breakfast Innkeepers of Colorado, Professional Association of Innkeepers International, Colorado Hotel and Lodging Association
RATED	AAA 3 Diamonds, Mobil 3 Stars, Breckenridge Resort Chamber 5 Peaks

LITTLE MOUNTAIN LODGE

98 Sunbeam Drive, Breckenridge, CO 80424　　　970-453-1969
Lynn Esmond, Resident Owner　　　800-468-7707
EMAIL *lml@colorado.com*　　　*FAX 970-453-1919*
WEBSITE *www.littlemountainlodge.com*

LOCATION	Two blocks from main street in Breckenridge.
OPEN	All year
DESCRIPTION	A whitewashed logpole lodge.
NO. OF ROOMS	Ten rooms with private bathrooms.
RATES	Year-round rates are $130-300.
CREDIT CARDS	American Express, MasterCard, Visa
BREAKFAST	Full breakfast is served in the dining room.
AMENITIES	TV/VCRs in all rooms, fine artwork.
RESTRICTIONS	No smoking, no pets, children over 12 are welcome.

KUDOS/COMMENTS "Outstanding, beautiful log house." "Romantic, very charming; Lynn is very friendly and helpful." (1997) "Great views." (1999)

MUGGINS GULCH INN

4023 Tiger Road, Breckenridge, CO 80424   970-453-7414
Beth Anne & Tom Hossley, Resident Innkeepers   800-275-8304

KUDOS/COMMENTS   "Hard to get to, but worth it." "My favorite. Owners built a fabulous log and beam, filled with antiques and art." (1996) "Incredible views; good people." (1997)

RIDGE STREET INN BED & BREAKFAST

212 North Ridge Street, Breckenridge, CO 80424   970-453-4680
Carol Brownson, Resident Owner   800-452-4680
EMAIL ridge@colorado.net   WEBSITE www.colorado.net/ridge

LOCATION	Downtown Breckenridge, one block east of Main Street. From Main Street, turn east onto Lincoln.
OPEN	All year
DESCRIPTION	An 1890 two-story Victorian inn with antiques and French country furnishings located in the heart of the historic district. Listed on the Colorado Historic Register.
NO. OF ROOMS	Four rooms with private bathrooms and two rooms share one bathroom. The best room is the Parlor Suite.
RATES	Year-round rates are $75-150 for a single or double with a private bathroom and $55-115 for a single or double with a shared bathroom. There is a minimum stay from December through April and during weekends from June through October. Cancellation requires 30 days' notice and a $10 fee.
CREDIT CARDS	MasterCard, Visa
BREAKFAST	Full breakfast is served in the dining room and includes a variety of cereals, homemade granola, yogurt, fresh fruit, coffee, tea, orange juice, and an entrée such as waffles and sausage, cheese omelet, or French toast with bacon.
AMENITIES	TVs in rooms, phone in living room, fireplace, guide service for hiking and biking, fresh flowers, ski and bike storage.
RESTRICTIONS	No smoking, no pets, children over six are welcome. There are two springer spaniels called Tilly and Simon.
REVIEWED	*Frommer's Colorado*

Breckenridge Bed & Breakfast Association, Bed & Breakfast
Innkeepers of Colorado, Summit County Bed & Breakfast
Association

SWAN MOUNTAIN INN

16172 Highway 9, Breckenridge, CO 80424   970-453-7903
Steve Gessner, Resident Owner   800-578-3687
WEBSITE *www.colorado-bnb.com/swanmtn*

LOCATION	From Denver, take I-70 west approximately 70 miles to exit 203 at Frisco; take Route 9 south about four miles. The inn is halfway between Frisco and Breckenridge at the corner of Highway 9 and Swan Mountain Road.
OPEN	All year
DESCRIPTION	A 1986 three-story log home with cathedral and vaulted ceilings, a fireside bar and candlelit dining room; furnished with antiques, Waverly fabrics, and light cedar walls.
NO. OF ROOMS	Three rooms with private bathrooms and one room shares one bathroom. The best room is the Blue River Hideaway.
RATES	The inn has three rate schedules. During high season in Christmas and March rates are $100-135 for a single or double with a private bathroom, $60 for a single or double with a shared bathroom, and $220 for the suite. During low season, from July 1 to September 15 and January 3 to April 15, rates are $75-100 for a single or double with a private bathroom, $50 for a single or double with a shared bathroom, and $165 for the suite. There is a minimum stay on weekends, Christmas, and in March. Cancellation requires two weeks' notice (less a 10% service charge).
CREDIT CARDS	Discover, MasterCard, Visa
BREAKFAST	Full gourmet breakfast, served in the dining room, includes a choice of entrée, orange juice, coffee, tea, granola, fresh breads, and pastries. Lunch and dinner are available in summer and winter.
AMENITIES	Outdoor hot tub, TV/VCR, two fireplaces, two decks, large front porch, afternoon tea, weddings and private parties, croquet in the summer, bath amenities, robes, handicapped access on lower level.
RESTRICTIONS	No smoking, no pets
REVIEWED	*Rocky Mountain News, Westword*
MEMBER	Bed & Breakfast Innkeepers of Colorado, Summit County Bed & Breakfast Association
AWARDS	Voted Best New Restaurant in 1992 and Best Brunch in 1993 and 1994 by the local paper, the *Summit Daily News*.

THE WALKER HOUSE

211 East Lincoln Street, Breckenridge, CO 80424   970-453-2426
Sue Ellen Strong, Resident Owner   FAX 970-468-6222
Polish spoken

LOCATION	Going south, turn left at the corner of Main Street and Lincoln (opposite the ski area), proceed two blocks, turn right on French, first driveway on the right.
OPEN	November 1 to May 30
DESCRIPTION	An 1875 three-story log Victorian with original Victorian furnishings.
NO. OF ROOMS	One room with a private bathroom and one room shares one bathroom. Check out the Boudoir Suite.
RATES	Regular rates are $89 for a single or double with a shared bathroom and $119 for the suite. Christmas rates are 10% more. There is a two-day minimum stay and a cancellation policy.
CREDIT CARDS	No
BREAKFAST	Full breakfast, served in the dining room, includes informal vegetarian dishes. Dinner and special meals are available.
AMENITIES	Very quiet and private, snacks, tea and coffee anytime.
RESTRICTIONS	No smoking, no pets, quiet atmosphere encouraged, no alcohol, children over 16 are welcome.
REVIEWED	*Feather Beds & Flap Jacks*
MEMBER	Breckenridge Bed & Breakfast Association

THE WELLINGTON INN

200 North Main Street, Breckenridge, CO 80424   970-453-9464
Hollie & Bill VanderHoeven, Resident Owners   800-655-7557

WILLIAMS HOUSE BED & BREAKFAST

303 North Main Street, Breckenridge, CO 80424   970-453-2975
Diane Jaynes & Fred Kinat, Resident Owners   800-795-2975

LOCATION	In the first block of Main Street on the west side of the street.

The Wellington Inn, Breckenridge

OPEN	Closed three weeks in May, two weeks in October, and one week in November
DESCRIPTION	An 1885 one-and-a-half-story boomtown Victorian inn with an 1880 one-story Victorian cottage, decorated romantically with antiques.
NO. OF ROOMS	Five rooms in the main house with private bathrooms. One room in Victorian Cottage. Owners recommend the Victorian Cottage.
RATES	High-season (December, February, March) rates are $110-140 for a single or double with a private bathroom in the main house and $175-200 for the cottage. There is a minimum stay requirement during ski season, summer, and autumn. There is a 45-day cancellation policy and a $20 charge.
CREDIT CARDS	American Express
BREAKFAST	Full breakfast, served in the dining room, varies daily but includes a theme entrée such as a breakfast taco, frittata, quiche, or Polynesian delight.
AMENITIES	Outdoor hot tub with view, two parlors with Victorian mantled fireplaces, afternoon refreshments, assorted area guidebooks and menus, lock-up ski and bike racks. The cottage has a Victorian mantled fireplace, Jacuzzi for two, and a small kitchenette.
RESTRICTIONS	No smoking, no pets, children over 14 are welcome.
REVIEWED	*The Colorado Guide, Frommer's Colorado, Best Places to Stay in the Rockies, Recommended Country Inns Rocky Mountain Region, America's Wonderful Little Hotels & Inns, The Non-Smokers Guide to Bed & Breakfasts*

MEMBER	Bed & Breakfast Innkeepers of Colorado, Professional Association of Innkeepers International, Breckenridge Bed & Breakfasts, Summit County Bed & Breakfasts, Colorado Hotel & Motel Association
RATED	AAA 2 Diamonds, Mobil 3 Stars

BUENA VISTA

Ringed by a bounty of fourteeners in the soaring Sawatch and Collegiate ranges, Buena Vista is anything but a misnomer. Must-do's during July and August include rafting the Arkansas River, checking out the fun of Gold Rush Days and the Burro Jamboree (the Kentucky Derby of pack-burro racing), being distracted by shiny objects at the Gem and Mineral Show, and hanging out at the Folklife Festival. Later in the year, enjoy Octoberfest and Moonlight Madness, or visit one of two major hot springs in the area. From Denver, 117 miles southwest via Highway 285.

THE ADOBE INN

303 North Highway 24, Buena Vista, CO 81211   719-395-6340
Paul, Majorie, & Michael Knox, Resident Owners

LOCATION	Two blocks north of the stoplight at Highway 24 and Sterling Avenue.
OPEN	All year
DESCRIPTION	A 1982 southwestern adobe hacienda and Mexican restaurant.
NO. OF ROOMS	Five rooms with private baths. Try the Indian Room.
RATES	May through October, rates are $69-89 for a single or double. November through April, rates are $59-79 for a single or double. There is no minimum stay and cancellation requires seven days' notice.
CREDIT CARDS	MasterCard, Visa
BREAKFAST	Full breakfast is served in the dining room and includes eggs, meat, croissants, fruit, and drinks.
AMENITIES	Cable TV in all rooms, two-person Jacuzzi, solarium with piano, fireplace, and library.
RESTRICTIONS	No smoking, no pets
REVIEWED	*The Colorado Guide, Recommended Country Inns Rocky Mountain Region, America's Wonderful Little Hotels & Inns*

The Adobe Inn, Buena Vista

MEMBER	Bed & Breakfast Innkeepers of Colorado
RATED	AAA 3 Diamonds, Mobil 2 Stars

BLUE SKY INN

719 Arizona Street, Buena Vista, CO 81211   719-395-8862
Butch & Marge Henley, Resident Owners   800-654-6297

LOCATION	Turn right at the one traffic light from Highway 24 to East Main, take a right on Court Street, and go 0.25 mile to the B&B.
OPEN	All year
DESCRIPTION	A 1960 contemporary mountain home furnished with antiques on 25 acres along the Arkansas River and Cottonwood Creek.
NO. OF ROOMS	One room with a private bathroom and three rooms share one bathroom. The best room is the Master Bedroom.
RATES	Year-round rates are $75 for the room with a private bathroom and $65 for a room with a shared bath. There is no minimum stay and a three-day cancellation policy.
CREDIT CARDS	MasterCard, Visa
BREAKFAST	Full country breakfast is served on the sun porch or the patios.
AMENITIES	Hot tub on the Arkansas River, outdoor dining, beautiful professional landscaping, fishing on the Arkansas River, hiking trails.
RESTRICTIONS	No smoking, no pets, children are welcome.
REVIEWED	*The Colorado Guide*

BUENA VISTA BED & BREAKFAST

230 North Gunnison, Buena Vista, CO 81211   *719-395-3170*
Jackie Melvin, Innkeeper   *FAX 719-395-3167*
Portuguese spoken
WEBSITE *www.bbonline.com/co/buenavista*

LOCATION	Go north on Highway 24. There is one stoplight in town—proceed one long block past it and turn left at Sterling. Go one more long block.
OPEN	All year
DESCRIPTION	An 1897 two-story Victorian country inn with comfortable Victorian furnishings.
NO. OF ROOMS	One bedroom with a private bathroom and four bedrooms with two shared bathrooms. Jackie recommends the Magenta Room, with a private Jacuzzi bath, skylights, and king-size bed.
RATES	High-season rates are $125 for a single or double with a private bathroom, $65-75 for a single or double with a shared bathroom, and $405 for the entire B&B. Regular rates are $115 for a single or double with a private bathroom, and $55-75 for a single or double with a shared bathroom. There is no minimum stay and cancellation requires 15 days' notice, 30 days during holidays, less a $15 fee.
CREDIT CARDS	MasterCard, Visa
BREAKFAST	Full breakfast is served in the dining room and includes fruit, orange juice, and coffee, with either famous oatmeal pancakes, bacon, and hashbrowns or gourmet eggs, sausage, and muffins. Special meals may be arranged.
AMENITIES	Cookies in the afternoons, meeting facilities, handicapped access.
RESTRICTIONS	No pets, children over eight are welcome. Smoking is permitted outside on the porch swing.
MEMBER	Bed & Breakfast Innkeepers of Colorado
RATED	AAA 2 Diamonds

MEISTER HOUSE BED & BREAKFAST

414 East Main Street, Buena Vista, CO 81211   *719-395-9220*
Barbara & Frank Hofmeister, Resident Owners   *888-395-9220*
EMAIL *meisterhouse@vtinet.com*   WEBSITE *www.vtinet.com/meister*

LOCATION	From Highway 24, go two blocks east on East Main Street.

Meister House Bed & Breakfast, Buena Vista

OPEN	All year
DESCRIPTION	An 1879 two-story western Victorian inn and brick hotel, completely renovated in 1994, with old and new western and ranch furnishings. Listed on the Colorado Historic Register.
NO. OF ROOMS	Four bedrooms with private bathrooms and two rooms share one bathroom. The owners' favorite is the Spanish Peaks Room.
RATES	High-season rates are $80-125 for a single or double with a private bathroom, $75 for a single or double with a shared bathroom, and $155 for a suite. The guesthouse rents for $125, and the entire B&B rents for $475 per night. During low season, October through April, rates are about $10 less for the rooms. The guesthouse rents for $115 during low season and the entire B&B for $425. There is no minimum stay and a 10-day cancellation policy.
CREDIT CARDS	MasterCard, Visa
BREAKFAST	Full breakfast, served in the dining room or courtyard, includes juice, fresh fruit, yogurt, and a main dish of crab bake, stuffed French toast, waffle boats with fruit, whole-grain pancakes, and frittatas, plus local coffee. Dinners are available upon request.
AMENITIES	Bottled water, sauna, a sink in each room, robes, shared refrigerator, afternoon treats, common area, game space and fireplace, library, large yard with flower garden, great views, wonderful courtyard.
RESTRICTIONS	No smoking, no pets, children over 10 are welcome. The resident miniature dachshund is called Bruno.
REVIEWED	*Denver Post, Rocky Mountain News*

THE POTTER'S HOUSE BED & BREAKFAST

28490 Chaffee County Road 313, Buena Vista, CO 81211   719-395-6458
Veryl Rember, Resident Owner

LOCATION	One mile south of town.
OPEN	May 1 through October 15
DESCRIPTION	A 1986 adobe home with antique furnishings.
NO. OF ROOMS	One room with a private bathroom and two rooms share one bathroom.
RATES	Rates are $75 for a double with a private bathroom and $69 for a single or double with a shared bathroom. There is a reservation/cancellation policy.
CREDIT CARDS	MasterCard, Visa
BREAKFAST	Full breakfast is served in the dining room or on garden patios. Sack lunches are available.
AMENITIES	Fireplace in one room, complimentary refreshments.
RESTRICTIONS	No smoking, small dogs welcome, children over 12 are welcome.

TROUT CITY INN

PO Box 431, Buena Vista, CO 81211   719-395-8433
Juel & Irene Kjeldsen, Resident Owners

LOCATION	On Trout Creek Pass, five miles east of Johnson Village (two miles south of Buena Vista) at Highways 24 and 285 and McGee Gulch Road.
OPEN	June 15 through September 15
DESCRIPTION	A 1987 reconstruction of a historic railroad depot, with Victorian furnishings, located in the San Isabel National Forest. Also a breeding and training farm for registered horses.
NO. OF ROOMS	Four rooms with private bathrooms, two rooms in depot, one suite in Pullman Car, one suite in Drover's Caboose. Choose the private Pullman Car.
RATES	Seasonal rates are $50-70 for a single or double with a private bathroom. There is no minimum stay and cancellation requires 72 hours' notice.

CREDIT CARDS	MasterCard, Visa
BREAKFAST	Full breakfast, served in the dining room, includes an egg entrée, meats, fresh-baked breads or muffins, biscuits and gravy, a dozen homemade preserves, and a number of house specialties.
AMENITIES	Fishing, gold panning, handcar rides, railroad museum, Victorian saloon game room, VCR library.
RESTRICTIONS	No smoking indoors, no pets, children over 10 are welcome—all ages welcome in the caboose.
REVIEWED	*America's Wonderful Little Hotels & Inns, Recommended Country Inns Rocky Mountain Region, Great Affordable B&B Getaways*
MEMBER	Bed & Breakfast Innkeepers of Colorado

CAÑON CITY

ACORN LEAF BED & BREAKFAST

138 Wilmoor Court, Cañon City, CO 81212   719-275-3833

DE WEESE LODGE

1226 Elm Avenue, Cañon City, CO 81212   719-269-1881

CARBONDALE

An independent and spirited community at the base of towering Mount Sopris. A few good reasons to visit: Gold Medal fishing in the Roaring Fork and Crystal Rivers; polo at the Roaring Fork Polo Club; the exceptional Mountain Fair during the last weekend in July; and the summer-long Performance in the Park Series. And, of course, this is prime skiing country: Aspen is 30 minutes away and cross-country enthusiasts will enjoy the Spring Gulch Cross-Country Center. Looking for something less strenuous? Yampah Spa offers total pampering.

AMBIANCE INN BED & BREAKFAST

66 North Second Street, Carbondale, CO 81623   970-963-3597
Norma & Robert Morris, Resident Owners   800-350-1515
EMAIL *ambiance@compuserve.com*   FAX 970-963-3130
WEBSITE *www.ambianceinn.com*

LOCATION	At Main Street turn left, go to 2nd Street, turn left, and go to the second house on the right.
OPEN	All year
DESCRIPTION	A 1975 two-story contemporary manor.
NO. OF ROOMS	Four rooms with private bathrooms. Norma suggests the Aspen Suite.
RATES	Year-round rates are $50-120 for a single or double, $90-120 for a suite, and the entire B&B rents for $330. There is a minimum stay during holidays. Ask about a cancellation policy.
CREDIT CARDS	MasterCard, Visa
BREAKFAST	Full breakfast is served in the dining room and includes fresh-ground coffee; juices; fruit bowl; homemade breads and muffins; special egg dish, waffles, or French toast; and bacon or sausage. Lunch and "picnics to go" are also available.
AMENITIES	Library, afternoon tea and coffee, TV, radio, phone, robes, and sitting room.
RESTRICTIONS	No smoking, no pets. Children over seven are welcome.
REVIEWED	*The Colorado Guide*
MEMBER	Bed & Breakfast Innkeepers of Colorado, Colorado Hotel and Lodging Association

MT. SOPRIS INN

0165 Mt. Sopris Ranch Road, Carbondale, CO 81623   970-963-2209
Barbara Fasching, Resident Owner   800-437-8675
EMAIL mt.soprisinn@juno.com   FAX 970-963-8975
WEBSITE www.colorado-bnb.com/mtsopris

LOCATION	Three miles southwest of the intersection of Highways 82 and 133. Turn right on Mt. Sopris Ranch Road.
OPEN	May 28 through October 15. Call during the rest of the year.
DESCRIPTION	A 1997 two-story contemporary log country inn with contemporary furnishings on 14 acres along the Crystal River, 40 feet above the Crystal Valley.
NO. OF ROOMS	Fourteen rooms with private bathrooms.
RATES	Year-round rates are $120-175 for a single or double. The guesthouse rents for $500. There is a minimum stay during weekends and holidays. Cancellation requires seven days' notice.
CREDIT CARDS	MasterCard, Visa
BREAKFAST	Full breakfast, served in the dining room, includes orange juice, fruit plate, and a hot entrée with meat. Advance notice is required for other meals.
AMENITIES	Swimming pool, grand piano, hot tubs, all rooms with telephones and TVs, pool table, fireplaces, VIP board room, rooms with handicapped access.
RESTRICTIONS	No smoking, no pets, no children
REVIEWED	The Colorado Guide, Recommended Country Inns Rocky Mountain Region
MEMBER	Bed & Breakfast Innkeepers of Colorado, Professional Association of Innkeepers International

ROARING FORK RIVER BED & BREAKFAST

16613 Highway 82, Carbondale, CO 81623   970-963-8853
Lou & Diana Moore, Resident Owners   800-328-9337
                                               FAX 970-963-8853 (call first)

LOCATION	Three-and-a-half miles south of Carbondale on Highway 82.
OPEN	All year
DESCRIPTION	A country house.

NO. OF ROOMS	Three rooms with private bathrooms.
RATES	Year-round rate is $75 for a single or double.
CREDIT CARDS	MasterCard, Visa
BREAKFAST	Full country-style breakfast is served in the dining room.
AMENITIES	Outdoor hot tub.
RESTRICTIONS	No smoking, no pets, children are welcome.

VAN HORN HOUSE AT LIONS RIDGE

0318 Lions Ridge Road, Carbondale, CO 81623   970-963-3606
Susan & John Laatsch, Innkeepers   888-453-0395
EMAIL jlaatsch@aol.com   FAX 970-963-1681

LOCATION	Exit I-70 at Glenwood Springs. Take Highway 82 east toward Aspen. Approximately 15 miles out of Glenwood Springs, take a left at the stoplight at a crossroads. Go about one long block and turn right onto Lions Ridge Road. Take two switchback turns and the B&B is the first house on the right. Look for the oversized wildflower-patterned mailbox.
OPEN	All year
DESCRIPTION	A 1980 three-story European cottage decorated with antiques and old family items, with a superb view of Mount Sopris.
NO. OF ROOMS	Two bedrooms with private bathrooms and two rooms with one shared bathroom. Susan and John suggest the Minnie Maud Room.
RATES	Year-round rates are $65-80 for a single or double and $55-60 for a single or double with a shared bathroom. There is a minimum stay during the last full weekend of July and some holiday weekends. Cancellation requires 10 days' notice for full refund; 50% charge if notice is not given within 10 days and the room cannot be rebooked.
CREDIT CARDS	MasterCard, Visa
BREAKFAST	Full breakfast is served in the dining room and includes a first course of fresh fruit; an entrée that may include meat; lots of hot coffee; and tea or other beverages. A summer breakfast might feature nectarines with yogurt and honey sauce, fresh blueberry baked pancakes, turkey sausage and melon garnish. Winter breakfasts are heartier. Dietary restrictions and preferences can be accommodated with prior notice.
AMENITIES	Guest lounge with satellite TV/VCR and a library of videos; lots of books, magazines, and games for those few days when the weather isn't perfect; each room has bathrobes (warm ones in winter, lighter ones in summer); wonderful hot tub under the stars; extensive library of menus of area restaurants, as well as local restaurant

	reviews; flowers and perhaps a card for special occasions such as anniversaries, honeymoons, or birthdays (with advance notice); fresh flowers from the beautiful garden in summer.
RESTRICTIONS	No smoking, no pets, children over eight are welcome. "Under special circumstances, we will consider younger children," says Susan. Sophia (Sofi) and Alexis (Alex) are the American multibreed cats (a breed of our creation). "Our 'girls' are rather timid, but will make their appearances if coaxed properly!"
REVIEWED	*Recommended Inns*
MEMBER	Bed & Breakfast Innkeepers of Colorado

CASCADE
(COLORADO SPRINGS)

A small residential mountain community in the Ute Pass area, Cascade offers access to the Pikes Peak Highway toll road. Wind your way up to the 14,100-foot summit—or enjoy something only slightly less down-to-earth: explore Santa's Village and theme park at the North Pole. About 15 miles west of downtown Colorado Springs on Highway 24.

BLACK BEAR INN OF PIKES PEAK

5250 Pikes Peak Highway, Cascade, CO 80809   719-684-0151
Christi Heidenreich, Innkeeper   877-732-5232

LOCATION	Ten miles west of I-25 on Highway 24. From downtown Colorado Springs, follow signs to the Pikes Peak Highway and go approximately one mile.
OPEN	All year
DESCRIPTION	A 1994 two-story New England farmhouse with mountain views and comfortable furnishings.
NO. OF ROOMS	Nine rooms with private bathrooms. Try room 8.
RATES	Year-round rates for a single or double are $70-100, and the entire inn rents for $685. There is no minimum stay and cancellation requires 10 days' notice.
CREDIT CARDS	Discover, MasterCard, Visa
BREAKFAST	Full breakfast is served in the dining room and includes a buffet with fruit platters, fresh rolls, pastries, cereal, yogurt, and a main dish, such as breakfast burritos, stuffed French toast, or breakfast pizza.
AMENITIES	Hot tub in the woods, hiking trails from the inn, wine and beer, cookies, large deck, great views from all rooms, handicapped access, robes.

RESTRICTIONS	No smoking, no pets, children over 10 are welcome. Tytus is the resident Lab.
REVIEWED	*The Colorado Guide*
MEMBER	Colorado Bed & Breakfast Association
RATED	AAA 3 Diamonds

EASTHOLME IN THE ROCKIES

4445 Haggerman Street, Cascade, CO 80809   800-672-9901
Terry Thompson & Family, Innkeepers
EMAIL *eastholm@rmi.net*   WEBSITE *www.eastholme.com*

LOCATION	From I-25 in Colorado Springs, take exit 141 to Highway 24 and go west for 11 miles. Exit to the right at the Cascade exit, drive one-and-a-half blocks, turn right on Topeka, go one block, and turn right onto Haggerman Street.
OPEN	All year
DESCRIPTION	A restored 1885 three-story Victorian with front porch and balcony, listed on the Colorado Historic Register.
NO. OF ROOMS	Four rooms with private bathrooms and two rooms share one bathroom. Pick the Marriott Suite.
RATES	Year-round rates are $79-89 for a single or double with a private bathroom, $69 for a single or double with a shared bathroom, $99 for a suite, $135 for a cottage, and $784 for the entire B&B. There is no minimum stay and cancellation requires seven days' notice less 10% of the deposit.
CREDIT CARDS	American Express, Discover, MasterCard, Visa
BREAKFAST	Full gourmet breakfast is served in the dining room and includes fresh-from-the-oven breads, pastries, main courses such as frittatas, and fruit juice, coffee, and tea.
AMENITIES	Guest parlor with fireplace, library, piano, TV/VCR, guest kitchen, 40-foot balcony, and hiking trails nearby.
RESTRICTIONS	No smoking. The resident dogs are Chessie and Ebony and the cat is called Owen.
REVIEWED	*Recommended Country Inns Rocky Mountain Region*
MEMBER	Bed & Breakfast Innkeepers of Colorado
AWARDS	1989 Preservation Excellence Award by Colorado Preservation, Inc.; Ute Pass Landmark designated by 1976 Bicentennial Committee
KUDOS/COMMENTS	"A wonderful tribute to western hospitality!" "Terry is making the place look like new." (1996)

Rocky Mountain Lodge & Cabins

4680 Haggerman Road, Cascade, CO 80205   719-684-2521

CEDAREDGE

Known as the southern gateway to the Grand Mesa, this is slightly off the beaten path . . . and worth the detour. The Apple Festival in October is a major event. From Grand Junction, six miles southeast at the southern terminus of Scenic Highway 65.

CEDARS' EDGE LLAMAS BED & BREAKFAST

2169 Highway 65, Cedaredge, CO 81413   970-856-6836
Ray & Gail Record, Resident Owners
EMAIL rrecord2@juneau.com   WEBSITE *www.llamabandb.com*

LOCATION	Five miles north of Cedaredge on Highway 65.
OPEN	All year
DESCRIPTION	A 1990 two-story contemporary cedar country inn and cottage located on a working llama farm and decorated with country furnishings.
NO. OF ROOMS	Four rooms with private bathrooms. Try the Hummingbird Suite.
RATES	Year-round rates are $50-85 for a double, $85 for the suite, and $285 for the entire B&B. There is a minimum stay during July 4th and Labor Day weekends and a two-week cancellation policy.
CREDIT CARDS	MasterCard, Visa
BREAKFAST	Full "hearty country fare" is served in the dining room or guestrooms, or on decks. Entrées may be whole-wheat blueberry pancakes, sausage casserole, mushroom scramble, or French toast, served with hashbrowns, bacon or sausage, fresh fruit, and beverages.
AMENITIES	Llamas, llamas, llamas, "all the llama petting you can stand," private decks. "Plus, llamas!"
RESTRICTIONS	No smoking, no pets, children are welcome. There is an outdoor golden retriever named Woody (Sir Woodward of Cedars' Edge).
REVIEWED	*Recommended Country Inns Rocky Mountain Region, Frommer's Colorado, The Non-Smokers Guide to Bed & Breakfasts*
MEMBER	Bed & Breakfast Innkeepers of Colorado

EAGLE'S NEST HUNTING LODGE

2450 Highway 65, Cedaredge, CO 81413   970-856-3521
Ron Moore, Resident Owner

CENTRAL CITY

This small Victorian mining town and National Historic District is known for its summer opera, limited-stakes gambling, and its Jazz Festival. Other worthwhile festivals include Freedomfest and Madame Lou Bunch Days. Thirty miles west of Denver on Highway 119.

CHATEAU L'ACADIENNE

325 Spring Street, Central City, CO 80427   303-582-5209
James & Shirley Voorhies, Innkeepers   800-834-5209
Some French and Spanish spoken
EMAIL *72202.456@compuserve.com*

LOCATION	Approximately 35 miles from Denver, take I-70 west to Central City (exit 244). Follow Highway 119 north to Black Hawk. Turn left at the third traffic light (Highway 279) and drive one mile up to Central City. Turn left at Spring Street (emergency signal) and proceed past the Big T parking lot to the first Y in the road. Bear left at the Y. Park in front of the blue garage doors.
OPEN	All year
DESCRIPTION	An 1876 one-story brick Victorian host home beautifully restored to reflect the architecture and style of the early pioneers of Central City. Chateau L'Acadienne means "Big House of the Cajun." Three rooms are adorned in the elegance of Louisiana French, English Victorian, and mountain decor. Listed on the National Historic Register.
NO. OF ROOMS	Three rooms share one bathroom. Try the Emerald Room.
RATES	High-season rates are $60-94 for a single or double and $180-230 for the entire B&B. Low-season rates are $55-89 for a single or double and $160-224 for the entire B&B. There is no minimum stay and cancellation requires 72 hours' notice.
CREDIT CARDS	Discover, MasterCard, Visa
BREAKFAST	Full gourmet breakfast is served in the dining room or the guestrooms. Selections may include baked eggs L'Acadienne, Grand Marnier French toast, crispy potato quiche, and German apple pancakes.

| AMENITIES | Fresh-baked bread and muffins with homemade jams; bottomless cookie jar with hot cocoa, tea, cider, and coffee; fresh fruit is also available; casino gambling and opera are within walking distance. |
| RESTRICTIONS | Bear Cat is the resident cat. |

GREGORY INN

341 Gregory, Central City, CO 80205   303-582-5561

HIGH STREET INN

215 West High Street, Central City, CO 80427   303-582-0622
Patrick & Selina Hughes, Resident Owners

LOCATION	In Central City go right on County Road (next to St. James Church), take the first left onto West High Street.
OPEN	All year
DESCRIPTION	An 1890 Victorian with front porch and comfortable furnishings.
NO. OF ROOMS	Three rooms with private bathrooms. The Hughes' like the Stained-Glass Room.
RATES	Rates are $65-85 for a double. There is no minimum stay and cancellation requires 72 hours' notice.
CREDIT CARDS	Discover, MasterCard, Visa
BREAKFAST	Full breakfast, served in the dining room, includes ham and cheese omelets, meats, hash browns, homemade bread and biscuits, fruit, coffee, tea, and juice.
AMENITIES	Fresh flowers, terry robes, turndown service, carafe of ice water, chocolates, cookies, fruit and beverages always available, TV in all rooms, free parking, walking distance to casinos and opera.
RESTRICTIONS	No pets (resident dog is Toby), supervised children are welcome, smoking allowed on porch and in front room.

THE PRIMROSE INN

310 East First High Street, Central City, CO 80427   303-582-5808
Janice Ward, Resident Owner

| LOCATION | Two blocks northeast of the central business district. |

OPEN	All year
DESCRIPTION	An 1864 two-story Victorian with Victorian furnishings.
NO. OF ROOMS	Three rooms share one bathroom. Choose the front room upstairs.
RATES	Year-round rates are $85 for a single or double with a shared bathroom and $150 for a three-room suite. There is no minimum stay and cancellation requires seven days' notice.
CREDIT CARDS	No
BREAKFAST	Continental breakfast is served in the dining room or kitchen.
AMENITIES	Oversized towels, robes, TV in den, piano in parlor, lawn chairs in the garden, off-street parking.
RESTRICTIONS	Smoking restricted to kitchen, no pets

WINFIELD SCOTT GUEST QUARTERS

210 Hooper Street, Central City, CO 80427   303-582-3433
Patty & Scott Webb, Resident Owners   FAX 303-582-3434
EMAIL *winfields@aol.com*

LOCATION	At the traffic light (there is only one), turn left and follow Spring Street up the hill past two parking lots and three houses on the right. You will then come to an open lot, at the end of which is Hooper Street; turn right and go up the hill.

Winfield Scott Guest Quarters, Central City

OPEN	All year
DESCRIPTION	A 1985 two-story Victorian guest house with country and southwestern decor, situated on one acre of beautiful grounds.
NO. OF ROOMS	All rooms have private bathrooms.
RATES	Year-round rates are $84 for a one-bedroom suite and $159 for a two-bedroom suite. There is a three-day minimum stay during weekends and cancellations require one weeks' notice.
CREDIT CARDS	Discover, MasterCard, Visa
BREAKFAST	Continental plus is served in the guestrooms and includes baked breads and muffins, fresh fruit salad, hot and cold cereals, milk, orange juice, coffee, tea, and hot chocolate.
AMENITIES	On quiet grounds with an excellent view. TV/VCR, fireplaces, kitchens, and phones are in the suites. Deck with barbecue grill, fax and copier are available.
RESTRICTIONS	No smoking, no pets, children over two are welcome. Please inquire about children under two. The English setter is Winnie.
REVIEWED	*The Colorado Guide*
MEMBER	Bed & Breakfast Innkeepers of Colorado

CHIPITA PARK
(COLORADO SPRINGS)

One of a cluster of small mountain towns in the Ute Pass area, Chipita Park is handy to the entrance of Pikes Peak Highway and lies at the edge of Pike National Forest. About 15 miles west of Colorado Springs on Highway 24.

TOP OF TIMPA

5620 Timpa Road, Chipita Park, CO 80809   719-684-2296
Dick & Elizabeth Dolbee, Resident Owners
EMAIL *dolbee@pciswis.com*

LOCATION	Between Cascade and Green Mountain Falls, take Highway 24 west to the Pikes Peak/Cascade exit, head northwest on Chipita Park Road, then go south on Timpa Road all the way to the top.
OPEN	All year
DESCRIPTION	A 1957 mountain compound with eclectic furnishings.
NO. OF ROOMS	Three suites and a honeymoon cottage with private bathrooms.
RATES	Year-round rates are $75-80 for a single or double. The honeymoon cottage is $90. There is a reservation/cancellation policy.

CREDIT CARDS	No
BREAKFAST	Full breakfast is served in the dining room.
AMENITIES	Eight-person hot tub; robes and cable TV in every room; radio, phone, refrigerators in rooms; one suite and the cottage have fireplaces; complimentary evening snacks; picnic, laundry, and meeting facilities.
RESTRICTIONS	No smoking, no pets

COALMONT

A little hideaway 45 miles northeast of Steamboat Springs and south of Walden off Highway 14, Coalmont is the southern jumping-off place for Delany Butte Lakes (big fish!), the North Platte and North Forks Rivers, and various creeks.

SHAMROCK RANCH

4363 County Road 11, Coalmont, CO 80430   *970-723-8413*
Cindy Wilson, Resident Owner

LOCATION	Highway 14 north from Highway 40, 16 miles to County Road 28, right on County Road 28. Go one mile and take a right fork onto a gravel road. The sign for the ranch is 4.5 miles on the left.
OPEN	Memorial Day through September 30
DESCRIPTION	A 1934 rustic lodge inn with cabins decorated with Western furnishings and situated on 400 acres.
NO. OF ROOMS	Two rooms with private bathrooms and two rooms share one bathroom. Try the Corner Room.
RATES	Seasonal rate is $100 for a single or double with a private bathroom and there is no minimum stay.
CREDIT CARDS	Visa
BREAKFAST	Full breakfast, served in the dining room, includes a variety of egg dishes, meats, and baked goods. Dinner is also included in the rates.
AMENITIES	Private trophy trout fishing on property, hot tub, beverages and hors d'oeuvres, large rock fireplace, wet bar, refrigerator, horseback riding.
RESTRICTIONS	No pets. A managerie of pets and farm animals lives on the ranch. Children over 10 are welcome.
MEMBER	Professional Association of Innkeepers International, Colorado Hotel and Lodging Association

COLLBRAN

SPRUCE INN BED & BREAKFAST

112 Main Street, Collbran, CO 81624   970-487-0225

COLORADO SPRINGS

Purple mountain's majesty pretty much begins right here at the base of Pikes Peak. The state's second largest city is a major tourist, sports, and military-industrial center. Some places to explore: the Olympic Training Center, US Air Force Academy, Garden of the Gods, the Cheyenne Mountain Zoo, Pro Rodeo Hall of Fame, and competitive cycling events at the velodrome. In July, racecar drivers, possessed of less sense than the rest of us, take to the clouds in the grueling Pikes Peak Hill Climb. In August the Pikes Peak or Bust Rodeo kicks into gear, and in September the Hot Air Balloon Classic takes off. Check out the Pikes Peak Cog Railway. From Denver, 65 miles south on I-25.

AWARENEST VICTORIAN B&B

1218 West Pikes Peak Avenue   719-630-8241
Colorado Springs, CO 80904
Rex & Karla Hefferan, Resident Owners

KUDOS/COMMENTS   "The perfect spot for a secluded getaway. Only one room but Karla dotes on her guests." "Charming, comfortable parlor and beautiful dining room with stained glass." (1996) "Great Victorian decor, attention to detail, excellent service, and many amenities." (1999)

BLACK FOREST BED & BREAKFAST

11170 Black Forest Road, Colorado Springs, CO 80908   719-495-4208
Robert & Susan Putnam, Innkeepers   800-809-9901
"Survival Spanish" spoken   FAX 719-495-0688
EMAIL *blackforestbandb@msn.com*   WEBSITE *www.blackforestbb.com*

LOCATION   From I-25, take Woodmen exit 149 east for six miles to Black Forest Road. Turn left and go north for three miles—at the Baptist

Black Forest Bed & Breakfast, Colorado Springs

church on the right, look 0.25 mile farther north for an orange mailbox on the left side of the road. Turn left between stone pillars and drive up the road another 0.25 mile.

OPEN	All year
DESCRIPTION	A massive 1998 two-story log gambrel host home with rustic, romantic, country decor, on 20 acres of pines with views of the mountains and city lights.
NO. OF ROOMS	Five bedrooms with private bathrooms. Try the Haven Room.
RATES	Year-round rates are $75-100 for a single or double, $125-175 for a suite, and $625 for the entire B&B. There is a minimum stay during holidays and cancellation requires one weeks' notice less a $15 fee.
CREDIT CARDS	American Express, Discover, MasterCard, Visa
BREAKFAST	A breakfast tray of hot muffins and fresh fruit is brought to guestrooms. All rooms have kitchens stocked with milk, juice, assorted coffees, teas, cocoas, and cereals.
AMENITIES	Microwave popcorn and cocoa stocked in kitchens; whirlpool tubs; fireplaces; indoor lap pool; sauna; fitness center; playground; copy machine, fax, and modem hookups; laundry room; wheelchair access; areas suitable for small receptions, meetings, or retreats.
RESTRICTIONS	No smoking, no pets, children are welcome. Honey is the resident golden retriever; Lynx and Little Orphan Andy are the cats. Honey will take you on a guided tour of "her" 20 acres.
MEMBER	Bed & Breakfast Innkeepers of Colorado, Bed & Breakfasts of the Pikes Peak Area

CHALICE HOUSE, A BED & BREAKFAST

1116 North Wahsatch Avenue
Colorado Springs, CO 80903
LoriLane Duke, Innkeeper
EMAIL *chalice@aol.com*

719-475-7505
888-475-7505
FAX 719-633-4686
WEBSITE *www.bbonline.com/co/chalicehouse/*

LOCATION	Take I-25 to exit 143 (Uintah Street) and go east 0.7 mile, turn right (south), and the B&B is the fifth house on the right.
OPEN	All year
DESCRIPTION	A 1922 two-story Georgian colonial inn with eclectic, turn-of-the-century decor, original lighting, moss-rock fireplace, oak hardwood floors, and sunny colonial windows.
NO. OF ROOMS	Two bedrooms with private bathrooms and two rooms with one shared bathroom. Try the Avebury Suite.
RATES	High-season rates are $78-98 for a single or double with a private bathroom, $58-78 for a single or double with a shared bathroom, $108-118 for a suite, and $118-128 for the cottage. Regular rates are $68-88 for a single or double with a private bathroom, $48-68 for a single or double with a shared bathroom, $108-118 for a suite, and $108-118 for the cottage. Discounts are available for stays of three nights or more and seven nights or more. There is a minimum stay during holidays and special events.
CREDIT CARDS	American Express, Discover, MasterCard, Visa
BREAKFAST	Full hearty breakfast is served in the dining room and includes juice, fresh fruit, muffins, and a main dish such as baked omelets,

Chalice House, A Bed & Breakfast, Colorado Springs

waffles, or French toast surprise. Vegan, vegetarian, and lactose-free diets are accommodated.

AMENITIES	Fresh flowers; fluffy terry robes; hot tub on patio; space for small intimate meetings, weddings, and workshops; guestrooms and cottage are air-conditioned; snacks in the dining room; tea and homemade shortbread available daily.
RESTRICTIONS	No smoking, children are welcome. Guinevere is the resident tabby/Maine coon cat. "She's the queen and is very loving, but she's shy and usually stays in the basement."
MEMBER	Bed & Breakfast Innkeepers of Colorado, Authentic Inns of the Pikes Peak Region, Pikes Peak Region Bed & Breakfasts

CHEYENNE CANON INN

2030 West Cheyenne Road, Colorado Springs, CO 80906   719-633-0625
Steve & Nancy Stannard, Innkeepers   800-633-0625
EMAIL *75552.2251@compuserve.com*   FAX 719-633-8826
WEBSITE *www.cheyennecanoninn.com*

LOCATION	From I-25, take exit 141B, then Tejon Street south to West Cheyenne Boulevard. Go west for 2.6 miles and turn right into Cheyenne Canyon Park. The driveway is 200 feet past the gate on the right.
OPEN	All year
DESCRIPTION	A 1921 two-story Mission-style mansion with international decor at the foot of Pikes Peak. This 12,000-square-foot inn was originally built as a casino and bordello.
NO. OF ROOMS	Ten rooms with private bathrooms. Your hosts recommend the Petite Maison.
RATES	Year-round rates are $90-150 for a single or double, a suite is $175-190, and the entire B&B rents for $1300. A multinight stay is required during some weekends. Cancellation requires five days' notice.
CREDIT CARDS	American Express, Discover, MasterCard, Visa
BREAKFAST	Full breakfast is served in the dining room or on the front porch and generally includes fresh fruit, quiche, or waffles.
AMENITIES	Bathrobes, hot tub, library, cookies, wine and cheese, meeting facilities, air conditioning.
RESTRICTIONS	No smoking, no pets
MEMBER	Bed & Breakfast Innkeepers of Colorado, American Bed & Breakfast Association, Professional Association of Innkeepers International

Cheyenne Canon Inn, Colorado Springs

RATED	AAA 4 Diamonds, ABBA 4 Crowns
KUDOS/COMMENTS	"Most striking location, great house with important history and unique decor." "Spectacular mansion with theme rooms." "Very spacious, well-appointed rooms. Great location." (1996) "Unbelievable, breathtaking location; huge rooms, historic setting; a real gem." (1997)

CRESCENT LILY INN

6 Boulder Court, Colorado Springs, CO 80903   *719-442-2331*
Lin Moeller, Innkeeper   *800-869-2721*
EMAIL moeller@pcisys.net   *FAX 719-442-6947*
WEBSITE www.crescentlilyinn.com

LOCATION	In downtown Colorado Springs between Boulder and Platt Streets, just west of Cascade facing Boulder Crescent Park.
OPEN	All year
DESCRIPTION	An 1898 three-story Queen Anne Victorian with original tiger's eye oak, beveled leaded glass, Van Briggle tile fireplaces, wraparound porch, French doors, and Victorian decor.
NO. OF ROOMS	Five bedrooms with private bathrooms. Lin suggests the Day Lily Suite.

RATES	Year-round rates are $80-125 for a single or double and $125 for a suite. There is no minimum stay and cancellation requires seven days' notice, 30 days during holidays and special events.
CREDIT CARDS	American Express, Discover, MasterCard, Visa
BREAKFAST	Full breakfast is served in the dining room or guestrooms and includes an assortment of beverages, cereal, biscotti, and a unique gourmet hot entrée.
AMENITIES	Fresh flowers, each room decorated with antiques, small meeting space, wine and cheese with hors d'oeuvres each evening, Jacuzzi tubs, big-screen TV/VCR and music system available, wedding package, in-room fireplace.
RESTRICTIONS	No smoking, no pets, children over 12 are welcome, younger children may be welcome with prior arrangements.
MEMBER	Bed & Breakfast Innkeepers of Colorado, Bed & Breakfasts of the Pikes Peak Region, Elegant Business Inns

DOGS' BEST FRIEND BED & BREAKFAST

7305 Maine Lane, Colorado Springs, CO 80922   719-495-2983
Bill Fuqua, Resident Owner
Dog spoken

LOCATION	From I-25, go east on Woodman Road for approximately six miles, turn south onto Maine Lane, and go one block.
OPEN	All year
DESCRIPTION	A 1990 country inn doghouse with a clean and comfortable interior.
NO. OF ROOMS	Forty units with private baths, heating, and air conditioning.
RATES	Year-round rates are $9-11 for a single. There is a three-day cancellation policy.
CREDIT CARDS	No
BREAKFAST	Full lamb and rice breakfast is served.
AMENITIES	Large open outside play areas for social gatherings, organized sports. Private in-home lessons, pre-puppy consultations.
RESTRICTIONS	No smoking, proof of current innoculations must be on file.
REVIEWED	*The Best Dog B&Bs in the World; Dog B&Bs, USA and Canada*
RATED	AAA 3 Bowls

THE HEARTHSTONE INN

506 North Cascade Avenue, Colorado Springs, CO 80903   *719-473-4413*
Dot Williams & Ruth Williams, Owners   *800-521-1885*
FAX 719-473-1322

LOCATION	On the corner of Cascade and Saint Vrain, four blocks from downtown.
OPEN	All year
DESCRIPTION	Two three-story 1885/1900 Victorian inns decorated with Victorian furnishings and listed on both the National and State Historic Registers.
NO. OF ROOMS	Twenty-three rooms with private bathrooms and two rooms share one bathroom.
RATES	Year-round rates are $90-150 for a single or double with a private bathroom, $70-75 for a single or double with a shared bathroom, and $160-170 for a suite. There is a two-night minimum stay on Memorial Day, Labor Day, and during college graduation. There is a reservation/cancellation policy.
CREDIT CARDS	American Express, MasterCard, Visa
BREAKFAST	Full breakfast, served in the dining room, includes a unique egg entrée, homemade bread, fresh fruit, and beverages. Group luncheons prepared with advance notice.
AMENITIES	Some rooms have fireplaces and private porches, early breakfast available, conference space for 48, one room is wheelchair accessible.
RESTRICTIONS	No smoking, no pets. Watch out for the resident squirrel, Jaws.
REVIEWED	*Country Inns & Backroads, Recommended Country Inns Rocky Mountain Region*
MEMBER	Independent Innkeepers Association, Professional Association of Innkeepers International, Distinctive Inns of Colorado, Colorado Hotel and Lodging Association
RATED	AAA 3 Diamonds, Mobil 3 Stars
KUDOS/COMMENTS	"Dot and Ruth have been in business for 20 years and have perfected the 'art' of innkeeping better than anyone else I know." "Wonderful antiques, located on one of the most beautiful streets in Colorado Springs." "Delightful food." "The Hearthstone Inn was the inspiration for the decor, hospitality, etc. of our inn." "Great breakfasts and impeccable housekeeping." (1997)

Holden House 1902 Bed & Breakfast Inn, Colorado Springs

HOLDEN HOUSE 1902 BED & BREAKFAST INN

1102 West Pikes Peak Avenue, Colorado Springs, CO 80904   719-471-3980
Sallie & Welling Clark, Resident Owners   *FAX 719-471-4740*
EMAIL *HoldenHouse@worldnet.att.net*
WEBSITE *www.bbonline.com/co/holden/*

LOCATION	One mile west of downtown near the Historic District. From I-25, take exit 141 (Highway 24) and go west. Take a right onto 8th Street, left on West Colorado, right on 11th, and go down one block.
OPEN	All year
DESCRIPTION	A 1902 two-story Victorian Colonial Revival, a carriage house, and an 1898 Victorian inn, all furnished with antiques and family heirlooms.
NO. OF ROOMS	Five suites with private bathrooms. Sallie suggests the Independence Suite.
RATES	Year-round rates are $120-135 for a single or double. There is a minimum stay of two to three nights during holidays, weekends, special events, and from May 15 through October 15. Cancellation requires eight days' notice, 30 days for holidays and special events with a $15 fee.
CREDIT CARDS	American Express, Diners Club, Discover, MasterCard, Visa

BREAKFAST	Full breakfast, served in the dining room, includes fresh fruit; muffins such as blueberry corn or oatmeal raspberry; a main entrée such as southwestern eggs fiesta, German puff pancakes, or ruffled crepes Isabel; plus juice, freshly ground coffee, or tea.
AMENITIES	Suites with fireplaces and tubs for two, telephones, TV in the parlor, guest refrigerator, 24-hour coffee/tea service, bottomless cookie jar, turndown service, fax and copier available, complimentary bottled water, air conditioning, off-street parking, and one suite with limited handicapped access. Some suites offer a "breakfast in suite" romance package for an extra $10 and a two-night minimum.
RESTRICTIONS	No smoking, no pets. "The inn is unsuitable for children." The two resident cats, Muffin and Mingtoy, have been featured in *Cats* magazine and *Cat Fancy*.
REVIEWED	*America's Wonderful Little Hotels & Inns, Recommended Country Inns of the Rocky Mountain Region,, The Colorado Guide, Fodor's Colorado, Frommer's Colorado, Best Choices in Colorado*
MEMBER	Bed & Breakfast Innkeepers of Colorado, Professional Association of Innkeepers International, Colorado Hotel and Lodging Association
RATED	AAA 3 Diamonds, Mobil 3 Stars
AWARDS	*Country Inns* magazine, 1993 Best Inn Buys; Waverly Country Inns' Inn of the Year (Independence Suite); Inn Times' Top 50 Inns.
KUDOS/COMMENTS	"They have the best B&B inn in the entire state." (1994) "Premiere B&B in the area, quality of service and design maintained at highest standards." (1999)

HUGHES HACIENDA B&B

12060 Calle Corvo, Colorado Springs, CO 80926   719-576-2060
Wayne Hughes, Resident Owner
EMAIL *hacienda@kktv.com*   WEBSITE *www.hugheshacienda.com*

LOCATION	Twenty minutes from downtown in the Broadmore Hotel area.
OPEN	All year
DESCRIPTION	A Spanish hacienda in a mountain setting on 19 acres.
NO. OF ROOMS	Two bedrooms with private bathrooms.
RATES	Year-round rates are $100-150 for a single or double.
CREDIT CARDS	American Express, MasterCard, Visa
BREAKFAST	Full gourmet, southwestern-style breakfast is served.

AMENITIES   Hot tub, hiking trails, fireside and patio dining.

RESTRICTIONS   No smoking, no pets, children negotiable.

KUDOS/COMMENTS   "A unique B&B in a truly spectacular spot, exceptional host and
                  food." "Great breakfast spot." (1996)

MONACO'S LODGE BED & BREAKFAST

1116 West Pikes Peak Avenue   719-475-8853
Colorado Springs, CO 80904

OLD TOWN GUEST HOUSE

115 South 26th Street, Colorado Springs, CO 80904   719-632-9194
Kaye & David Caster, Innkeepers   888-375-4210
EMAIL *oldtown@rmi.net*   FAX 719-632-9026
WEBSITE *www.bbonline.com/co/oldtown*

LOCATION   Take exit 141 off I-25 onto Highway 24, go to 26th Street and turn
                  right. The guest house is two blocks north on the right.

OPEN   All year

DESCRIPTION   A 1997 three-story red-brick federal-style guest house with upscale
                  eclectic decor.

NO. OF ROOMS   Eight bedrooms with private bathrooms.

RATES   Year-round rates are $95-175 for a single or double. There is a
                  minimum stay during holidays and cancellation requires two weeks'
                  notice.

CREDIT CARDS   American Express, Discover, MasterCard, Visa

BREAKFAST   Full breakfast is served in the dining room or on the patio and
                  includes fruit, pastry, an entrée, side dishes, juices, coffee, and tea.
                  Special dietary requests are accommodated.

AMENITIES   Wine and hors d'oeuvres during check in, all rooms air conditioned,
                  dedicated voice and data ports, ADA room, elevator, soundproof
                  walls, TV/VCR, fireplaces, private hot tubs, steam showers, private
                  conference facility.

RESTRICTIONS   No smoking inside, no pets, children over 16 are welcome.

REVIEWED   *America's Favorite Inns, B&Bs and Small Hotels*

MEMBER   Bed & Breakfast Innkeepers of Colorado, Professional Association
                  of Innkeepers International, Colorado Hotel & Lodging
                  Association

RATED   AAA 4 Diamonds

Old Town Guest House, Colorado Springs

OUR HEARTS INN OLD COLORADO CITY

2215 West Colorado Avenue, Colorado Springs, CO 80904   719-473-8684
Andy & Pat Fejedelem, Resident Owners   800-533-7095
WEBSITE *www.bbonline.com/co/ourhearts/*   FAX 719-634-4954

LOCATION	Highway 24 to 21st Street, go north three blocks to Colorado Avenue and turn right.
OPEN	All year
DESCRIPTION	An 1895 two-story Victorian inn with hand-stenciled interior, original plaster walls, curved vaulted ceilings, and antique furnishings.
NO. OF ROOMS	Four rooms with private bathrooms. "Hearts Out West," a cottage, is the owner's favorite.
RATES	May through October, rates are $85-120 for a single or double. Off-season rates are discounted. There is a minimum stay during holiday weekends and special events. Cancellation requires seven days' notice.
CREDIT CARDS	American Express, Diners Club, Discover, MasterCard, Visa
BREAKFAST	Full hearty breakfast, served in the dining room, includes juice, fruit, sweet treat, home-baked bread, and an entrée.

Our Hearts Inn Old Colorado City, Colorado Springs

AMENITIES	Air conditioning in all rooms, cable TV in two rooms, separate sleeping quarters in two rooms, Jacuzzi, fireplace, cookies around the clock, carafe for hot drinks in each room, gourmet coffee and grinder in cottage, guest refrigerator, guest phone line.
RESTRICTIONS	No smoking, no pets, children in cottage only. BB is the resident Parakeet. BB stays in the cage at all times.
REVIEWED	*Victorian Voyages: US Travel Guide for Victorian Era Enthusiasts*
MEMBER	Bed & Breakfast Innkeepers of Colorado, Authentic Inns of the Pikes Peak Region, Westside Innkeepers Association
KUDOS/COMMENTS	"Quaint country decor, homey hand stenciling adds a personal touch." (1996) "Beautiful French garden, friendly atmosphere, good breakfast." (1997)

THE PAINTED LADY BED & BREAKFAST INN

1318 West Colorado Avenue, Colorado Springs, CO 80904   719-473-3165
Valerie & Zan Maslowski, Innkeepers   800-370-3165
EMAIL *paintedladyinn@worldnet.att.net*   FAX 719-635-1396
WEBSITE *www.bbonline.com/co/paintedlady/*

LOCATION	From I-25, take exit 141 (Cimarron Street). Turn left onto Cimarron Street and take a right at the first intersection onto 8th Street. Turn left onto Colorado Avenue, right onto 14th Street, and

go half a block before turning right into the alleyway. The parking lot is midblock on the right. Come to the front door.

OPEN	All year
DESCRIPTION	An 1894 three-story Victorian inn featuring gingerbread trim, a wraparound porch and balcony, and eclectic, relaxed Victorian furnishings.
NO. OF ROOMS	Three bedrooms with private bathrooms. Try Violet's Suite.
RATES	Year-round rates are $100-150 for a single or double and $250-500 for a suite. There is a minimum stay during holidays and special events. Cancellation requires 10 days' notice, 30 days during holidays and special events.
CREDIT CARDS	American Express, Discover, MasterCard, Visa
BREAKFAST	Full hearty breakfast is served in the dining room and includes fruit, juice, baked goods, and a hot entrée that is different each day. Special dietary needs can be accommodated with advance notice. There is a special off-season (November through March) dinner-in-suite package available as well.
AMENITIES	Private outdoor hot tub; in-suite fireplace; oversized or two-person soaking tub; 24-hour coffee, tea, and cookies; cool summer drinks in afternoon.
RESTRICTIONS	No smoking, no pets, children over four are welcome. Zandra is the resident cat of the overfed variety who is "as much a partner in the innkeeping business as the human innkeeper . . . a true silent partner."
MEMBER	Bed & Breakfast Innkeepers of Colorado, Authentic Inns of the Pikes Peak Region, Westside Innkeepers Association

ROOM AT THE INN BED & BREAKFAST

618 North Nevada Avenue, Colorado Springs, CO 80903   719-442-1896
Jan & Chick McCormick, Resident Owners   800-579-4621
EMAIL *roomatinn@pcisys.net*   FAX 719-442-6802
WEBSITE *www.roomattheinn.com*

LOCATION	Half a mile north of downtown and 0.5 mile east and south of the Uintah Street exit (143) off I-25.
OPEN	All year
DESCRIPTION	An 1896 three-story Queen Anne Victorian inn with a wraparound porch, turret, fish-scale siding, wood floors, ornate staircase, and four original fireplaces. The furnishings are Victorian-era antiques.
NO. OF ROOMS	Seven rooms with private bathrooms. The owners recommend the High Tower Suite.

Room at the Inn Bed & Breakfast, Colorado Springs

RATES	Year-round rates are $70-140 for a single or double. The rate for a suite is $140. There is a minimum stay during high-season weekends, holidays, and special events. Cancellation requires 14 days' notice.
CREDIT CARDS	American Express, Diners Club, Discover, MasterCard, Visa
BREAKFAST	Full breakfast, served in the dining room by candlelight on English china with sterling silver, includes a hot entrée, baked goods, fresh fruit, freshly squeezed orange juice, coffee, and 85 kinds of tea.
AMENITIES	Hot tub on the deck, air conditioning, fresh-cut flowers, robes, custom soaps, turndown service with chocolates, in-room snacks, afternoon tea with fresh-baked goodies, designer linens, adventure and romance packages, on-site massage, fax, handicapped accessible room.
RESTRICTIONS	No smoking, no pets, children over 12 are welcome.
REVIEWED	*Recommended Country Inns Rocky Mountain Region, The Colorado Guide, The Official Guide to American Historic Inns*
MEMBER	Bed & Breakfast Innkeepers of Colorado, Professional Association of Innkeepers International, Bed & Breakfasts of the Pikes Peak Area, Elegant Business Inns of the Pikes Peak Area

RATED	Mobil 3 Stars
AWARDS	Finalist for Bed & Breakfast Innkeepers of Colorado's Inn of the Year award in 1997
KUDOS/COMMENTS	"Wonderful Victorian, great antiques, great location; romantic." (1997) "Fantastic hosts and old-downtown location." (1999)

SERENITY PINES GUESTHOUSE

11910 Windmill Road, Colorado Springs, CO 80908   *719-495-7141*
Bob & Kathy, Innkeepers   *FAX 719-495-7141 (call first)*
EMAIL serenpines@aol.com   *WEBSITE www.colorado-bnb.com/serenpines*

LOCATION	From I-25, take exit 149 and head east on Woodmen Road for 5.5 miles. Go left at Black Forest Road and make an immediate right onto Vollmer Road. Go right at the first blinking light onto Burgess Road, then go 1.4 miles to Windmill and turn left. From the Colorado Springs airport, take Powers Boulevard north, take a right onto Woodmen, go one mile to Black Forest, take a left and follow above directions. Call for directions if coming from the west.
OPEN	All year
DESCRIPTION	A 1997 one-story country ranch cottage with country-Victorian decor, situated on acres of pines.
NO. OF ROOMS	Two suites with private bathrooms.
RATES	Year-round rate is $129 per couple for a suite. Add $10 per additional person. There is a two-night minimum stay on weekends and cancellation requires 14 days' notice.
CREDIT CARDS	American Express, MasterCard, Visa
BREAKFAST	Kathy describes breakfast as "hot and hearty cook-your-own." The kitchen is stocked with milk, eggs, sausage, muffins, breads, croissants, orange juice, homemade jam, specialty coffees and teas, fresh fruit, and hot and cold cereals. The breakfast items are delivered the evening before. A candlelight pasta dinner is also available.
AMENITIES	Shower for two; shampoo, soap, lotion provided; fireplace; evening snacks; sun deck; picnic area with gas barbecue; acres of pines in parklike setting with total privacy; full modern kitchen with dishwasher and microwave; cable TV/VCR, video library; two phones and answering machine; hiking, biking trails; unlimited parking for RVs and horse trailers; badminton and volleyball; evening campfires; games and books; Red Cross-trained babysitter; licensed neuromuscular massage therapist available; will decorate or bake a cake for special occassion; crib; handicapped accessible.
RESTRICTIONS	No smoking, no pets, children are welcome.

Serenity Pines Guest House, Colorado Springs

MEMBER	Bed & Breakfast Innkeepers of Colorado, Bed & Breakfasts of Pikes Peak Area
RATED	Bed & Breakfast Innkeepers of Colorado, Award of Excellence, 1998

VALLEY VIEW HOMESTAY BED & BREAKFAST

2839 Valley Hi Avenue, Colorado Springs, CO 80910   *719-635-2859*
Norm & Norma Merritt, Resident Innkeepers   *FAX 719-635-2859*
(call first)

LOCATION	From Interstate 25 (exit 138), turn left onto Circle Drive and head northeast to Airport Road, turn right (east) for a short block to Valley Hi Avenue, and take a right.
OPEN	April 15 through November 15
DESCRIPTION	A 1960s ranch-style home with contemporary furnishings.
NO. OF ROOMS	One room with a private bathroom and two rooms share one bathroom. The King Suite is the best room.
RATES	Seasonal rates are $85 for a single or double with a private bathroom and $65-75 for a single or double with a shared bathroom. There is a bunkhouse for kids (four bunks renting for $20 each). There is a 25 percent senior discount.

CREDIT CARDS	No
BREAKFAST	Full "western gourmet" breakfast is served in the dining room "to meet your schedule."
AMENITIES	Balcony overlooking the ninth green of the golf course, croquet, swing set and toy room for children, wine and hors d'oeuvres on arrival.
RESTRICTIONS	No smoking, no pets. Children of all ages are welcome.

WEDGEWOOD COTTAGE BED & BREAKFAST INN

1111 West Pikes Peak Avenue, Colorado Springs, CO 80904   719-636-1829
Shannon & Karen Jones, Resident Owners
WEBSITE *www.bbonline.com/co/wedgewood/*

LOCATION	Take Highway 24 westbound and exit at 8th Street; turn left on West Colorado Avenue. Go two-and-a-half blocks to 11th Street, turn right, and continue down one block, then turn left at West Pikes Peak Avenue.
OPEN	All year
DESCRIPTION	An 1899 Victorian cottage with antique furnishings.
NO. OF ROOMS	One two-room luxury suite with private bathroom.
RATES	Year-round rate is $110 for a single or double. There is a minimum stay on weekends and during May through September.
CREDIT CARDS	MasterCard, Visa
BREAKFAST	Full gourmet breakfast, served in the guestroom, includes a main course, fresh fruit, muffins, and beverages.
AMENITIES	Fireplaces, Jacuzzi tub for two, cable TV, self-serve coffee and tea, stereo and refrigerator in room.
RESTRICTIONS	No smoking, no pets, no children. The resident cat, Cabernet, is not allowed in the guest area.
KUDOS/COMMENTS	"Very homey; great food!" (1996)

COMO

Railroad buffs will love this place, a partial ghost town of the 1870s railroad era. Glimpses of its colorful past can be seen at the Old Como Eatery, Como Mercantile, and the restored Como Depot. A rare, historic roundhouse still stands here. In the South Park Valley, 75 miles southwest of Denver and 25 miles northeast of Fairplay on Highway 285.

COMO DEPOT

PO Box 110, Como, CO 80432   719-836-2594
Keith & Jo Hodges, Resident Owners

LOCATION	Nine miles north of Fairplay, 0.25 mile west of Highway 285.
OPEN	March through December
DESCRIPTION	A restored 1898 railroad depot with restaurant and eclectic furnishings, listed on the National Historic Register.
NO. OF ROOMS	Four rooms share one bathroom.
RATES	Rates are $30 for a single and $55 for a double.
CREDIT CARDS	No
BREAKFAST	Full breakfast is served in the dining room. Other meals are available in the restaurant.
AMENITIES	One room with fireplace and clawfoot bathtub.
RESTRICTIONS	No pets
REVIEWED	*The Colorado Guide*

CORTEZ

Cortez lies a mere 10 miles to the west of Mesa Verde National Park and the heart of the Anasazi ruins, forty-five miles from Durango on the scenic San Juan Skyway.

A BED & BREAKFAST ON MAPLE STREET

102 South Maple Street, Cortez, CO 81321   970-565-3906
Roy & Nonnie Fahsholtz, Resident Owners   800-665-3906
EMAIL *maple@fone.net*   FAX 970-565-2090
WEBSITE *www.subee.com/maple/home.html*

A Bed & Breakfast on Maple Street, Cortez

LOCATION	Take Highway 160 (main street) into downtown Cortez, turn south on South Maple, and go one block.
OPEN	All year
DESCRIPTION	A 1920 two-story log and rock home with country decor and antiques, surrounded by flower gardens.
NO. OF ROOMS	Four rooms with private bathrooms.
RATES	April through October, rates for a single or double are $79-109. November through March, rates for a single or double are $69-99. There is no minimum stay and cancellation requires 14 days' notice (30 days during holidays and special events).
CREDIT CARDS	American Express, Discover, MasterCard, Visa
BREAKFAST	Full breakfast is served in the dining room and includes fresh fruit, blueberry upside-down pancakes with almond and whipped topping, hot maple syrup, bacon, cold cereal, yogurt, juice, coffee, and hot tea. Sack lunches are available.
AMENITIES	Gazebo-enclosed hot tub, homemade cookies, games to play, air conditioning, piano, limited handicapped access.
RESTRICTIONS	No smoking, no pets
MEMBER	Professional Association of Innkeepers International, Bed & Breakfast Innkeepers of Colorado, Southwest Colorado Bed & Breakfast Association
RATED	Mobil 2 Stars
KUDOS/COMMENTS	"Very comfortable, excellent hosts." (1996)

GRIZZLY ROADHOUSE BED & BREAKFAST

3450 Highway 160, Cortez CO 81321

970-565-7738
800-330-7286

KUDOS/COMMENTS "Great food! Tops in cleanliness." (1996)

KELLY PLACE

14663 Road G, Cortez, CO 81321
Rodney & Kristie Carriker, Innkeepers
EMAIL kellypl@fone.net
WEBSITE www.kellyplace.com

970-565-3125
800-745-4885
FAX 970-565-3540

LOCATION	Ten-and-a-quarter miles west of Highway 160 on Road G (toward Hovenweep National Monument).
OPEN	All year
DESCRIPTION	A 1965 two-story adobe-style lodge and cabins with southwestern decor on 100 acres of archaeological preserve.
NO. OF ROOMS	Ten bedrooms with private bathrooms. Try the Casita Room.
RATES	Year-round rates are $59-120 for a single or double, $110-120 for a suite, and $59-89 for a cabin. There is no minimum stay and cancellation requires 10 days' notice.
CREDIT CARDS	Discover, MasterCard, Visa
BREAKFAST	Full breakfast is served in the dining room and includes a hot entrée of the day, homemade granola, hot bread, muffins, fruit, juices, and cereals. Lunch and dinner are also available.
AMENITIES	Self-guided tour to over 25 on-site archaeological ruins, horseback riding and stabling available, fireplace in lodge and in some cabins, air conditioning, owned and operated by the Carrikers for the past 18 years.
RESTRICTIONS	No smoking, no pets
REVIEWED	*Journey to the High Southwest; Adventure Guide to the High Southwest; The Colorado Guide; North American Horse and Travel Guide; Colorado Cabins, Cottages and Lodges; Sleeping with Literary Lions*
MEMBER	Southwest Colorado Bed & Breakfast Association

CRAWFORD

BLACK CANYON RANCH

7600 B-76 Road, Crawford, CO 81415   970-921-4252
Dennis Grieve, Resident Owner

CREEDE

An 1892 mining boom built this town from scratch. The last mine closure here
was in 1985. Events of note include the Taste of Creede over Memorial Day
weekend and the Days of '92 celebration over July 4th weekend. Check out the
Creede Repertory Theater, and the underground mining museum and
underground fire station.

CREEDE HOTEL

120 North Main Street, Creede, CO 81130   719-658-2608
Cathy & Rich Ormsby, Resident Owners   FAX 719-658-2608 *(call first)*
Some Spanish spoken

LOCATION	Take Highway 149 to Creede (22 miles north of South Fork). Jog left (west) to Main Street. The hotel is four miles up on the right, next to the Creede Repertory theater.
OPEN	May through November, limited rooms available from December through April.
DESCRIPTION	An 1892 two-story mining-town hotel with "old hotel" furnishings and a full-service restaurant.
NO. OF ROOMS	Seven rooms with private bathrooms. The best room is 4, "unless you don't mind the noise of Main Street, then choose 3."
RATES	High-season (Memorial Day through September) rates are $59-79 for a single or double. Low-season rates are $35-69 for a single or double. Guesthouse rooms are $100-220. There is no minimum stay and cancellation requires seven days' notice plus a $15 charge.
CREDIT CARDS	Discover, MasterCard, Visa
BREAKFAST	Full breakfast, served in the dining room, varies depending on whether the hotel restaurant is serving breakfast. If it is open, choose anything off the menu, such as salsa eggs, hot grains and fruit, scones, and beverages. Lunch, dinner, and special meals are also available.
AMENITIES	Cross-country ski guides, great restaurant, "unspoiled" mining

town, room for small meetings, some rooms handicapped accessible, bike storage.

RESTRICTIONS   No smoking inside, no pets during high season, children of all ages are welcome. The resident Siamese cat is called Beer Can. The golden retriever is called Bear.

REVIEWED   *The Colorado Guide, Recommended Country Inns Rocky Mountain Region, Colorado Restaurants and Recipes, Non-Smokers Guide to Bed & Breakfasts*

THE OLD FIREHOUSE NO. 1

Creede Avenue, Creede, CO 81130   719-658-0212
R. Katherine Brennand, Resident Owner
Spanish and French spoken

LOCATION   Across from the Creede Repertory Theatre on Main Street. "Since Main Street is only two blocks long, it is very easy to find anything in Creede."

OPEN   All year

DESCRIPTION   A renovated 1892 two-story western Victorian firehouse with Victorian furnishings and a main floor ice-cream parlor and restaurant.

NO. OF ROOMS   Five rooms with private baths. Katherine Brennand recommends room 5.

RATES   Summer rates are $65-75 for a single or double and $130 for the two bedroom suite. Winter rates are $15 less. There is no minimum stay and cancellation requires seven days' notice.

CREDIT CARDS   Discover, MasterCard, Visa

BREAKFAST   Continental breakfast is served in the dining room.

AMENITIES   Ice-cream parlor, gift shop, library, and games for children.

RESTRICTIONS   No smoking except on the outside balcony, no pets. Children are welcome.

CRESTED BUTTE

This old mining town, with original buildings on historic Elk Avenue dating back
to 1860, has transformed itself into a world-class ski resort. Local celebrations
include the Wildflower Festival, Vinotok Storytelling Festival, Mountain Biking
Festival, Aerial Weekend, and the Arts Festival. In the summer, enjoy a feast of
outoor activities. About 30 miles north of Gunnison on Highway 135.

BUCKHORN RANCH HOUSE

42 Earhart Lane, Crested Butte, CO 81224   970-349-1340

THE CLAIM JUMPER BED & BREAKFAST

704 Whiterock Avenue, Crested Butte, CO 81224   970-349-6471
Jerry Bigelow, Innkeeper

LOCATION	As you enter town, a carved wooden sign says, "Welcome to Crested Butte." Turn right at the sign and go two blocks; we are on the right across from the town park.
OPEN	All year
DESCRIPTION	This rebuilt historic log home is on the National and Colorado Historic Registers and features six theme rooms, each with its own unique collection of antiques, heirlooms, and treasures.
NO. OF ROOMS	Six rooms with private baths.
RATES	High-season rates (November 15 through April 15 and June 15 through October 15) are $89-129. Off-season rates are $69-89 for a double. There is a minimum stay during high season and cancellation requires 30 days' notice.
CREDIT CARDS	Discover, MasterCard, Visa
BREAKFAST	Hearty gourmet breakfast, served in the dining room, includes homemade buckwheat waffles, sausages, breads, fruits, and pastries stuffed with eggs and feta. Special meals are also available.
AMENITIES	European sauna with pine water, antique game room, book and classic movie library, glassed-in hot tub, TV/VCR in rooms, telephone, and wedding ceremonies performed by Reverend Jerry Bigelow.
RESTRICTIONS	No smoking, children over the age of 12 are welcome. Otis, the resident Newfoundland, is large and loveable and may join guests on outdoor activities.
REVIEWED	*America's Small Inns, The Colorado Guide*

MEMBER   Bed & Breakfast Innkeepers of Colorado

KUDOS/COMMENTS   "More 'stuff' than the Smithsonian." "An incredible experience!
                      Very warm welcome and service." "Jerry does a great narrative
                      breakfast." "The decorations are really fun." "Words can't describe
                      it." (1996) "The inn is unique and filled with fun memorabilia."
                      (1999)

CRISTIANA GUESTHAUS

621 Maroon Avenue, Crested Butte, CO 81224   970-349-5326
Rosemary & Martin Catmur, Innkeepers   800-824-7899
Some Spanish spoken   FAX 970-349-1962
EMAIL *cristian@rmi.net*

LOCATION   In Crested Butte, go one block north of Elk Avenue (the main
                  street).

OPEN   All year

DESCRIPTION   A 1962 two-story European-style alpine lodge with country interior,
                  including pine furniture and rocking chairs.

NO. OF ROOMS   Twenty-one rooms with private bathrooms.

RATES   Ski season (November through April), rates are $67-91 for a single
                  or double. May through October, rates are $58-69 for a single or
                  double. There is a minimum stay during ski season, Christmas,
                  spring break, and some weekends and holidays in summer.
                  Cancellation requires 45 days' notice during ski season and by noon
                  the day of arrival during the summer.

CREDIT CARDS   American Express, Discover, MasterCard, Visa

BREAKFAST   Continental plus is served fireside in the lobby and includes
                  homemade granola and muesli, fresh fruit, a selection of freshly
                  baked pastries, juices, and hot drinks (teas, coffee, hot chocolate,
                  spiced cider).

AMENITIES   Cozy lobby with couches around a large stone fireplace; outdoor
                  hot tub with great mountain views; indoor sauna; large sun deck;
                  hot drinks available throughout the day; award-winning rock
                  gardens. Rooms do not have TVs or phones. The TV is in a separate
                  area off the lobby.

RESTRICTIONS   No smoking, no pets. Piglet and Tigger are the resident cats.

REVIEWED   *The Colorado Guide, Colorado Handbook*

MEMBER   Colorado Hotel and Lodging Association

CRYSTAL INN BED & BREAKFAST

624 Gothic Avenue, Crested Butte, CO 81224
Charlene & Dennis Goree, Innkeepers
EMAIL abs@crystalinn.com
WEBSITE www.colorado-bnb.com/crystal

970-349-1338
800-390-1338
FAX 970-349-1942

LOCATION	Entering Crested Butte on Highway 135, go to the third stop sign (Gothic Avenue) and turn right. The B&B is on the right.
OPEN	All year
DESCRIPTION	A 1993 two-and-a-half-story cedar mountain home with antique furnishings.
NO. OF ROOMS	Five rooms with private bathrooms.
RATES	Winter rates are $79-119 for a single or double. Summer rates are $79-99. There is a minimum stay during holidays and special events, and cancellation requires 14 days' notice in summer, 30 days in winter.
CREDIT CARDS	American Express, Discover, MasterCard, Visa
BREAKFAST	Full hearty breakfast is served family-style in the sunny dining room and includes juices, fresh fruits, breads and muffins, an entrée of the day, and breakfast meat.
AMENITIES	Indoor hot tub, phone and TV in rooms, balconies and decks, majestic views, guest icebox and microwave, ski storage, bottomless cookie jar, 24-hour coffee and tea bar, two common areas, and warm, friendly hospitality.
RESTRICTIONS	No smoking, no pets
MEMBER	Bed & Breakfast Innkeepers of Colorado

ELIZABETH ANNE B&B

703 Maroon Avenue, Crested Butte, CO 81224
Kirk & Karen Smith, Resident Owners
EMAIL elizabethannbnb@hotmail.com

970-349-0147
888-745-4620

LOCATION	As you enter town, take the first right on 7th Avenue and drive to the intersection of 7th and Maroon. The inn is on the northeast corner.
OPEN	Open late-May through mid-October and mid-November through mid-April
DESCRIPTION	A 1992 two-story Victorian with period furniture, wallpaper, and accessories.

NO. OF ROOMS	Four rooms with private bathrooms. The T&K Room is the best.
RATES	Winter rates, mid-November to mid-April, are $95-110 for a single or double. Summer rates, late-May through mid-October, are $90 for a single or double. There is a $16 per-person additional charge for up to six people in the large room. There is a two-day minimum on weekends. Cancellation requires 30 days' notice for a full refund.
CREDIT CARDS	American Express, MasterCard, Visa
BREAKFAST	Full breakfast, served in the dining room, includes buttermilk waffles, stuffed French toast, blueberry pancakes, coffee, fruit juice, and other offerings.
AMENITIES	TV in rooms, indoor hot tub, refreshments each afternoon, refrigerator, washer, dryer, ski and bike storage, telephone in parlor, fireplace, wet bar.
RESTRICTIONS	No smoking, no pets, children are welcome in the T&K Room only. The resident Australian shepherd is called Jake.
REVIEWED	*Non-Smokers Guide to Bed & Breakfasts, America's Wonderful Little Hotels & Inns*
MEMBER	Bed & Breakfast Innkeepers of Colorado

THE ELK MOUNTAIN LODGE

129 Gothic Avenue, Crested Butte, CO 81224 970-349-7533
J. Pyper Lund, Resident Owner 800-374-6521
WEBSITE *www.elkmountainlodge.net* FAX 970-349-5114

LOCATION	The corner of Second Street and Gothic Avenue, two blocks north of the Old Town Hall.
OPEN	Almost year-round
DESCRIPTION	A 1919 three-story Victorian lodge (originally a miners' lodge) with traditional furnishings.
NO. OF ROOMS	Nineteen rooms with private bathrooms. J. Pyper recommends rooms 4, 20, or 9.
RATES	Winter rates are $70-133 for a single or double with a private bath and summer rates are $70-115. There is a minimum stay during winter and summer holidays and cancellation requires 30 days' notice in winter and seven days in summer.
CREDIT CARDS	American Express, Discover, MasterCard, Visa
BREAKFAST	Full breakfast, served in the dining room, features a home-cooked buffet with many southern and Swedish specialties.
AMENITIES	Telephones, cable TV, hot tub, rustic bar, and library for guests.

RESTRICTIONS   No smoking, no pets, children over 12 are welcome. The resident
                   dog is a Malamute.

INN AT CRESTED BUTTE

510 White Rock Avenue, Crested Butte, CO 81224   970-349-1225
M. Claybaugh, Resident Owner   800-949-4828
                                                    FAX 970-349-1825

OPEN   All year

DESCRIPTION   A small two-story hotel.

NO. OF ROOMS   Sixteen rooms with private baths.

RATES   High-season rates are $110-130 for a single or double; low-season
                   rates are $55.

CREDIT CARDS   American Express, MasterCard, Visa

BREAKFAST   Continental breakfast is served in the dining room and includes
                   cereal, muffins, bagels, juice, coffee, and tea.

AMENITIES   Hot tub.

RESTRICTIONS   No smoking, no pets, children are welcome.

THE LAST RESORT

213 Third Street, Crested Butte, CO 81224   970-349-0445
Rita Wengrin, Resident Owner   800-349-0445
French and Spanish spoken

LOCATION   Entering Crested Butte, turn left onto Elk Avenue (main street)
                   and take a right at Third Street; the road dead ends at the inn.

OPEN   All year

DESCRIPTION   Begun in 1887 and finished in 1991, a two-story contemporary log
                   cabin overlooking Crested Butte, with dark woods, lots of glass, and
                   overstuffed furniture.

NO. OF ROOMS   Seven rooms with private bathrooms.

RATES   High-season (every month except May and October) rates are
                   $95-105 for a single or double with private bathroom. Low-season
                   (May and October) rates are $65-75 for a single or double. There is
                   no mininimum stay and a seven-day cancellation policy.

CREDIT CARDS   MasterCard, Visa

BREAKFAST	Full hearty, all-you-can-eat breakfast is served "any time you want it" in the dining room, and includes homemade baked goods.
AMENITIES	Steam room, two solariums, private Jacuzzis in selected rooms, coffee delivered to rooms in the morning, robes, limited access to kitchen, guided cross-country skiing and hiking, plus coffee, tea, and hot chocolate in each room.
RESTRICTIONS	No smoking, no pets, no children
REVIEWED	*Fodor's Ski Guide*
KUDOS/COMMENTS	"Great location and warm, casual atmosphere." (1996)

PURPLE MOUNTAIN

714 Gothic Avenue, Crested Butte, CO 81224 970-349-5888
Paul & Marilyn Caldwell, Resident Owners 800-286-3574
EMAIL *mailbox@purple-mountain.com* FAX 970-349-7194
WEBSITE *www.purple-mountain.com*

LOCATION	In the town of Crested Butte, two blocks north and one-and-a-half blocks east of the four-way stop.
OPEN	All year
DESCRIPTION	A renovated 1927 two-story miners' lodge with French country furnishings.
NO. OF ROOMS	Five rooms with private bathrooms.
RATES	Year-round rates for a single or double are $75-103. Weekends and holidays are about 10% higher. There is a minimum stay on holidays and cancellation requires 30 days' notice and a $15 fee.
CREDIT CARDS	Discover, MasterCard, Visa
BREAKFAST	Full gourmet breakfast, served in the dining room, includes fruit, homemade breads, meats, egg dishes, waffles, and pancakes. "Nothing ordinary to be found."
AMENITIES	Thick robes, foot warmers, down comforters, sun room with hot tub, fresh flowers in season, stone fireplace, après-ski served year-round with hot appetizers daily.
RESTRICTIONS	No smoking, no pets
MEMBER	Crested Butte Bed & Breakfast Association

CRESTONE

The Sangre de Cristo range towers over this tiny hamlet at the base of Crestone Peak and Crestone Needle. Technical climbers love this place, and spelunkers will want to explore the seven limestone caves in Marble Mountain. From Alamosa, 40 miles north on Highway 17, 12 miles on County Road T.

CREST-DOME BED & BREAKFAST

4179 Rarity Way, Crestone, CO 81131   719-256-4370

RAINBOW BED & BREAKFAST

223 Rainbow Overlook, Crestone, CO 81131   719-256-4110
                                              FAX 719-256-4110

SLICE OF HEAVEN BED & BREAKFAST

Carefree Way, Crestone, CO 81131   719-256-4150
Lea Black, Resident Manager

CRIPPLE CREEK

A historic mining and gambling town, today's Cripple Creek features Donkey Derby Days, Gold Hill Days, Historic Victorian modeling shows, boundless hiking, and Jeep tours of the aspen in the fall.

CHERUB HOUSE BED & BREAKFAST

415 Main Street, Cripple Creek, CO 80813   719-689-0526
Eyvonne & Johnny Harding, Innkeepers   800-679-7366

LOCATION	Three blocks north of Highway 67 (Bennette Street).
OPEN	All year
DESCRIPTION	An 1892 two-story log cabin with a two-story Victorian addition, with Victorian and western decor. Guest rooms are decorated in themes.

NO. OF ROOMS	Two rooms with private bathrooms and two rooms share one bathroom. Try the Victorian Rose Room.
RATES	Year-round rates are $79.95 for a single or double with a private bathroom and $69.95 for a single or double with a shared bathroom. Rates for New Year's Eve are $100-125. There is no minimum stay and cancellation requires 24 hours' notice.
CREDIT CARDS	MasterCard, Visa
BREAKFAST	Full breakfast is served in the dining room or guestrooms, or on the deck, and includes quiche, fresh fruit, biscuits and gravy, eggs, giant cinnamon rolls, pancakes, French toast, Belgian waffles, juice, milk, coffee, tea, and hot chocolate. Breakfast layout depends on the number of guests and guests' requests.
AMENITIES	Two robes in each room; champagne for birthdays, anniversaries, and weddings; outdoor private hot tub with music and low lighting; billiard room with TV and music (pool table can double as a large dining or meeting table); fresh-baked goods for snacking; room service.
RESTRICTIONS	No pets, children over eight are welcome. Jazz is the cockatiel—she thinks the guests come to see her.
KUDOS/COMMENTS	"Beautifully decorated, interesting hosts." (1999)

THE COZY CABINS

---

232 & 234 Thurlow, Cripple Creek, CO 80813   719-689-3351
Rita Mason, Innkeeper

LOCATION	Six blocks from downtown Cripple Creek. Enter town on Bennett Avenue (main street) and turn south on A Street. Go to Thurlow and turn right (west).
OPEN	All year
DESCRIPTION	Two log cabins, one built in 1901 (the Cozy Cabin) and the other in 1995 (the Cowboy Cabin), both with Victorian decor, combining today's conveniences with the romance and charm of the West.
NO. OF ROOMS	Two cabins with kitchens and private bathrooms.
RATES	Based on season, holidays, number of guests, and duration of stay. Cabins rent from $75-180. There is no minimum stay and no refunds.
CREDIT CARDS	No
BREAKFAST	Cupboards are stocked with breakfast foods for guests to prepare.
AMENITIES	Complimentary breakfast items and snacks; the Cozy Cabin has a fireplace; both cabins have phones, TV/VCRs, irons and ironing boards, microwaves, and no stairs. Special decorations, candies, and

candles; complimentary champagne for honeymoons, anniversaries, and birthdays.

RESTRICTIONS	None. Children are welcome.

GREYHOUND RANCH BED & BREAKFAST

401 South Second Street, Cripple Creek, CO 80813   719-689-2599
Barbara & Wil Wray, Resident Owners   888-987-0029

LOCATION	Four blocks south of Bennet Street on the corner of Second and El Paso.
OPEN	All year
DESCRIPTION	An 1895 two-story brick boarding house with Victorian interior, decorated with antiques, family memorabilia, and Native American pictures and beadwork.
NO. OF ROOMS	Four rooms share two bathrooms. The best rooms are the balcony rooms, 1 and 2.
RATES	May through September, rates are $75 for a single or double. Low-season rates are $65 for a single or double. The entire B&B rents for $240 per night. Cancellation requires 48 hours' notice.
CREDIT CARDS	MasterCard, Visa, Discover
BREAKFAST	Full breakfast includes honeybaked ham, sourdough pancakes, home-baked breads, fresh fruit platter, juice, coffee or tea, and chile soufflé.
AMENITIES	Fresh flowers or balloons for special occasions.
RESTRICTIONS	The resident dogs are Italian greyhounds named Fancy, Foxy, and Moe. This breed was originally bred for royalty in 500 B.C.

IRON GATE INN

204 North 2nd Street, Cripple Creek, CO 80813   719-689-3384
Arlia McManis, Innkeeper   800-315-3384
EMAIL *arliaj@worldnet.att.net*   WEBSITE *www.cripple-creek.co.us*

LOCATION	One-and-a-half blocks north of the corner of Bennett Avenue (Highway 67) and 2nd Street.
OPEN	All year
DESCRIPTION	An 1898 two-story Victorian cottage with antiques, Victorian touches, and oak floors.

NO. OF ROOMS	Two rooms share one bathroom.
RATES	Rates vary seasonally; call for details.
CREDIT CARDS	MasterCard, Visa
BREAKFAST	Continental breakfast is served in the dining room.
AMENITIES	Location for small weddings and receptions, privacy, snacks, fully equipped kitchen, access to laundry, deck and hot tub, cable TV.
RESTRICTIONS	No smoking, no pets, no children

THE LAST DOLLAR INN

315 East Carr Avenue, Cripple Creek, CO 80813   719-689-9113
Rick & Janice Wood, Resident Owners   888-429-6700
EMAIL packy578@concentric.net   FAX 719-689-0868
WEBSITE www.cripple-creek.co.us/lastdinn.htm

LOCATION	From Highway 24 at Divide, turn south onto Highway 67 and go 18 miles to Cripple Creek. In the center of town, turn right onto 3rd Street, go one block and turn right on Carr Avenue.
OPEN	All year
DESCRIPTION	An 1898 two-story brownstone with a Victorian addition added in 1995, decorated with period Victorian furnishings and antiques.
NO. OF ROOMS	Six rooms with private bathrooms. Try the Wood Room.
RATES	Year-round rates are $50-120 for a single or double. Discounts are available for renting the entire B&B. There is no minimum stay and cancellation requires seven days' notice.
CREDIT CARDS	MasterCard, Visa
BREAKFAST	Full breakfast is served in the dining room and includes Belgian waffles and eggs with sausage, fruit, coffee, tea, and more.
AMENITIES	Bottomless cookie jars and snack trays, soda pop and coffee around the clock.
RESTRICTIONS	No smoking, no pets, no children. Tahoe and Blue are the resident dogs and Smoky is the cat. They do not venture into guest areas.
MEMBER	Bed & Breakfast Innkeepers of Colorado, Pikes Peak Area Bed & Breakfasts, Lodging at Cripple Creek
KUDOS/COMMENTS	"Elegant, business-like, very professional." (1998) "Friendly hosts, lovely decorating, very clean." (1999)

Thurlow House Bed & Breakfast

319 Thurlow Avenue, Cripple Creek, CO 80813   719-689-3074
John & Jenny Lord, Resident Owners

Cuchara

This tiny town is tucked into San Isabel National Forest near the Spanish Peaks and breathtaking Cucharas Pass. About 30 miles southwest of Walsenburg via Highway 12.

Quarter Circle W Lazy H Ranch

PO Box 276, Cuchara, CO 81055   719-742-3912
EMAIL wlsonrch@rmi.net

Rivers Edge Bed & Breakfast

90 East Cuchara Avenue, Cuchara, CO 81055   719-742-5169
Michael Moore, Innkeeper   FAX 719-742-3111
Limited Spanish and French spoken
EMAIL rebb@rmi.net

LOCATION	From Walsenburg, go west on Highway 160 for 11 miles, then 13 miles southwest on Highway 12 to Cuchara. The B&B is the last building on the right in downtown Cuchara.
OPEN	All year
DESCRIPTION	A 1945 cabin and 1998 addition ("Alpine without the froufrou.") that matches the style of historic downtown Cuchara, with southwestern decor.
NO. OF ROOMS	Three bedrooms with private bathrooms and two rooms with two shared bathrooms. Try the Ponderosa Room.
RATES	June through September and December through March, rates are $125 for a single or double with a private bathroom, $100 for a single or double with a shared bathroom, $225 for a suite, and $500 for the entire B&B. The remainder of the year, rates are $75 for a single or double with a private bathroom, $65 for a single or double with a shared bathroom, $140 for a suite, and $375 for the entire

B&B. There is no minimum stay and cancellation requires 30 days' notice.

CREDIT CARDS	No
BREAKFAST	Full breakfast is served in the dining room and includes coffee, juice, fruit cup, and an entrée such as oatmeal almond pancakes, eggs Florentine, an omelet, or eggs Benedict, with breakfast meat and potatoes.
AMENITIES	Trout fishing; hot tub; robes; wine; mountain biking, horseback riding and championship golf nearby in summer; cross-country and downhill skiing, snowboarding, and snowshoeing two miles away.
RESTRICTIONS	No smoking

DEL NORTE

An agricultural treasure on the Rio Grande River, at the western edge of the beautiful San Luis Valley and bounded by the La Garita Mountains. Visit the Museum and Cultural Center for interesting exhibits and lectures, and don't miss a visit to the Monte Vista Wildlife Refuge or the Crane Festival in mid-March. August offers the Mountainman Rendezvous, Covered Wagon Days, and the Heritage Fair. From Alamosa, 31 miles west on Highways 285 and 160.

LA GARITA CREEK RANCH

38145 County Road E-39, Del Norte, CO 81132   719-754-2533
Dee & Lee Bates & John Engle, Resident Owners   888-838-3833
EMAIL dude@lagarita.com   FAX 719-754-2533 (call first)
WEBSITE www.lagarita.com/

LOCATION	From Del Norte, take Highway 112 northeast for three miles to La Garita turnoff, turn left and drive seven miles, then turn left at the ranch sign and go one mile.
OPEN	B&B in the winter only
DESCRIPTION	A 1970s two-story contemporary log inn with a mixture of southwestern and country furnishings, on 155 acres along La Garita Creek.
NO. OF ROOMS	Fourteen rooms with private bathrooms. Try the Deluxe Cabin or the Family Cabin.
RATES	Winter rates are $79 for a double, $89 for a cabin, and $10 for each additional person. There is a two-day minimum stay (cabins only) and cancellation requires 30 days' notice.
CREDIT CARDS	Discover, MasterCard, Visa
BREAKFAST	Full "delicious and healthy" breakfast, served in the dining room,

includes huevos rancheros (a specialty), homemade muffins, rolls, and beverages. Lunch, dinner, and special meals available.

AMENITIES   Outdoor hot tub by the creek, tennis court, sauna, pool, volleyball, horseshoes, weekend wine and cheese welcome hour, fresh flowers, reading and TV rooms, piano and bar, moss-rock fireplace, secluded location, facilities for retreats, family reunions, weddings.

RESTRICTIONS   No smoking in rooms, no pets

DELTA

An agricultural center with acre upon acre of local orchards and ranches. From Grand Junction, 61 miles southeast on Highway 50.

ESCALANTE RANCH BED & BREAKFAST

701 650 Road, Delta, CO 81416   970-874-4899
Dick Miller, Resident Owner   800-426-2191
Spanish spoken   FAX 970-426-0366

LOCATION   Approximately 14 miles northwest of Delta. From Highway 50, turn south at Road 650 and go three miles to Escalante Canyon.

OPEN   All year

DESCRIPTION   A working cattle ranch on 100,000 acres. The main ranch house is on the Gunnison River and features contemporary western furnishings.

NO. OF ROOMS   Two rooms share one bathroom and there is a three-bedroom suite. Remote cabins are also available. The best room is the Grand Mesa Room.

RATES   Year-round rate is $48 per person. There is no minimum stay. Ask about a reservation/cancellation policy.

CREDIT CARDS   MasterCard, Visa

BREAKFAST   Full breakfast is served in the dining room.

AMENITIES   Common room with TV/VCR, complete kitchen.

RESTRICTIONS   None. This is a working ranch with livestock and all sorts of wildlife including deer, bear, mountain lions, and elk.

REVIEWED   Several books have been written about the ranch including *Red Hole in Time* and *Trails and Trials*.

MEMBER   Colorado Hotel and Lodging Association

DENVER

America's Mile High City and Colorado's capitol, with the flatlands to the east and the Rockies to the west, Denver is a major cosmopolitan, cultural, manufacturing, financial, and transportation center (boasting one of the world's most controversial and expensive airports). Things to see and do include the State Capitol atrium; the 16th Street pedestrian mall; the historic and well-restored Larimer Square; the Molly Brown house; the Denver Art Museum and the Museum of Natural History; the Cherry Creek Arts Festival in July; and the National Western Stock Show in January. City Park includes the terrific Denver Zoo, Gates Planetarium, and the Museum of Natural History. And lest we forget, Denver is crazy about its major league pro sports teams, most notably the champion Broncos and Avalanche, slightly less notably the Rockies and Nuggets.

ADAGIO BED & BREAKFAST

1430 Race Street, Denver, CO 80206   303-370-6911
Amy & Jim Cremmins (and Abby, the dog), Innkeepers   800-533-3241
EMAIL *cremmins@sni.net*   FAX 303-377-5968
WEBSITE *www.sni.net/adagio*

LOCATION	Take I-25 to Speer Boulevard south. Go left onto 14th, drive 1.3 miles, and take a left onto Race. The inn is between 14th and Colfax.
OPEN	All year
DESCRIPTION	An 1892 three-story Victorian inn with an interior that blends contemporary and Victorian decor.
NO. OF ROOMS	Five bedrooms with private bathrooms. Try the Brahms Suite.
RATES	Year-round rates are $94-145 for a single or double. There is a two-night minimum stay during holidays and cancellation requires three days' notice.
CREDIT CARDS	American Express, Discover, MasterCard, Visa
BREAKFAST	Full breakfast is served in the dining room and includes a fruit course, yogurt course, and a hot entrée such as quiche or breakfast burritos, plus juice, coffee, breads, and muffins.
AMENITIES	Hot tubs in room; fireplaces; air conditioning; CD players; robes; patio for outdoor breakfast in summer; beautiful gardens; Midweek Music Getaways (on Wednesday evenings from January through March), a package deal that includes catered dinner, informal concert in the parlor, and full breakfast (prices begin at $150/couple).
RESTRICTIONS	No smoking, no pets
MEMBER	Bed & Breakfast Innkeepers of Colorado, Professional Association of Innkeepers International

"The owners are very personable. Their rooms are large with interesting themes." "Large mansion in the heart of Capitol Hill. Wonderful atmosphere and large suites." (1999)

CAPITOL HILL MANSION BED & BREAKFAST

1207 Pennsylvania, Denver, CO 80203   303-839-5221
Bill & Wendy Pearson, Innkeepers   800-839-9329
Spanish spoken   FAX 303-839-9046
EMAIL capitol_hill@earthlink.net   WEBSITE www.capitolhillmansion.com

LOCATION	Two blocks south and two blocks east of the State Capitol.
OPEN	All year
DESCRIPTION	An 1891 three-story ruby-sandstone Victorian in the Richardsonian Romanesque style with high turrets and soaring chimneys, listed on the National and State Historic Registers.
NO. OF ROOMS	Eight rooms named after western wildflowers, each with a private bathroom. Try the Shooting Star Room.
RATES	May through October, rates are $95-175 for a single or double. November through April, rates are $85-155 for a single or double.

Capitol Hill Mansion Bed & Breakfast, Denver

There is no minimum stay and cancellation requires three days' notice.

CREDIT CARDS	American Express, Discover, MasterCard, Visa
BREAKFAST	Full breakfast is served in the dining room and includes a hot entrée, fresh-baked items, breads, fruit, juices, yogurt, teas, and a special blend of coffee.
AMENITIES	Air conditioning, handicapped access, whirlpool tubs in three rooms, fresh flowers, modem-ready jacks, free local phone calls, complimentary beverages, iron/ironing board, hair dryer, hot pot and a variety of instant beverages, cable TV, clock radio, refrigerator.
RESTRICTIONS	No smoking, no pets. Petone and Tutti are the resident poodles.
REVIEWED	*Recommended Country Inns*
MEMBER	Professional Association of Innkeepers International, American Bed & Breakfast Association
RATED	AAA 3 Diamonds
AWARDS	American Bed & Breakfast Association's Highest Award, *Westword's* Best of Denver 1994.

CASTLE MARNE

1572 Race Street, Denver, CO 80206   303-331-0621
Diane & Jim Peiker, Resident Owners   800-926-2763
Hungarian, Spanish, and French spoken   303-331-0623
EMAIL *themarne@ix.netcom.com*   WEBSITE *www.castlemarne.com*

LOCATION	From the State Capitol, go east 20 blocks on Colfax to Race Street. Turn right at Race Street and go one block north to Race and 16th Avenue.
OPEN	All year
DESCRIPTION	An 1889 three-story Richardsonian Romanesque with Victorian furnishings. The inn is on the National and State Historic Registers and is "the finest example of the work of America's most eclectic architect, William Lang."
NO. OF ROOMS	Nine rooms with private bathrooms. Pick the Presidential Suite.
RATES	Year-round rates are $85-180 for a single or double and $225 for a suite. There is no minimum stay. Reservations are recommended and cancellation requires 48 hours' notice.
CREDIT CARDS	American Express, Diners Club, Discover, MasterCard, Visa
BREAKFAST	Full breakfast, served in the dining room, includes homemade breads and muffins, juice, at least five different kinds of fruit, a hot

entrée that changes daily, "Marne blend" coffee, and a variety of teas.

AMENITIES	Fresh flowers in the rooms in season, robes in some rooms, Jacuzzis in two rooms, hot tubs on private balconies of three rooms, telephones in all rooms, afternoon tea served daily in the parlor, game room with pool table and darts, guest office with computer and meeting facilities for up to 12, free parking.
RESTRICTIONS	No smoking, no pets, children over 10 are welcome.
REVIEWED	*Frommer's Denver, Boulder and Colorado Springs; The Colorado Guide*
MEMBER	Independent Innkeepers of America, Carter Collection of Inns, Distinctive Inns of Colorado, American Historic Hotels of the West, Bed & Breakfast Innkeepers of Colorado
RATED	AAA 3 Diamonds, ABBA 3 Crowns, Mobil 3 Stars
AWARDS	Country Inns Magazine, One of the top 12 inns in the US, 1994; Colorado State Historical Society, Stephen H. Hart Preservation Award
KUDOS/COMMENTS	"Elegant rooms, elegant breakfast, and friendly down-to-earth innkeepers." "Sheer elegance and wonderful hospitality." "Castle Marne and the Peikers are 11.5 on a scale of one to ten." "Castle Marne is so exquisite you feel like a princess in a beautiful castle." (1994) "An impressive stone mansion in the Denver historical district near parks and museums. An absolutely immaculate inn, beautiful rooms, and exceptionally warm innkeepers." (1996) "Stunning Victorian decor, friendly and helpful owners and staff, gourmet food." "Considered a landmark in Colorado. Great place to stay in Denver!" (1999)

FRANKLIN HOUSE B&B

1620 Franklin Street, Denver, CO 80218   303-331-9106
George & Sharon Bauer, Resident Owners   FAX 303-320-6555
German, Spanish, and some French spoken

LOCATION	One-and-a-half miles east of Denver and two blocks south of St. Joseph's Hospital.
OPEN	All year except closed Christmas
DESCRIPTION	An 1890 three-story brick Queen Anne with antique furnishings.
NO. OF ROOMS	One room with private bathroom, seven rooms share three bathrooms. The Bauer's favorite room is the Franklin Room.
RATES	Year-round rates are $30 for a single and $50 for a double with a private bathroom (additional guests are $10 each). A single with a shared bathroom is $30, and a double with a shared bathroom is

$40. There is no minimum stay. Ask about a reservation/cancellation policy.

CREDIT CARDS	Discover, MasterCard, Visa
BREAKFAST	Full breakfast is served in the dining room and includes quiche, breads, pastry, fruit, juices, tea, and coffee.
AMENITIES	Lounge with TV, books, brochures, and restaurant menus; pay phone in the lobby; backyard patio with umbrella tables.
RESTRICTIONS	No pets, children are welcome. There are three resident cats, Spiffer, S. Klause, and Checkers.
KUDOS/COMMENTS	"Sharon and George Bauer were most gracious and hospitable and provided excellent service at all times. George was an excellent breakfast host, learning quickly what I enjoyed for breakfast and providing it." (1996)

GREGORY INN LODO

2500 Arapahoe Street, Denver, CO 80205   303-295-6570

HAUS BERLIN

1651 Emerson Street, Denver, CO 80218   303-837-9527
Christiana & Dennis Brown, Resident Owners   800-659-0253
German spoken   FAX 303-837-9527 (call first)
EMAIL haus.berlin@worldnet.att.net   WEBSITE www.hausberlinbandb.com

LOCATION	Nine blocks east of Broadway (downtown) on 17th Avenue and Emerson Street.
OPEN	All year
DESCRIPTION	An 1892 three-story Victorian townhouse decorated with a mix of upscale European furnishings and antiques, listed on the National Historic Register.
NO. OF ROOMS	Four rooms with private bathrooms.
RATES	Year-round rates are $95-135 for a double. Cancellation requires seven days' notice.
CREDIT CARDS	American Express, Discover, MasterCard, Visa
BREAKFAST	Full breakfast is served in the dining room, the suite, or the courtyard and includes fresh-squeezed orange juice, fruit plate, and a choice of entrées such as wild mushroom quiche or German pancakes, plus fresh rolls, homemade scones and tarts, cold meats, and cheeses.

AMENITIES	Flowers, TV, phones, fax, complimentary beverages, air conditioning, ceiling fans, courtyard, and fine cotton linens.
RESTRICTIONS	No smoking, no pets, no children. The resident cat is named Ophelia.
REVIEWED	*America's Wonderful Little Hotels & Inns, Recommended Country Inns Rocky Mountain Region, Non-Smokers Guide to Bed & Breakfasts, American Cities Bed & Breakfast Guide*
MEMBER	Bed & Breakfast Innkeepers of Colorado

HOLIDAY CHALET, A VICTORIAN HOTEL

1820 East Colfax Avenue, Denver, CO 80218　　303-321-9975
Margot Crowe, Resident Owner　　800-626-4497
Some French, Polish, and German spoken　　FAX 303-377-6556

LOCATION	On the corner of Colfax Avenue and High Street, 18 blocks east of the State Capitol and two blocks from Cheesman Park.
OPEN	All year
DESCRIPTION	A restored 1896 Queen Anne brownstone, owned and operated by the same family for three generations, decorated with Victorian furnishings and family heirlooms.
NO. OF ROOMS	Ten suites/rooms have private bathrooms and kitchens.
RATES	Year-round rates are $84-130 for a single or double. There is no minimum stay and cancellation requires 48 hours' notice.
CREDIT CARDS	American Express, Diners Club, Discover, MasterCard, Visa
BREAKFAST	Continental breakfast is served in the music room or brought to the guestrooms.
AMENITIES	TV, radio, grand piano and upright piano, phone, flowers and plants, courtyard with flowers, barbecues available in the summer, and a small meeting space available with catered meals.
RESTRICTIONS	No smoking. Pets are $5 extra. The resident schnauzer goes by "Dixie." Children are welcome.
REVIEWED	*The Colorado Guide*
MEMBER	Colorado Hotel and Lodging Association, Professional Association of Innkeepers International
RATED	AAA 3 Diamonds

THE LUMBER BARON INN

2555 West 37th Avenue, Denver, CO 80211   *303-477-8205*
Maureen & Walter Keller, Resident Owners   *FAX 303-477-0269*
EMAIL *Stay@LumberBaron.com*   WEBSITE *www.LumberBaron.com*

LOCATION	Located in a residential neighborhood two miles west of downtown Denver. Take Speer Boulevard north from I-25 for 0.5 mile to Federal Boulevard. Turn right and go seven blocks to 37th Avenue. Turn right and go four blocks.
OPEN	All year
DESCRIPTION	An 1890 three-story Queen Anne Victorian mansion restored with period furnishings.
NO. OF ROOMS	Five rooms with private bathrooms. The Kellers suggest the Helen Keller Suite.
RATES	Year-round rates are $125-195 for a single or double. There is no minimum stay and cancellation requires seven days' notice.
CREDIT CARDS	American Express, Discover, MasterCard, Visa
BREAKFAST	Full breakfast is served in the dining room, the guestrooms, or on porches and in gardens. Breakfast includes fresh fruit, baked goods, juice, coffee, and a hot entrée such as eggs, waffles, or bread pudding. Meals are also served for Dinner Theater Fridays.
AMENITIES	Complimentary beverages, radios, and phones in rooms; TV available upon request; all rooms with Jacuzzis and showers; individual heat and air conditioning controls.
RESTRICTIONS	No smoking
REVIEWED	*Recommended Country Inns Rocky Mountain Region*
MEMBER	Distinctive Inns of Colorado, Professional Association of Innkeepers International
AWARDS	Community Preservation Award—Historic Denver; 2nd Place in Great American Home Award—Washington DC National Trust for Historic Preservation; Best Place for a Romantic Night—*Westword* magazine
KUDOS/COMMENTS	"A magnificent restoration of a great old mansion. Immense third floor ballrooms and outside garden/yard for weddings and special events. The wallpapered ceilings and walls are unbelievable. Walter and Maureen are very nice people." (1997) "Great all-around value. One of Colorado's ten best as rated by respected travel journalist Doris Kennedy." (1999)

MERRITT HOUSE BED & BREAKFAST INN

941 East 17th Avenue, Denver, CO 80218   303-861-5230
Cathy Kuykendall, Innkeeper   *877-861-5230 (reservations)*
EMAIL *merritthouse@earthlink.net*   WEBSITE *www.merritthouse.com*

LOCATION	Take I-70 to Colorado Boulevard south. Go west for three miles on 17th Avenue (17th becomes 18th). Turn left at Ogden. The inn is one-and-a-half blocks south on the right.
OPEN	All year
DESCRIPTION	An 1889 three-story Queen Anne Victorian with Victorian decor, listed on the State Historic Register.
NO. OF ROOMS	Ten rooms with private bathrooms. Try room #17.
RATES	Year-round rates are $90-100 for a single or double and $105-140 for a single or double with a Jacuzzi. There is no minimum stay and cancellation requires 72 hours' notice.
CREDIT CARDS	American Express, Diners Club, Discover, MasterCard, Visa
BREAKFAST	Full breakfast is served in the dining room and includes 15 menu items, such as Florentine scramble, French toast, homemade breads, and a variety of juices. Catering is also available.
AMENITIES	Fresh flowers in rooms, meeting facilities, special events, catering, air conditioning, telephones, voice mail, cable TV, honor bars, free parking available.
RESTRICTIONS	No smoking, no pets, children are welcome.
MEMBER	Professional Association of Innkeepers International

QUEEN ANNE BED & BREAKFAST INN

2147-51 Tremont Place, Denver, CO 80205   303-296-6666
The King Family, Innkeepers   800-432-4667
Some Spanish and French spoken   FAX 303-296-2151
EMAIL *queenanne@bedandbreakfastinns.org*
WEBSITE *www.bedandbreakfastinns*

LOCATION	At the east end of downtown Denver facing Benedict Fountain Park. From Denver International Airport, take I-70 west to Colorado Boulevard; left to 17th Avenue; right to Logan; then right to 20th; and left to Tremont Place.
OPEN	All year
DESCRIPTION	Two side-by-side 1886/1979 Victorians facing a quiet park in front and lighted skyscrapers in back, furnished with comfortable,

Queen Anne Bed & Breakfast Inn, Denver

antique period pieces. Both buildings are listed on the National and State Historic Registers.

NO. OF ROOMS	Fourteen rooms with private baths, including four suites. Tom King favors the Rooftop Suite with its private deck and two-person tub.
RATES	May through October, rates for a single or double are $85-175, and suites are $165-175. November through April, rates for a single or double with a private bathroom are $75-155, and suites are $145-155. There is a minimum stay during some holiday weekends and cancellation requires 72 hours' notice.
CREDIT CARDS	American Express, Diners Club, Discover, Eurocard, MasterCard, Visa
BREAKFAST	Full breakfast is served in the dining room, guestrooms, or gardens during nice weather. Breakfast includes various hot entrées, all-natural granola, croissants, fresh fruit, special coffee blends, breads, and muffins.
AMENITIES	Fresh flowers, chamber music, special tubs in some rooms, free on- and off-site parking, air conditioning in the summer, Colorado wine and hors d'oeuvres, meeting room for up to 15, outdoor reception for up to 75, cable TV in rooms, dedicated outgoing phone lines for modems, and concierge.

RESTRICTIONS	No smoking, no pets. Children over 12 are welcome.
REVIEWED	"In all regional and national books that include Colorado."
MEMBER	Distinctive Inns of Colorado, Professional Association of Innkeepers International, American Bed & Breakfast Association, National Tourist Home Association, Colorado Hotel & Motel Association
RATED	AAA 3 Diamonds, Mobil 3 Stars
AWARDS	Since 1990, 32 awards for excellence
KUDOS/COMMENTS	"Very accommodating innkeepers and staff, delightful social hour, wonderful breakfasts, everything business travelers could need at their fingertips." (1996)

VICTORIA OAKS INN

1575 Race Street, Denver, CO 80206
Clyde Stephens, Innkeeper

303-355-1818
800-662-6257
FAX 303-331-1095

LOCATION	One mile east of downtown Denver, just north of Colfax between Cheesman and City Parks in the Capitol Hill Historic District.
OPEN	All year
DESCRIPTION	An 1897 three-story Denver Square with antique furnishings, hanging staircase, plaster decorated ceilings, and leaded-glass windows.
NO. OF ROOMS	Seven rooms with private bathrooms and two rooms share one bathroom.
RATES	Year-round rates are $75-95 for a single or double with a private bathroom, $60-70 for a single or double with a shared bathroom, and the entire B&B rents for $850. There is a seven-day cancellation policy.
CREDIT CARDS	American Express, Diners Club, Discover, MasterCard, Visa
BREAKFAST	Continental plus is served in the dining room.
AMENITIES	Telephones/radios/TVs in the rooms, two rooms with fireplaces, refreshments in the afternoon, concierge, meeting and special-occasion facilities, kitchen and laundry privileges.
RESTRICTIONS	No pets, no children
REVIEWED	*The Colorado Guide; Frommer's Denver, Boulder and Colorado Springs*
RATED	Mobil 2 Stars

DILLON
(SUMMIT COUNTY)

A bustling year-round vacation destination on the shores of Lake Dillon Reservoir. This is a summer mecca for fishing and sailing. August is known for Dillonfest, the Sailing Regatta, and nearby Montezuma Downs horse racing.

SNOWBERRYHILL BED & BREAKFAST

0236 Snowberry Way, Dillon, CO 80435   970-468-8010
George & Kristi Blincoe, Resident Owners
EMAIL bigsnow@sni.net   WEBSITE www.colorado-bnb.com/snowbry

LOCATION	Between Dillon and Keystone, off Swan Mountain Road.
OPEN	All year
DESCRIPTION	A 1984 three-story contemporary mountain host home with eclectic furnishings and filled with antiques.
NO. OF ROOMS	One suite with a private bathroom.
RATES	Thanksgiving through Easter, rates are $115-130 for the suite. Off-season rate is $75 for the suite. There is no minimum stay and cancellation requires 14 days' notice.
CREDIT CARDS	MasterCard, Visa

Snowberryhill Bed & Breakfast, Dillon

BREAKFAST	The suite is stocked with a variety of continental breakfast items such as fresh-baked breads, fruit bowl, yogurt, cereals, freshly ground coffee, beverages, and more.
AMENITIES	Daily maid service, full kitchen in suite, robes, TV/VCR, phone, ski locker, laundry facilities, crib and baby equipment.
RESTRICTIONS	No smoking, no pets. Ian is the resident cat. He is not permitted in the guest suite.
MEMBER	Bed & Breakfast Innkeepers of Colorado, Summit County Bed & Breakfast Association

WESTERN SKIES— A MOUNTAIN BED & BREAKFAST

5040 Montezuma Road, Dillon, CO 80435 970-468-9445
Kent & Lynne Lange, Resident Owners FAX 970-262-6466
EMAIL skiesbnb@aol.com WEBSITE www.colorado-bnb.com/westernskies

LOCATION	From Highway 6 exit on Montezuma Road, 4.8 miles east of Keystone Resort.
OPEN	All year
DESCRIPTION	A 1987 remodeled two-story country lodge and cabins with antique furnishings, situated on 37 acres.
NO. OF ROOMS	Three cabins with private bathrooms and four rooms with private bathrooms. Choose the cabin with the hot tub.
RATES	Rates vary from $75-185; call for details. There is a three-night minimum stay over the Christmas holidays; ask about a cancellation policy.
CREDIT CARDS	American Express, Discover, MasterCard, Visa
BREAKFAST	Continental plus includes homemade cinnamon rolls and breads, fruit, hot and cold cereals, coffee, tea, hot chocolate, spiced cider, and orange juice.
AMENITIES	Outside cedar-wood-fired hot tub, cross-country skiing, hiking and biking from the lodge.
RESTRICTIONS	No smoking, no pets, children are welcome.
REVIEWED	The Colorado Guide
MEMBER	Summit County Bed & Breakfast Association

DIVIDE
(COLORADO SPRINGS)

This small mountain community in the Ute Pass area is the main access route to Cripple Creek and the splendid Mueller State Park. Rock climbers itching for a challenge should take their best shot at conquering Penitente Canyon. On the high road to Florissant Fossil Beds National Monument, 30 miles west of Colorado Springs and seven miles west of Woodland Park on Highway 24.

MOUNTAIN MAN BED & BREAKFAST

603 Kutsu Ridge Road, Divide, CO 80814   719-687-2796
Dean & Jeanne Wilson, Resident Owners   888-687-2796
EMAIL *alpinefolk@aol.com*

LOCATION	Rural mountain homestay.
OPEN	All year
DESCRIPTION	A mountain lodge with western and southwestern artwork.
NO. OF ROOMS	Two guest rooms with private bathrooms.
RATES	Year-round rate is $89 for the first night and $85 thereafter.
CREDIT CARDS	American Express, MasterCard, Visa
BREAKFAST	Full breakfast is served in the dining room.
AMENITIES	Hot tub, decks, telescopes, hiking and biking trails close by, near a casino and Pikes Peak.
RESTRICTIONS	Smoking on deck, no pets

SILVER WOOD BED & BREAKFAST AT DIVIDE

463 County Road 512, Divide, CO 80814   719-687-6784
Larry & Bess Oliver, Innkeepers   800-753-5592
Texan spoken
EMAIL *silver1007@aol.com*   WEBSITE *www.silverwoodinn.com*

LOCATION	Drive north from the only traffic signal in Divide. Half a mile north of the signal, take the left fork and follow the paved road for 3.5 miles. The B&B is 0.25 mile past the Golden Bell Camp sign.
OPEN	All year
DESCRIPTION	A 1990 contemporary two-story home with four levels, located in the mountains and featuring eclectic furnishings, outstanding views, and abundant hiking trails.

NO. OF ROOMS	Two rooms with private bathrooms.
RATES	Year-round rates for a single or double are $65-95, extra twin beds are $20 each. There is a minimum stay during holiday weekends.
CREDIT CARDS	American Express, Discover, MasterCard, Visa
BREAKFAST	Full breakfast, served in the dining room, includes juice, homemade breads, seasonal fresh fruit, various quiches, French toast, or gourmet sausage with gravy and angel biscuits.
AMENITIES	TV in rooms; queen beds; private decks; complimentary coffee, tea, soft drinks, and homebaked goods.
RESTRICTIONS	No smoking, no pets. The resident cats, Lucy and Frisco, are the "comfort assurance engineers." Children are welcome.
REVIEWED	*The Colorado Guide*
MEMBER	Bed & Breakfast Innkeepers of Colorado

DOLORES

This little hamlet on the beautiful Dolores River, at the edge of McPhee Reservoir and the San Juan National Forest in the southwestern Four Corners area, is also situated in a prime spot for exploring the Anasazi ruins. Two well-preserved ruins are only a half-mile away. Check out the excellent exhibits and interpretive displays at the Anasazi Heritage Center. In September, enjoy the spectacular colors of fall during Colorfest. Other good reasons to be here: Mesa Verde National Park is only 20 miles southeast of town; Telluride is a pretty 50 miles north on Scenic Highway 145. From Cortez, 11 miles northeast on Highways 145 and 160.

HISTORIC RIO GRANDE SOUTHERN HOTEL

101 South Fifth Street, Dolores, CO 81323   970-882-7527
Fred & Cathy Green, Innkeepers   800-258-0434

LOCATION	One block off the town square and 10 miles northeast of Cortez.
OPEN	March through December 21
DESCRIPTION	An 1893 three-story German Gothic hotel with Victorian furnishings and turn-of-the-century antiques, listed on the National and State Historic Registers.
NO. OF ROOMS	Three rooms with private bathrooms and four rooms share two bathrooms. Try room 4.
RATES	Year-round rates are $55-75 for a single or double with a private bathroom, $45-69 for a single or double with a shared bathroom, and $140 for a suite. There is no minimum stay and cancellation

requires 48 hours' notice (two weeks at holidays).

CREDIT CARDS	Discover, MasterCard, Visa
BREAKFAST	Full breakfast is served in the dining room and includes a choice of meat, eggs to order, potatoes, pancakes, French toast, hot or cold cereal, and a fruit plate. Lunch and special meals are also available.
AMENITIES	Homey atmosphere and cooking, large deck, quiet.
RESTRICTIONS	No smoking, no pets. Children of all ages are welcome.
REVIEWED	*Hidden Secrets of the Southwest, Historic Inns, 101 Best Restaurants in Colorado*

LEBANON SCHOOLHOUSE BED & BREAKFAST

24925 County Road T, Dolores, CO 81323   970-882-4461
Bob & Penny Richardson, Resident Owners   800-349-9829
WEBSITE *www.subee.com/sch_house/home.html*

LOCATION	Seven miles north of Cortez in the country.
OPEN	All year.
DESCRIPTION	A fully restored 1907 historic landmark of Greek Revival architecture with country furnishings.
NO. OF ROOMS	Three rooms with private bathrooms and two share one bathroom.
RATES	Year-round rates are $69-120.
CREDIT CARDS	MasterCard, Visa
BREAKFAST	Full gourmet breakfast is served in the dining room.
AMENITIES	Two common areas for seminars, high ceilings, cheery wood-burning stove, artwork, TV/VCRs in all rooms, pool table. Views from porch, patio, and Jacuzzi. Merry-go-round for children. Close to Anasazi Heritage Center and Mesa Verde National Park. Half-price vouchers for skiing at Telluride.
RESTRICTIONS	No smoking, pets OK (have a dog kennel), children are very welcome.

MOUNTAIN VIEW BED & BREAKFAST

28050 County Road P, Dolores, CO 81323   970-822-7861
Brenda & Cecil Dunn, Resident Owners   800-228-4592
WEBSITE *www.subee/mtnviewhome.html*   FAX 970-882-4321

LOCATION	From Cortez go 4.3 miles north toward Dolores on Highway 145. Turn right on County Road P and travel one mile. When Country Road P curves left, take the gravel road to the right. The inn is the second house.
OPEN	All year
DESCRIPTION	A 1984 two-story ranch-style inn with southwestern furnishings, wraparound porches, and decks, on 22 wooded acres.
NO. OF ROOMS	Eight rooms with private bathrooms.
RATES	Year-round rates are $60 for a double, $70-80 for a suite, $90 for the cabin, and $500 for the entire B&B. There is no minimum stay and cancellation requires seven days' notice.
CREDIT CARDS	Discover, MasterCard, Visa
BREAKFAST	Full breakfast is served in the dining room or on the enclosed porch or the deck, and includes hot entrées such as southwestern casserole, bacon and eggs, sausage, French toast, specialty pancakes (blueberry, banana nut, honey whole wheat), and beverages. Special meals are available for groups.
AMENITIES	Guest TV room and kitchen, hot tub, handicapped access, evening refreshments.
RESTRICTIONS	No smoking, no pets, and no alcohol. There are two resident Arabians called Moriah and Misty, but they are not for guest use.
MEMBER	Southwest Colorado Bed & Breakfast Association, Colorado Hotel and Lodging Association

PRIEST GULCH LODGE BED & BREAKFAST

27646 Highway 145, Dolores, CO 81323   970-562-3810
Margaret Allsup, Resident Owner
EMAIL *gulch@phone.net*

LOCATION	In San Juan National Forest, 24 miles from Dolores.
OPEN	May 1 through October
DESCRIPTION	A modern home with three rooms, surrounded by a campground, and five cabins that are for rent (but don't include breakfast).

NO. OF ROOMS	Three rooms with private bathrooms.
RATES	Year-round rates are $55-65 for a single or double.
CREDIT CARDS	Discover, MasterCard, Visa
BREAKFAST	Continental breakfast is served in the dining room.
AMENITIES	Balconies, views of the river.
RESTRICTIONS	No smoking in house, no pets, children are welcome.

DURANGO

Midway between Purgatory ski resort and Mesa Verde National Park, Durango is well positioned to accommodate a grand diversity of tastes and interests, year-round. Excellent skiing is up the road in the San Juan National Forest, and Anasazi ruins lie to the east. Hop on the Durango-Silverton narrow-gauge railroad or hang out and enjoy one of Durango's many festivals: Snowdown in January, the Bluegrass Festival in April, the Iron Horse Bicycle Classic in May, Music in the Mountains in July and August, the Main Avenue Juried Arts Festival in August, the Four Corners Iron Horse Motorcycle Rally in September, and the Durango Cowboy Gathering in October. Twenty miles from the New Mexico border in southwest Colorado.

APPLE ORCHARD INN

7758 County Road 203, Durango, CO 81301   970-247-0751
John & Celeste Gardiner, Innkeepers   800-426-0751
Portuguese spoken   FAX 970-385-6976
EMAIL apple@frontier.net   WEBSITE *www.appleorchardinn.com*

LOCATION	Six miles north of Durango on Highway 550; turn west on Trimble Lane, turn north on County Road 203, drive 1.4 miles, and the inn is on the right.
OPEN	All year
DESCRIPTION	A 1993 two-story farmhouse inn and six cottages with elegant country furnishings, complete with porches and rocking chairs, located in an apple orchard with views of the mountains.
NO. OF ROOMS	Ten bedrooms with private bathrooms. John and Celeste suggest the Cortland Cottage.
RATES	June through September, rates are $105-150 for a single or double. October through May, rates are $85-130 for a single or double. There is a minimum stay during holidays and cancellation requires two weeks' notice.
CREDIT CARDS	American Express, Discover, MasterCard, Visa
BREAKFAST	Full breakfast is served in the dining room or on the patio in the

110

summer and includes something fresh out of the oven such as sourdough Belgian waffles topped with sautéed cinnamon apples, breakfast burritos, "light" eggs Benedict, or filled savory crepes. Lunch, dinner, and special meals are also available.

AMENITIES   Fresh flowers in room, robes in some rooms, wine, hors d'oeuvres, bottomless cookie jar, dining room with handicapped access, feather beds throughout, TV and fireplace in common room, three cottages are wheelchair accessible, hot tub in the garden, and apples to take home in the fall.

RESTRICTIONS   No smoking, no pets. Woody is the resident golden retriever; 18-year-old Newman is the orange-spotted tabby.

REVIEWED   *Fodor's Colorado; Fodor's The Rockies; America's Favorite Inns, B&Bs and Small Hotels; Great Towns of America*

MEMBER   Bed & Breakfast Innkeepers of Colorado, Professional Association of Innkeepers International

RATED   AAA 3 Diamonds, Mobil 2 Stars

AWARDS   1997 Inn of the Year in the " New, Large Inn" category, awarded by the Bed & Breakfast Innkeepers of Colorado; America's 1998 Favorite Inns Award, awarded by America's Favorite Inns, B&Bs, and Small Hotels

KUDOS/COMMENTS   "Owners have incredible enthusiasm and a beautiful home." "Excellent cook, wonderful gourmet breakfasts." "Warm and open common area." "Beautiful landscaping." "Country setting but convenient to the city." "The cottages are adorable." (1996)

BLUE LAKE RANCH

16000 Highway 140, Durango, CO 81326   303-385-4537
David & Shirley Alford, Resident Owners   888-258-3525
German and French spoken   FAX 303-385-4088
EMAIL *bluelake@frontier.net*   WEBSITE *www.bluelakeranch.com*

LOCATION   From Highway 160 at Hesperus, go south 6.5 miles on Highway 140.

OPEN   All year

DESCRIPTION   A country estate with Victorian architecture and eclectic interiors overlooking the private Blue Lake and mountains, located on 200 very secluded acres with nationally publicized gardens.

NO. OF ROOMS   Twelve rooms, suites, or cabins—all have private baths. David recommends the Garden Room, but thinks the best accommodations are at the cabin on the lake.

RATES	May through October, rates are $60-275 for a single or double with a private bathroom. November through April, rates are $45-195 for a single or double with a private bathroom. There is a two-night minimum stay and cancellation requires 30 days' notice with a $30 handling fee.
CREDIT CARDS	No
BREAKFAST	Full European buffet is served in the dining room.
AMENITIES	Magnificent gardens, flowers, robes, telephones, TVs, peace, quiet, fishing, cross-country skiing, and afternoon tea.
RESTRICTIONS	No smoking, no pets. There is a resident cat called Fuzzy and a small flock of peacocks. Children are welcome at the innkeeper's discretion.
REVIEWED	*The Colorado Guide*
MEMBER	Bed & Breakfast Innkeepers of Colorado, Professional Association of Innkeepers International, Distinctive Inns of Colorado
RATED	AAA 3 Diamonds
KUDOS/COMMENTS	"A delightful country inn with acres of rolling hills and ponds." "Famous for fabulous mountain gardens! An exceptional retreat." "Interesting owner, nice facilities for the price." "Fabulous views of the LaPlata Mountains. The gardens are large and well-kept and the owners are very personable." "Great in every way." (1996).

COUNTRY SUNSHINE BED & BREAKFAST

35130 Highway 550 North, Durango, CO 81301   970-247-2853
Beanie & Gary Archie, Resident Owners   800-383-2853
EMAIL *inn@countrysunshine.com*   FAX 970-247-1203
WEBSITE *www.countrysunshine.com*

LOCATION	Twelve miles north of Durango on Highway 550. At mile marker 35 there is a large redwood mailbox with "35130" on the front and signs on the east side of the highway.
OPEN	All year
DESCRIPTION	A 1979 two-story ranch-style country inn with wraparound decks and rustic furnishings.
NO. OF ROOMS	Six rooms with private bathrooms.
RATES	Summer (May 15 to October 15), Christmas season, and spring break, the rate is $85 for a single or double with a private bathroom. Off-season rate is $70. During the holidays guests are requested to stay two nights and there is a 15-day cancellation policy.

CREDIT CARDS	American Express, Diners Club, Discover, MasterCard, Visa
BREAKFAST	Full breakfast is served in the dining room.
AMENITIES	Large outdoor spa, complimentary beer and wine, extensive library and bicycles for use, common area with TV/VCR.
RESTRICTIONS	No smoking, no pets, children over five are welcome. There is a resident dog and cat.
MEMBER	Bed & Breakfast Innkeepers of Colorado
KUDOS/COMMENTS	"Very friendly atmosphere, filled with country charm." "Very comfortable home, charming innkeepers." (1997)

FARMHOUSE VILLAGE AT EDGEMONT

281 The Silver Queen, Durango, CO 81301   970-259-2812

GABLE HOUSE

805 East 5th Avenue, Durango, CO 81301   970-247-4982
Heather Bryson, Resident Owner   FAX 970-247-1454
Spanish spoken
EMAIL *ghbb@frontier.net*
WEBSITE *www.creativelinks.com/gablehouse/gable.htm*

LOCATION	Three blocks north and five blocks east of the Narrow-Gauge Railroad station.
OPEN	All year
DESCRIPTION	An 1892 four-story Queen Anne Victorian with antiques, oriental furnishings, and a fine-art collection. The B&B is on both the State and National Historic Registers.
NO. OF ROOMS	Three rooms share two-and-a-half bathrooms. The owner suggests the room with the private balcony.
RATES	Year-round rates for a single or double with a shared bathroom are $75-100. There is no minimum stay and a two-week cancellation policy.
CREDIT CARDS	MasterCard, Visa
BREAKFAST	Full hot breakfast is served in the dining room on fine china with silver.
AMENITIES	Robes, fresh flowers, libations offered upon arrival, picnics in the private yard.

RESTRICTIONS	Smoking on porch and balconies only, no pets, children over 12 are welcome.
REVIEWED	*Non-Smokers Guide to Bed & Breakfasts*
MEMBER	Bed & Breakfast Innkeepers of Colorado

LELAND HOUSE B&B SUITES/ ROCHESTER HOTEL

721 East Second Avenue, Durango, CO 81301   970-385-1920
Kirk & Diane Komick, Resident Owners   800-664-1920
EMAIL *leland@frontier.net*   FAX 970-385-1967
WEBSITE *www.rochesterhotel.com*

LOCATION	Turn left off Highway 550 onto College Drive, cross over Main, turn left onto Second Avenue. Located between Seventh and Eighth streets.
OPEN	All year
DESCRIPTION	Historic inns built in 1892 and 1927 with Brick Craftsman architecture and Western and Victorian decor.
NO. OF ROOMS	Twenty-five rooms with private bathrooms. The owners favorite is the "Support Your Local Gunfighter" Room in the Rochester.
RATES	Year-round rates are $99-199 for a single or double with a private bath and $149-199 for a suite. There is a two-night minimum stay at Christmas and cancellation requires 14 days' notice.
CREDIT CARDS	American Express, Discover, MasterCard, Visa
BREAKFAST	Full breakfast, served in the lobby and courtyard of the Rochester, includes coffee, juices, fruit plate, baked goods, homemade granola, and a daily hot entrée. Boxed lunches available.
AMENITIES	Courtyard, robes, social hour with tea and fresh-baked cookies, meeting rooms, handicapped accessible room.
RESTRICTIONS	No smoking, no pets
REVIEWED	*Recommended Country Inns of the Rocky Mountain Region*
MEMBER	American Bed & Breakfast Association, Bed & Breakfast Inns of Colorado, Professional Association of Innkeepers International, Distinctive Inns of Colorado
RATED	AAA 3 Diamonds, Mobil 2 Stars
AWARDS	1995 Durango Historic Preservation Board Special Recognition; 1994 Durango Park & Forestry Board Award for Landscaping; September 1995 *Conde Nast Traveler's* Flagship Hotel of Colorado.

"Perfect location for exploring the heart of Durango, very comfortably furnished, excellent breakfast." (1997) "Clean, friendly. Can walk to every attraction in Durango." (1999)

LIGHTNER CREEK INN

999 County Road 207, Durango, CO 81301
Julie & Richard Houston, Innkeepers
EMAIL *lci@frontier.net*
WEBSITE *www.lightnercreekinn.com*

970-259-1226
800-268-9804
FAX 970-259-9526

LOCATION — From Durango, head west on Highway 160 for three miles and turn right on County Road 207 (also known as Lightner Creek Road). Go one mile and look for the big white house on the left.

OPEN — All year

DESCRIPTION — A 1903 three-story French country guest house set in the mountains with elegant, French country decor.

NO. OF ROOMS — Ten bedrooms with private bathrooms. Try the Lisa Ann Suite.

RATES — May through October, rates are $85-185 for a single or double with a private bathroom and $165-185 for a suite. November through April, rates are $75-148 for a single or double with a private bathroom and $132-148 for a suite. There is no minimum stay and cancellation requires two weeks' notice less a $20 fee per room.

CREDIT CARDS — American Express, Diners Club, Discover, MasterCard, Visa

BREAKFAST — Full breakfast is served in the dining room and includes juice, tea, coffee, and an elegant fruit dish, followed by either an egg-based dish, waffles, stuffed French toast, or pancakes.

AMENITIES — Friendly hospitality; baby grand piano; fireplace; robes; gazebo; handicapped access; fresh flowers from the gardens in summer; small gift shop; afternoon tea, lemonade, and cookies; weddings, receptions, showers, family reunions; dinner sleigh rides; snowmobiling; ski packages and gift certificates available.

RESTRICTIONS — No smoking, no pets, children over eight are welcome. Miss Whitney Houston is the resident golden retriever, George is the goose, and Bonnie and Les are the ducks. George is a celebrity, having been in several magazines.

REVIEWED — *Recommended Country Inns, Non-Smokers Guide to Bed & Breakfasts, Special Places, Most Romantic Inns, Complete Guide to American B&Bs, Official Guide to American Historic Inns, America's Wonderful Little Hotels and Inns, Bed & Breakfast Inns and Guesthouses, Adventure Guide to the High Southwest, Inside Guide to the Rockies, Southwest America on Wheels*

MEMBER	Bed & Breakfast Innkeepers of Colorado, Distinctive Inns of Colorado, Professional Association of Innkeepers International, San Juan Skyway Association, Durango Hotel and Motel Association
RATED	AAA 3 Diamonds, Mobil 3 Stars
KUDOS/COMMENTS	"Best decorated B&B I've ever seen; great hosts." "A dream come true. A perfect country getaway in a picture-perfect setting. We couldn't ask for nicer hosts." "Beautifully decorated, located only three miles from town but with a country atmosphere." "Breakfast was fantastic." (1997)

LOGWOOD BED & BREAKFAST

35060 US Highway 550 North, Durango, CO 81301   970-259-4396
Paul & Maggie Windmueller, Innkeepers   800-369-4082
EMAIL *logwood@frontier.net*   FAX 970-259-7812
WEBSITE *www.fsnw.com/logwood*

LOCATION	From Durango, go north for 13 miles and take a right at the Timberline Academy exit. Take an immediate right turn into the Logwood driveway.
OPEN	All year
DESCRIPTION	A 1988 three-story cedar-log lodge with southwestern and mountain decor, situated in the mountains along the banks of the Animas River.
NO. OF ROOMS	Eight rooms with private bathrooms. Try the Cliff Palace.
RATES	May through October and holidays, rates are $85-115 for a single or double, $135 for a suite, and $895 for the entire inn. November through April, rates are $75-105 for a single or double, $125 for a suite, and $550 for the entire B&B. There is no minimum stay and cancellation requires 30 days' notice less a $20 fee.
CREDIT CARDS	American Express, MasterCard, Visa
BREAKFAST	A full country breakfast is served in the dining room. Special meals are available upon request.
AMENITIES	Tickets to Trimble Hot Springs; discount lift tickets to Purgatory ski resort; recreation room with pool table, video library, piano, and CD stereo system; meeting facilities for corporate retreats; innkeepers help plan activities such as Jeep tours, fishing, hiking, and train rides.
RESTRICTIONS	No smoking, no pets, children over five are welcome. Ricky and Lucy are the resident dalmations and Big Bird is the canary. The dogs are kept next door in the innkeepers' home. Big Bird is kept in the Lodge.
REVIEWED	*Best Places to Stay in the Rockies, Log Home Living, Log Home*

Illustrated, Best Places to Stay in the Southwest, Journey to the High Southwest

MEMBER	Bed & Breakfast Innkeepers of Colorado, National Bed & Breakfast Association, American Bed & Breakfast Association
RATED	AAA 3 Diamonds
AWARDS	Award in the Romantic Category, by Log Home Living and Log Home Illustrated. 1997 "Award of Excellence" by the Bed and Breakfast InnKeepers of Colorado.

RIVER HOUSE BED & BREAKFAST

495 Animas View Drive, Durango, CO 81301   970-247-4775
Kate & Lars Enggren, Crystal Carroll, Resident Owners   800-254-4775
Some Spanish spoken   FAX 970-259-1465
EMAIL *riverhousebb@compuserve*
WEBSITE *www.durango.com/riverhouse*

LOCATION	Head north on Highway 550 and turn right on Animas View Drive (last right before heading out of town), go 0.5 mile north; the B&B is on the left side.
OPEN	All year
DESCRIPTION	A 1960 southwest-style ranch with southwestern and antique furnishings.
NO. OF ROOMS	Eight rooms with private bathrooms and one honeymoon cottage. Try the Crystal River Suite.
RATES	Year-round rates are $75-125 for a single or double, $125 for a suite for one and $170 for a suite for two, $170 for the honeymoon guesthouse, and $600 for the entire B&B. There is no minimum stay and cancellation requires 14 days' notice.
CREDIT CARDS	American Express, Discover, MasterCard, Visa
BREAKFAST	Full "healthy gourmet, sometimes decadent" breakfast is served buffet-style in the atrium. Lunch is also available and special diets can be accommodated.
AMENITIES	Hot tub, atrium with waterfall and skylights, game room with pool table, large-screen TV, big brass fireplace, library, massage and hypnotherapy available, large backyard with reading areas and chess table, Jeep tours are available. The entire house can be rented for wedding parties or reunions.
RESTRICTIONS	No smoking, no pets. Saygee is the resident pooch and Molly is the outside cat.
MEMBER	Bed & Breakfast Innkeepers of Colorado, Professional Association of Innkeepers International

RATED   ABBA 3 Crowns

RATED	ABBA 3 Crowns
KUDOS/COMMENTS	"Soothing, delightful stay, pleasant innkeepers." "Warm and homey, a good place for kids also." (1997)

SCRUBBY OAKS BED & BREAKFAST INN

PO Box 1047, Durango, CO 81302   **970-247-2176**
Mary Ann Craig, Resident Owner
WEBSITE *www.southwesterninns.com/scrubby.htm*

LOCATION	From the intersection of 3rd Avenue and Florida Road, take Florida 2.7 miles; the inn is on the left side.
OPEN	April 25 through October 20
DESCRIPTION	A 1959 ranch house with comfortable country antiques located on 10 acres overlooking the Animas Valley and the surrounding mountains.
NO. OF ROOMS	Three rooms with private bathrooms and four rooms share two bathrooms.
RATES	Rates are $65-80 for a single or double with a private bathroom and $55-70 for a single or double with a shared bathroom. There is no minimum stay and cancellation requires two weeks' notice for a 50% refund of deposit less a $10 fee.
CREDIT CARDS	No
BREAKFAST	Full breakfast, served in the country kitchen, includes 12 menu items plus beverages.
AMENITIES	Lemonade, tea, home-baked goodies, popcorn, and peanuts each afternoon.
RESTRICTIONS	No smoking, no pets
REVIEWED	*Non-Smokers Guide to Bed & Breakfasts, Journey to the High Southwest*
MEMBER	Bed & Breakfast Innkeepers of Colorado, Colorado Hotel and Lodging Association
AWARDS	"Beautiful location; run by a seasoned innkeeper who knows the area." (1996)

WATERFALL BED & BREAKFAST

4138 County Road 203, Durango, CO 81301　　　　970-259-4771
Joan & Hall Sippy, Resident Owners

ELDORA

In the Roosevelt National Forest, Eldora offers skiing at its namesake ski area and easy access to Boulder, 20 miles to the east.

GOLDMINER HOTEL

601 Klondike Avenue, Eldora, CO 80466　　　　303-258-7770
Scott Bruntjen, Innkeeper　　　　800-422-4629
　　　　FAX 303-258-3850

LOCATION	Three-and-a-third miles west of Highway 119 in the town of Eldora.
OPEN	All year
DESCRIPTION	An 1897 two-and-a-half-story Four Square log hotel with original false front and a gold rush interior. Listed on the National and State Historic Registers.
NO. OF ROOMS	Five rooms with private bathrooms and two rooms share one bathroom. Scott recommends Mount Sweet Room.
RATES	Year-round rates are $119-179 for a single or double with a private bathroom, $75-85 for a single or double with a shared bathroom, $139 for a suite, $149 for the guesthouse, and the entire hotel rents for $850. There is no minimum stay and a seasonal cancellation policy.
CREDIT CARDS	American Express, Discover, MasterCard, Visa
BREAKFAST	Full breakfast is served in the dining room and includes eggs, meat, bread, fruit, and beverages.
AMENITIES	Hot tub, lounge with wood-burning fireplace.
RESTRICTIONS	No pets
MEMBER	Professional Association of Innkeepers International, American Hotel and Motel Association

EMPIRE

A small mountain community in a star-shaped valley on the high road to Winter Park, Empire offers easy access to that town's year-round festivals and activities. At the foot of Berthoud Pass on Highway 40.

MAD CREEK BED & BREAKFAST

167 Park Avenue (US 40), Empire, CO 80438 303-569-2003
Heather & Mike Lopez, Resident Owners 888-266-1498
Some Spanish spoken

LOCATION	Exit 232 from I-70 and go two miles to Empire. The B&B is on the north side of Park Avenue going west.
OPEN	All year
DESCRIPTION	An 1875 two-story Victorian cottage offering both rustic atmosphere and mountain charm, decorated with country antiques and relics of the mining and skiing past.
NO. OF ROOMS	One room with a private bathroom, one room shares a bathroom, and one room with a half-bathroom.
RATES	Year-round rates for a single or double with a private bathroom are $75-85, a single or double with a shared bathroom is $55-65. Rates are $65-75 for a single or double with a half-bathroom. There is a 15% discount for renting the entire B&B. There is no minimum stay. Ask about a cancellation policy.
CREDIT CARDS	MasterCard, Visa
BREAKFAST	Full breakfast, served in the dining room, includes homemade "Mad Creek Crunch" granola, blueberry waffles, fresh fruit, orange juice, yogurt, gourmet coffee, and tea. Breakfast is served in the gazebo during the summer.
AMENITIES	Outdoor hot tub, robes, ceiling fans, TV/VCR and movie selection, library of books and maps for Colorado adventures, use of cross-country skis and snowshoes.
RESTRICTIONS	No smoking, no pets, children over 10 are welcome. The resident Samoyed is called Sequoya.
REVIEWED	*Inn for the Night, Great Affordable Bed & Breakfast Getaways*
KUDOS/COMMENTS	"Charming." "Wonderful owners." (1996)

THE PECK HOUSE

83 Sunny Avenue, Empire, CO 80438　　　　　　303-569-9870
Gary & Sally St. Clair, Resident Owners　　　　FAX 303-569-2743
French, Spanish, and Japanese spoken
WEBSITE *www.peckhouse.com*

LOCATION	Take exit 232 from I-70 and travel two miles on Highway 40 to Empire. We are a block or so up the hill.
OPEN	All year
DESCRIPTION	The oldest hotel in Colorado—an 1860-1862 two-story stagecoach stop and restaurant decorated with antiques.
NO. OF ROOMS	Eleven rooms with private bathrooms and one room shares one bathroom. Check out the Bridal Suite.
RATES	Year-round rates are $70-85 for a double with a private bathroom, $45 for a double with a shared bath, and $100 for a suite. The rates are $5 higher from December 23 through January 1, and $10 higher on Valentine's Day. Cancellation requires 48 hours' notice with special requirements for holidays, August, and September.
CREDIT CARDS	Yes
BREAKFAST	Continental breakfast is served in the dining room. Dinner is available in the restaurant and lunch is served in the summer only.
AMENITIES	Bar, five-star gourmet restaurant, hot tub.
RESTRICTIONS	No pets. Resident pets include Scruffy (dog), Abraham and Topper (cats), Boo and Red (horses), Daisy and Grover (donkeys), Jack (goat), and Henry the chicken. Children are welcome.
REVIEWED	*Best Places to Stay in the Rocky Mountain Region, The Colorado Guide, The Official Guide to American Historic Inns, Recommended Country Inns of the Rocky Mountain Region, Restaurants from 101 Colorado Small Towns*
RATED	AAA 3 Diamonds (for the restaurant)
AWARDS	Uncle Ben's Inc., finalist for the 10 Best Country Inns of the Year award; 1993, Colorado Department of Agriculture, winner of the Governor's Award for the Best All-Colorado Meal

ESTES PARK

At the eastern entrance to Rocky Mountain National Park, Estes Park is the perfect starting point for exploring majestic Longs Peak and the Continental Divide. In June, shop at the wool market for products made from the coats of llamas, sheep, angora rabbits, and goats. Equally wild and woolly is the Rooftop Rodeo and Western Week in July. Other major events include the Rocky Mountain Folk Festival in August and the Longs Peak Scottish-Irish Festival in September. Fall is spectacular around here—the aspen are dazzling and bugling elk are everywhere (in particular, they like to congregate on the golf course). From Denver, 65 miles northwest via I-25 and Highway 36.

THE ANNIVERSARY INN B&B

1060 Mary's Lake Road, Moraine Route　　　　　　　970-586-6200
Estes Park, CO 80517
Norma & Harry Menke, Resident Owners
Some German spoken

LOCATION	On Route 36, 1.5 miles west of town. Turn left at the stoplight on Mary's Lake Road. The driveway is 0.1 mile on the left.
OPEN	All year except for Thanksgiving and Christmas
DESCRIPTION	An 1890 two-story mountain log inn furnished with country antiques and situated on two acres.
NO. OF ROOMS	The main house has three rooms with private baths. The cottage has a private bath, fireplace, and whirlpool tub for two. The Sweetheart's Cottage is the most popular room.
RATES	Year-round rates are $90-150 for a single or double with a private bathroom. A two-night minimum stay is preferred. There is a cancellation policy.
CREDIT CARDS	MasterCard, Visa
BREAKFAST	Full breakfast, served on the wraparound glassed-in porch, includes a hot entrée, fresh-baked goods, and fresh fruit.
AMENITIES	Robes in rooms, evening hors d'oeuvres, beverages, custom toiletries, fresh cookies, turndown service, extra pillows and blankets in rooms, moss-rock fireplace in living room, library with books and games, TV/VCR, refrigerator use, and whirlpool-for-two in three rooms.
RESTRICTIONS	No smoking, no pets, children over 14 are welcome.
REVIEWED	*America's Wonderful Little Hotels & Inns, Best Places to Stay in the Rocky Mountain Region, Recommended Country Inns, Birder's Guide to Bed & Breakfasts, Official Guide to American Historic Inns: Bed & Breakfasts and Country Inns, Recommended Romantic Inns*

MEMBER	Bed & Breakfast Innkeepers of Colorado, Professional Association of Innkeepers International

AWARDS	1996 Bed & Breakfast Innkeepers of Colorado Award of Excellence
KUDOS/COMMENTS	"A beautiful old log home." "Honeymoon cottage is great as well." "Eating on porch with beautiful views is a special delight." "Quiet getaway." "Super-quiet setting and gorgeous decor." (1996)

THE BALDPATE INN

4900 South Highway 7, Estes Park, CO 80517   970-586-6151
Lois Smith, Resident Owner
EMAIL *baldpatein@aol.com*   WEBSITE *www.baldpateinn.com*

LOCATION	At the junction of Highway 36 and County Highway 7, turn south and go seven miles to the Lily Lake Area of Rocky Mountain National Park. Turn left at the sign.
OPEN	Memorial Day weekend to September 30
DESCRIPTION	A 1917 two-story western stick log inn and three cabins with log and lace decor, listed on the National and State Historic Registers.
NO. OF ROOMS	Two rooms have private bathrooms and 10 rooms share five bathrooms. Room 4 is the largest and has the best view; room 21 has a great view and private bath.
RATES	Seasonal rates (May through September) are $100 for a double with a private bathroom, $145 for a cabin, and $85 for a double with a shared bathroom. The main lodge may be reserved for $1100. The lodge has no minimum stay; the cabins require a two-night minimum stay. Cancellation requires seven days' notice.
CREDIT CARDS	Discover, MasterCard, Visa
BREAKFAST	Full three-course breakfast is served in the dining room and includes fresh fruit and muffins, a quiche entrée, and a cinnamon roll for dessert. Lunch and dinner are also available.
AMENITIES	Native-stone fireplaces in lodge and cabins, historic key and photo collections, front porch, homemade quilts in rooms, and evening snacks in the lobby.
RESTRICTIONS	No smoking, no pets. Duke is the resident German shepherd.
REVIEWED	*Frommer's Colorado*
MEMBER	Bed & Breakfast Innkeepers of Colorado

BARBARA'S BED & BREAKFAST

255 Cyteworth, Estes Park, CO 80517
Barbara Felte, Resident Owner

970-586-5871
800-597-7903

LOCATION	Half a mile south of the park on main street. Turn left from Elkhorn Avenue onto East Riverside Drive. Go about three blocks, then turn left onto Cyteworth and follow the paved road up the hill. The B&B is the fifth house on the left.
OPEN	All year
DESCRIPTION	A 1950 two-story western wood-frame home with knotty pine paneling, hardwood floors, and moss-rock fireplace.
NO. OF ROOMS	Four rooms with private bathrooms and two rooms share one bathroom. Try Arlene's Room.
RATES	Year-round rates for a single or double with a private bathroom are $100-125; a single or double with a shared bathroom is $90. There is no minimum stay. Ask about the cancellation policy.
CREDIT CARDS	American Express, Discover, MasterCard, Visa
BREAKFAST	Full country breakfast is served family style in the dining room and includes homemade breads, eggs, meats, and fruits.
AMENITIES	Robes in the rooms; antiques and crafts shop; sodas in the refrigerator; cookies and treats around the house; coffees, teas, and hot chocolate at all times.
RESTRICTIONS	No smoking, no pets, children over five are welcome.
MEMBER	Bed & Breakfast Innkeepers of Colorado

BLACK DOG INN BED & BREAKFAST

650 South Saint Vrain Avenue, Estes Park, CO 80517
Pete & Jane Princehorn, Resident Owners

970-586-0374

LOCATION	On Highway 7, 0.5 mile south of the Holiday Inn between Graves and Morgan Streets on the east side of the road. Look for oval sign and rail fence in front of inn.
OPEN	All year except Thanksgiving Day, Christmas Eve, and Christmas.
DESCRIPTION	A 1910 mountain inn with hardwood floors, knotty pine walls, antique furnishings, and original art, located on an acre surrounded by old aspen. Owners live in a cabin behind the B&B.
NO. OF ROOMS	Four rooms with private bathrooms. Try the Sundance Mountain Room.

RATES	May through September, plus holidays and weekends, rates are $85-150 for a single or double with a private bathroom and $105-140 for suites. Low-season (includes midweek specials) rates are $25 for all rooms. There is a minimum stay during the high season and on weekends and holidays. Cancellation requires 15 days' notice.
CREDIT CARDS	MasterCard, Visa
BREAKFAST	Full breakfast, served in the dining room, includes feather bed eggs, German puff pancakes, eggs olé, stuffed French toast with fruit sauce, homebaked breads, muffins, scones, potatoes Colorado, cereal, and beverages. Special meals, including those for guests with special dietary needs, are available by prior arrangement.
AMENITIES	In-room fireplaces, fireplace in the living room, Jacuzzi for two, TV/VCR and videos, full cookie jar, snacks and beverages available, footpath connects with river walk, outdoor seating, trail maps, bicycles, daypacks, water bottles, binoculars, and guest parking.
RESTRICTIONS	No smoking, no pets, no cooking, children over 12 are welcome. The inn is named after the resident Black Lab, Sara: "She is our celebrity."
REVIEWED	*Recommended Country Inns of the Rocky Mountain Region, The Birder's Guide to Bed & Breakfasts*
MEMBER	Bed & Breakfast Innkeepers of Colorado, Colorado Hotel and Lodging Association, Professional Association of Innkeepers International
KUDOS/COMMENTS	"Make yourself at home because you *are* home. I didn't want to leave. I never do. Jane and Pete make you feel like a family visiting." "Lovely antiques and decorations, very nice folks." (1997)

DRIPPING SPRINGS INN & CABINS

2551 US Highway 34, Estes Park, CO 80517   970-586-3406
Janie & Oliver Robertson, Innkeepers   800-432-7145
Some Spanish spoken   FAX 970-586-3035
EMAIL *innestes@aol.com*   WEBSITE *www.drippingsprings.com*

LOCATION	Three miles east of the visitor center in Estes Park on Highway 34 east.
OPEN	May 15 through October
DESCRIPTION	Mountain cabins and a two-story country inn on five acres of riverfront property.
NO. OF ROOMS	Five bedrooms with private bathrooms and one room with one shared bathroom. Try Grandma Lillian's Room.

RATES	June through August, rates are $110 for a single or double with a private bathroom, $69-79 for a single or double with a shared bathroom, and $115-200 for the guesthouse. September and October, rates are $89 for a single or double with a private bathroom, $69 for a single or double with a shared bathroom, and $115-200 for the guesthouse. There is a two-night minimum stay on weekends (more on holiday weekends) and cancellation requires two weeks' notice.
CREDIT CARDS	American Express, Diners Club, Discover, MasterCard, Visa
BREAKFAST	Full country breakfast is served family style and includes homemade breads, quiches, fruits, meats, muffins, juice, coffee, tea, and cocoa. Picnic basket lunches are also available.
AMENITIES	Robes; private hot tubs and fireplaces in cabins; hammocks on river; park; small refrigerator in rooms; champagne for birthdays, anniversaries, etc. on request.
RESTRICTIONS	No smoking. "We don't encourage children or pets at the B&B, but they're OK in the cabins." Jake is the resident Lab, Rutt is the cat, and Tecate is the parrot.
MEMBER	Colorado Cabins, Lodges and Campgrounds

EAGLE CLIFF HOUSE

2383 Highway 66, Estes Park, CO 80517   970-586-5425
Nancy & Mike Conrin, Resident Owners   800-414-0922
WEBSITE www.estes-park.com

LOCATION	Two miles west of the center of Estes Park. Follow signs for Highway 36, which connects with Highway 66, 0.75 mile before YMCA.
OPEN	All year
DESCRIPTION	A mountain home with guest cottage nestled in the ponderosa pines at the base of Eagle Cliff Mountain within walking distance to Rocky Mountain National Park.
NO. OF ROOMS	Two rooms with private baths and a cottage with a private bathroom and kitchenette. The cottage comes highly recommended.
RATES	Year-round rates are $80 for a single or double and $115 for the cottage. There is a two-day minimum stay at the cottage on weekends and cancellation requires three weeks' notice.
CREDIT CARDS	No
BREAKFAST	Full breakfast includes whole-grain pancakes and homemade granola.

AMENITIES	Flowers for birthdays and anniversaries, TV and extensive movie collection, snacks are always available. The Conrins are hiking and backpacking consultants and offer trailhead pick-up or delivery.
RESTRICTIONS	No smoking, no pets, children are welcome.
MEMBER	Bed & Breakfast Innkeepers of Colorado, Colorado Hotel and Lodging Association
KUDOS/COMMENTS	"Lovely, cozy home; exceptional hosts, breakfasts are superb! Excellent decor." (1996)

ESTES PARK BED & BREAKFAST

141 Courtney Lane, Estes Park, CO 80517 970-586-7781
Orie Vaye & Dick Williams, Resident Owners 800-492-3425
EMAIL *stay@estesparkbandb.com* FAX 970-586-7782
WEBSITE *www.eastesparkbandb.com*

LOCATION	Two blocks from the center of town.
OPEN	All year
DESCRIPTION	A remodeled log-style home located two miles from the Rocky Mountain National Park.
NO. OF ROOMS	Two suites with private bathrooms.
RATES	Summer rates are $125-150 for a single or double with a private bathroom. Winter rates have a variable off-season discount.
CREDIT CARDS	American Express, Discover, MasterCard, Visa
BREAKFAST	Full gourmet breakfast is served in the dining room.
AMENITIES	Outside hot tub, TV and VCRs in the rooms, close to town, wildlife viewing.
RESTRICTIONS	No smoking, no pets, no children

FRICKEY MCSHANE'S BED & BREAKFAST

1731 Avalon Drive, Estes Park, CO 80517 970-586-0872
Norm & Sharon Frickey, Resident Owners

Glenn's Mountain Vista Acre B&B, Estes Park

GLENN'S MOUNTAIN VISTA ACRE B&B

751 University Place, Estes Park, CO 80517 970-586-3547
Glenn & Judy Speece, Innkeepers
EMAIL *gmtnvista@aol.com* WEBSITE *www.estes-park.com/glenns*

LOCATION	From the intersection of Highways 36 and 7, go south 0.75 mile to Morgan. Turn right on Morgan and drive two blocks. Take a left on University Drive.
OPEN	May 15 through October
DESCRIPTION	A 1992 two-story cedar chalet with an eclectic combination of antiques, and Native American and southwestern decor.
NO. OF ROOMS	Two rooms with private bathrooms and one room shares one bathroom. The Speece's recommend the Twin Owls Room.
RATES	Rates are $85 for a single or double with a private bathroom and $65 for a single or double with a shared bathroom. There is a two-night minimum stay from June 15 through August 15. Cancellation requires 30 days' notice.
CREDIT CARDS	MasterCard, Visa
BREAKFAST	Full breakfast includes homemade breads and muffins, fresh fruit and juice, a baked egg dish and French toast or breakfast burritos.
AMENITIES	Kitchenettes, private patio or balcony, private entrances.
RESTRICTIONS	No smoking, no pets

HENDERSON HOUSE BED & BREAKFAST

5455 Highway 36, Estes Park, CO 80517
Carl & Vicki Henderson, Resident Owners
WEBSITE www.estes-park.com/henderson

970-586-4639
800-798-4639
FAX 970-586-5009

LOCATION	Five miles east of Estes Park on Highway 36.
OPEN	All year
DESCRIPTION	A 1988 three-story Cape Cod Victorian country inn on 11 acres and decorated with Victorian country furnishings.
NO. OF ROOMS	Five rooms with private bathrooms. The King and Queen suite is the most popular.
RATES	Summer rates are $125-145 for a double with a private bathroom and $155 for the suite. Off-season rates are $105-135 for a double with a private bathroom and $140 for the suite. There is a minimum stay on holidays and during weekends in the summer. Cancellation requires 14 days' notice.
CREDIT CARDS	MasterCard, Visa
BREAKFAST	Full breakfast is served in the dining room, gazebo, or on the deck. Dinner is also available.
AMENITIES	Gazebo spa, king- and queen-size beds, two rooms have whirlpool tubs, fresh flowers, robes, central TV room with phone, welcome trays, dinners on back deck or inside house, suite with TV and VCR, all rooms with fireplaces.
RESTRICTIONS	No smoking, no pets, no children. The resident dogs are Berry, Kodi, and Meila.

Henderson House Bed & Breakfast, Estes Park

MEMBER   Bed & Breakfast Inns of Colorado, Estes Valley Resort Association

KUDOS/COMMENTS   "The Hendersons are delightful and their home is beautiful and spacious." "Superb meals and wonderful snacks." "We loved every room." (1997) "Lots of extras." (1999)

HOLLYHOCK COTTAGE BED & BREAKFAST

5475 North Street Vrain, Highway 36   970-586-0785
Estes Park, CO 80517
Gini & Floyd Denton, Resident Owners

LOCATION   Five miles outside Estes Park down Highway 36 toward Boulder. Turn onto Hell Canyon Road between Henderson House B&B and Jellystone Park campground, and go 18 miles up Hell Canyon Road.

OPEN   Memorial Day until October

DESCRIPTION   A 1989 two-story country host home furnished with antiques and some Victorian decor.

NO. OF ROOMS   Two bedrooms with private bathrooms. The owner recommends the Roses & Ribbons Room.

RATES   Rates are $80-90 for a single or double with a private bathroom. There is a minimum stay during July 4 and a ten-day cancellation policy.

CREDIT CARDS   MasterCard, Visa

Hollyhock Cottage Bed & Breakfast, Estes Park

BREAKFAST	Full breakfast includes fresh fruit, homemade breads, and "something different every day."
AMENITIES	Covered porch to enjoy scenery and wildlife, spacious sitting room for relaxing, TV and VCR, hiking, a special sweet upon arrival.
RESTRICTIONS	No smoking, no pets. The cottage is set up for couples—"Sorry no children." Rusty is the resident poodle and Crissy is the house cat.

THE QUILT HOUSE BED & BREAKFAST

310 Riverside Drive, Estes Park, CO 80517   970-586-0427
Hans & Miriam Graetzer, Resident Owners
German spoken

LOCATION	From Elkhorn Avenue (the main street through town), turn south at the traffic light to Riverside Drive. Continue about one mile on Riverside Drive past a Pizza Hut to a large brown house on the left.
OPEN	All year
DESCRIPTION	A 1924 two-story mountain host home decorated with quilts and a large picture window facing the mountains. There is also a guesthouse with a fully equipped kitchenette.
NO. OF ROOMS	Three rooms with private bathrooms. Hans recommends the guesthouse.
RATES	Year-round rates for a single or double are $35-55. The guesthouse with a kitchenette rents for $65 for a double and the entire B&B rents for $230 for up to eight people. There is no minimum stay and cancellation requires five days' notice.
CREDIT CARDS	No
BREAKFAST	Full breakfast is served in the dining room and includes juice; hot dish; fruit plate; homemade bread or muffins; choice of coffee, tea, or hot chocolate; and friendly conversation.
AMENITIES	Guest lounge, games, books, snack area, homemade quilts on the beds, guesthouse is handicapped accessible, file of restaurant menus, hiking trail guidebook available.
RESTRICTIONS	No smoking, no pets, children over 10 are welcome.
MEMBER	Bed & Breakfast Innkeepers of Colorado

ROMANTIC RIVERSONG INN

PO Box 1910, Estes Park, CO 80517
Gary & Sue Mansfield, Innkeepers
Some Spanish spoken
EMAIL *riversng@frii.com*

970-586-4666
FAX 970-577-0699

WEBSITE *romanticriversong.com*

LOCATION	Take Highway 36 from Denver. Proceed through Estes Park to Moraine Avenue, at the stoplight at Mary's Lake Road turn left, go one block and cross bridge, then make an immediate right and proceed to the end.
OPEN	All year
DESCRIPTION	A collection of 1920s Craftsman cottages nestled on the hillside with spectacular views of the Continental Divide.
NO. OF ROOMS	Nine bedrooms with private bathrooms. The Mansfields suggest the Mountain Rose Room for its see-through fireplace and rooftop shower overlooking the snowcapped peaks of Rocky Mountain National Park.
RATES	Year-round rates are $135-250 for a single or double with a private bathroom. There is a two-night minimum stay (three nights during Christmas) and cancellation requires 15 days' notice (31 days during holidays) less a $25 fee.
CREDIT CARDS	MasterCard, Visa
BREAKFAST	Full multicourse breakfast is served in the dining room and includes entrées such as John Wayne casserole, giddy-up grits, old miners' potatoes, and fresh-from-the-oven cinnamon rolls (Sue's grandmother's recipe). Candlelight dinners are available by prior reservation.
AMENITIES	All rooms have fireplaces, romantic tubs and showers, and cozy robes; wildlife and flowers abound; located on 27 acres along a river with ponds, gazebo, hiking trails, and stunning mountain views; three rooms are wheelchair accessible; elopement and renewal ceremonies performed.
RESTRICTIONS	No smoking, no pets, children over 12 are welcome. Only two people per room except in the Cowboy's Delight. OBe (O Be Joyful!) is the resident golden retriever. Other critters on the property include elk, squirrels, rabbits, deer, beaver, and birds.
REVIEWED	*America's Romantic Inns, The Colorado Guide, Birders' Guide to Bed & Breakfast Inns, Recommended Country Inns of the Rocky Mountains, Great Towns of America, Special Places, America's Wonderful Little Hotels & Inns*

Independent Innkeepers Association, Distinctive Inns of Colorado, Professional Association of Innkeepers International

RATED   AAA 3 Diamonds, Mobil 3 Stars

KUDOS/COMMENTS   "Definitely a place for couples to make memories." "Beautiful rooms with unique furnishings. Peaceful setting for a great getaway." (1996)

TAHARAA MOUNTAIN LODGE

3110 South Saint Vrain Avenue, Estes Park, CO 80517   *970-577-0098*

EVERGREEN

This small foothills community is fast becoming a Denver suburb. Historical Evergreen features quaint shops and pretty Evergreen Lake. There are a number of art and music fairs each summer. About 30 miles west of Denver via I-70 and Highway 74.

BEARS-R-INN

27425 Spruce Lane, Evergreen, CO 80439   *303-670-1205*

KUDOS/COMMENTS   "Great place to stay. Wonderful location. Fantastic cookies and dog tricks." (1999)

HIGHLAND HAVEN CREEKSIDE INN

4395 Independence Trail, Evergreen, CO 80439   *303-674-3577*
Gail Riley & Tom Statzell, Innkeepers   *800-459-2406*
Some French spoken   *FAX 303-674-9088*
EMAIL thehaven2@earthlink.net   *WEBSITE www.highlandhaven.com*

LOCATION   Exit I-70 at Evergreen Parkway and continue for about eight miles into old Evergreen. Once you've passed Evergreen Lake, you will be on Main Street. Look for Cozy Cleaners on the right-hand side of the street and take an immediate right. Look for the blue sign.

OPEN   All year

DESCRIPTION	A 1960 two-story wood-sided lodge and separate wood-sided cottages nestled on Bear Creek and decorated with classic Colorado furnishings and Ralph Lauren bedding.
NO. OF ROOMS	Sixteen bedrooms with private bathrooms. Try the Gardener's Cottage.
RATES	May through August, rates are $80-200 for a single or double with a private bathroom, $130-150 for a suite, and $80-220 for a cottage. September through April, rates are $75-200 for a single or double with a private bathroom, $115-200 for a suite, and $75-200 for a cottage. There is a minimum stay for select rooms during summer months.
CREDIT CARDS	American Express, Discover, MasterCard, Visa
BREAKFAST	Continental plus is served in the dining room and includes bakery fresh bagels and flavored cream cheeses; muffins and/or sweet breads; hot dishes such as cheese and vegetable egg strata, raspberry and white chocolate bread pudding, or hot cranberry apple crisp; fresh fruit; hot oatmeal and cold cereal bar; custom-blended coffee; herbal teas; and juices.
AMENITIES	Bottled spring waters by bedside; custom chocolates; flowers and romantic poems on bed to celebrate weddings, anniversaries, and birthdays; landscaped grounds for picnics or just relaxing; robes in select cottages with Jacuzzis; happy hour each Friday and Sunday in lobby area.
RESTRICTIONS	No smoking, no pets
REVIEWED	Voted one of the top three inns of 1997 by *Conde Nast Traveler*; voted Best Honeymoon Getaway by *Colorado Homes and Lifestyles*
MEMBER	Bed & Breakfast Inns of Colorado
RATED	AAA 3 Diamonds, Mobil 3 Stars

FAIRPLAY

Situated in a high, grassy valley surrounded by mountain peaks, Fairplay was founded in 1859 by a group of idealistic prospectors intent on treating people with equity. As this was the height of the gold rush, such noble aspirations were not long endured. Do not miss the fascinating outdoor museum, South Park City Museum—a collection of furnished historic buildings, taken from around the South Park Area and arranged to recreate the feel of an old mining town at the end of the 19th century.

THE BEARS DEN

PO Box 1326, Fairplay, CO 80440   719-836-0921
Thelma Milburn, Resident Owner   800-585-4711

OPEN	All year
DESCRIPTION	A lodge-style log house located at 11,000 feet ("the highest B&B in North America").
NO. OF ROOMS	Four bedrooms with private bathrooms.
RATES	Rates are $110-150 for a single or double with a private bath and deck.
CREDIT CARDS	No
BREAKFAST	Full breakfast is served in the dining room and includes eggs Benedict, Belgian waffles, pancakes, French toast, pastry, fruit, orange juice, coffee, and tea.
AMENITIES	Slippers and bathrobes provided; library; recreation room with Ping-Pong, exercise equipment, TV; spa.
RESTRICTIONS	No smoking, no pets. Bears are seen frequently.

HAND HOTEL BED & BREAKFAST

531 Front Street, Fairplay, CO 80440   719-836-3595
Dale & Kathy Fitting, Resident Owners   FAX 719-836-1799
WEBSITE *www.handhotel.com/*

LOCATION	In Fairplay's Historic District.
OPEN	All year
DESCRIPTION	Built in the 1930s with eclectic, historical, theme-based rooms like the Miner, Trapper, Outlaw, Silverheels (after a dance hall girl), and School Marm rooms.

NO. OF ROOMS	Eleven rooms. Try the Silverheels Room.
RATES	Year-round rates are $45 for a single and $60 for a double.
CREDIT CARDS	American Express, MasterCard, Visa
BREAKFAST	Continental breakfast is served in the dining room and includes bagel, coffee, cereal, and fruit.
RESTRICTIONS	No smoking inside, pets are allowed for $5 extra, children are welcome.

FLORISSANT

Home of the Florissant Fossil Beds National Monument that features tropical fossils (believe that or not). From Colorado Springs, 30 miles west on Highway 24.

PINECREST LODGE

178 Palmer Drive, Florissant, CO 80816   719-687-3425
Cavin & Larry Harper, Resident Owners   800-265-8531
EMAIL pinecrest@compuserv.com   FAX 719-687-3496
WEBSITE www.comcenter.com/pinecrest

LOCATION	Thirty miles west of Colorado Springs.
OPEN	All year
DESCRIPTION	A lodge-style chalet.
NO. OF ROOMS	Eleven bedrooms with private baths and four cabins.
RATES	Year-round rates range from $85-$130 for a single or double with a private bath; cabins are $98.
CREDIT CARDS	Discover, MasterCard, Visa
BREAKFAST	Full breakfast is served in the dining room.
AMENITIES	Indoor pool and hot tub, fishing lake. The lodge borders Fossil Bed National Monument.
RESTRICTIONS	No smoking, no pets, children are welcome.

FORT COLLINS

A medium-size (and growing) city, Fort Collins has its roots in farming and ranching, though the presence of Colorado State University gives it a more sophisticated, "college town" flavor. The recently restored Old Town is a definite must to explore. There's art, theater, and music at the Lincoln Center. The Anheuser-Busch Clydesdales and Visitors Center are a kick, as is the New West Fest in August and the Balloon Festival in September. Head out of town to discover the wild and scenic Cache la Poudre (Poo-der) River and Canyon, Lory State Park, and Horsetooth Reservoir. From Denver, 60 miles north on I-25.

BENNETT HOUSE BED & BREAKFAST

314 East Mulberry Street, Fort Collins, CO 80524   970-482-0025
Carolyn Goodwin, Resident Innkeeper

LOCATION	From I-5, take Highway 14 into town. It becomes Mulberry Street at the railroad tracks. Continue west for 5.5 blocks. The B&B is on the right between Peterson and Mathews.
OPEN	All year
DESCRIPTION	A 1902 simplified Queen Anne inn furnished with family antiques and collectibles.
NO. OF ROOMS	One bedroom with a private bathroom.
RATES	Year-round rates are $55 for a single and $65 for a double.
CREDIT CARDS	No
BREAKFAST	Continental breakfast is served in the dining room and includes coffee or tea, juice, fruit, and a bakery item. Cereal is available upon request. Special dietary needs may be accommodated with prior notice.
RESTRICTIONS	No smoking, no pets, no children. Thirteen-year-old Orion is the resident cocker spaniel.
MEMBER	Northern Colorado Innkeepers Association, Northern Colorado Bed & Breakfast Association

THE EDWARDS HOUSE BED & BREAKFAST

402 Mountain Avenue, Fort Collins, CO 80521   *970-493-9191*
Gregory Belcher & Leslie Vogt, Resident Owners   *800-281-9190*
Spanish, French, and German spoken   *FAX 970-484-0706*
EMAIL *edshouse@edwardshouse.com*   WEBSITE *www.edwardshouse.com*

LOCATION	Three blocks west of College Avenue.

OPEN	All year
DESCRIPTION	A fully remodeled, neoclassical Denver Four Square with Victorian furnishings.
NO. OF ROOMS	Six rooms with private bathrooms and one room shares one bathroom. The owners recommend the Montezuma Fuller Suite.
RATES	Year-round rates are $105 for a single or double with a private bathroom, $85 for a single or double with a shared bathroom, and $135-145 for a suite. There is no minimum stay and cancellation requires two weeks' notice.
CREDIT CARDS	American Express, Discover, MasterCard, Visa
BREAKFAST	Full breakfast, served in the dining room, includes a special daily entrée, seasonal fruits, homemade baked goods, and beverages. Special meals are available on request.
AMENITIES	Fresh flowers; robes; private phones; TV/VCRs; evening hors d'oeuvres; use of library, parlor, exercise room, fax, copy machines, computer ports; large conference room for meetings and special events; fireplaces; air conditioning.
RESTRICTIONS	No smoking, no pets, children over 10 are welcome.
MEMBER	Bed & Breakfast Innkeepers of Colorado, Professional Association of Innkeepers International, Distinctive Inns of Colorado
RATED	AAA 3 Diamonds, Mobil 3 Stars
KUDOS/COMMENTS	"Wonderful variety of rooms, beautifully furnished and decorated." "Warm reception and great breakfast." (1997)

Elizabeth Street Guest House B&B, Fort Collins

ELIZABETH STREET GUEST HOUSE B&B

202 East Elizabeth Street, Fort Collins, CO 80524   970-493-2337
John & Sheryl Clark, Innkeepers   FAX 970-493-6662
WEBSITE www.bbonline.com/co/elizabeth

LOCATION	In the Historic District, one block east of Colorado State University campus on the northeast corner of Elizabeth and Remington.
OPEN	All year
DESCRIPTION	A restored 1905 two-story American Four Square brick home with oak woodwork, turn-of-the-century antiques, and folk art.
NO. OF ROOMS	One room with a private bathroom and two rooms share one bathroom. The Clarks' favorite room is the Alaska.
RATES	Year-round rates are $65-95 for a single or double with a private bathroom and $45-70 for a single or double with a shared bathroom. There is a minimum stay during Colorado State University events. Cancellation requires one weeks' notice.
CREDIT CARDS	American Express, Discover, MasterCard, Visa
BREAKFAST	Full breakfast, served in the dining room, includes tea and coffee, juice, three kinds of cereal, fruit, homemade muffins and breads, eggs, and specialty dishes.
AMENITIES	Robes and turndown service, TV in parlor, tea and coffee always available, books and games, guest refrigerator, airport shuttle, ironing board and iron.
RESTRICTIONS	No smoking, no pets. Louie, the resident blue heeler, plays Frisbee and loves to go on walks with guests and show off his food dispenser. Children over 10 years of age are welcome.
REVIEWED	*Recommended Country Inns of the Rocky Mountain Region, Best Places to Stay in the Rockies*
MEMBER	Tourist House Association, Northern Colorado Bed & Breakfast Association

FLYNN'S INN BED & BREAKFAST

700 Remington Street, Fort Collins, CO 80524   970-484-9984

MARIPOSA ON SPRING CREEK

706 East Stuart, Fort Collins, CO 80525   970-495-9604
Michele Kyle, Resident Owner   800-495-9604
EMAIL bandb@mariposaspa.com   WEBSITE www.mariposaspa.com

LOCATION	Near Colorado State University.
OPEN	All year.
DESCRIPTION	A Mediterranean-style building with three wings surrounding a tropical atrium.
NO. OF ROOMS	Six bedrooms with private bathrooms.
RATES	Year-round rates are $85-105 for a single or double.
CREDIT CARDS	American Express, Discover, MasterCard, Visa
BREAKFAST	Full breakfast is served in the atrium.
AMENITIES	TVs available, phones in rooms, full-service Aveda spa.
RESTRICTIONS	No smoking, no pets, children over 12 are welcome.
KUDOS/COMMENTS	"Lovely and unusual setting. It is a full-service day spa, hair salon, and B&B." (1999)

The West Mulberry Street Bed & Breakfast Inn, Fort Collins

THE WEST MULBERRY STREET
BED & BREAKFAST INN

616 West Mulberry Street, Fort Collins, CO 80521   *970-221-1917*
Michael & Rebecca Martin, Resident Owners   *FAX 970-490-2810*
Bits and pieces of French spoken
EMAIL becksbb@verinet.com
WEBSITE www.bbonline.com/co/westmulberry

LOCATION	Six miles west of I-25 from exit 269B (Highway 14) and two blocks north of Colorado State University between Loomis and Whitcomb Streets.
OPEN	All year
DESCRIPTION	A 1905 three-story American Four Square with quartersawn oak floors, beveled and stained-glass leaded windows, and turn-of-the-century furnishings.
NO. OF ROOMS	Four rooms with private bathrooms, plus a two-room business suite. Rebecca recommends the West Garden Room.
RATES	Year-round rates (including tax) are $66-110 for a single or double with a private bathroom. The business suite rents for $165. There is a minimum stay during holidays, graduation, and special events. Cancellation requires seven days' notice, 30 days during special events.
CREDIT CARDS	American Express, Diners Club, Discover, MasterCard, Visa
BREAKFAST	Full breakfast, served in the dining room, includes quiche, omelets, waffles, crepes, homemade baked goods, and beverages.
AMENITIES	Fresh flowers, evening snack, bicycles, robes, TV room, down comforters, and reading material on the area's history.
RESTRICTIONS	No smoking, no pets, children over 12 are welcome.
REVIEWED	*Recommended Country Inns*
MEMBER	Bed & Breakfast Innkeepers of Colorado, Northern Colorado Bed & Breakfast Association, Professional Association of Innkeepers International, Northern Colorado Innkeepers Association
KUDOS/COMMENTS	"The B&B makes you feel very comfortable and the rooms are beautiful." "The house is very nicely done; the innkeepers are delightful, kind, caring, gracious, and lovely." (1997) "Beautiful Victorian, lovely and tasteful decor, friendly hosts, excellent location, fabulous woodwork." (1999)

FRISCO
(SUMMIT COUNTY)

On the south shores of Lake Dillon, Frisco lies at the crossroads of Summit County's year-round resorts. From here, it's a quick trip to Breckenridge, Copper Mountain, Keystone, and handy enough to Vail. The Frisco Nordic Ski Center offers lovely cross-country skiing through a pine forest along the lake shore. Heartier souls will want to enter the Frisco Gold Rush, the biggest citizens' cross-country race in the Rocky Mountains. Frisco's Fantastic Fourth features laser light shows, live music, parades, and spectacular fireworks over Lake Dillon. From Denver, 75 miles west on I-70 and Highway 9.

THE FINN INN

0224 Highwood Terrace, Frisco, CO 80443 970-668-5108
Bill & Edith Anttila, Innkeepers
Finnish spoken
EMAIL anttila@colorado.net

LOCATION	Take exit 201 off I-70 and an immediate left onto Forest Drive. Stay on Forest for 0.33 mile until it ends at Aspen Drive. Turn left onto Aspen and go up a slight incline to the stop sign on Highwood Terrace. Turn right onto Highwood and go to the fourth driveway on the right.
OPEN	All year
DESCRIPTION	A 1971 three-story host home with redwood siding, a cedar shake roof, rustic decor, and antiques.
NO. OF ROOMS	One bedroom with private bathrooms and two rooms with one shared bathroom.
RATES	December through March, rates are $80 for a single or double with a private or shared bathroom. April through November, rates are $60 for a single or double with a private bathroom. There is a two-night minimum stay during high season and cancellation requires 15 days' notice.
CREDIT CARDS	No
BREAKFAST	Full hearty breakfast is served in the dining room. The menu changes daily.
AMENITIES	Hot tub on the deck; TV/VCR and videos in all rooms (over 500 videos in all); detailed information and maps for the eight major ski areas within a radius of 40 miles.
RESTRICTIONS	No smoking, children over 10 are welcome. Mustaa is the resident mixed cat and Ariel is the calico.

FRISCO LODGE

321 Main Street, Frisco, CO 80443	970-668-0195
Susan Wentworth, Resident Owner	800-279-6000
EMAIL info@friscolodge.com	FAX 970-668-0149

LOCATION   On the corner of 4th and Main.

OPEN   All year

DESCRIPTION   An 1885 Tyrolean with rustic furnishings.

NO. OF ROOMS   Ten rooms with private bathrooms and eight rooms with three shared bathrooms.

RATES   Winter rates are $60-130 for a single or double with a private bathroom and $30-90 for a single or double with a shared bathroom. Summer rates are $35-85 for a single or double with a private bathroom and $30-65 for a double with a shared bathroom. Inquire about a minimum stay requirement. There is a reservation/cancellation policy.

CREDIT CARDS   American Express, Discover, MasterCard, Visa

BREAKFAST   Continental is served in the dining room.

AMENITIES   Hot tub, fireplace, TV, radio and phone in rooms, complimentary après-ski, small meeting facilities.

RESTRICTIONS   No smoking, no pets, children are welcome.

LARK MOUNTAIN INN

109 Granite Street, Frisco, CO 80443	970-668-5237
Sheila Morgan, Resident Owner	800-668-5275
EMAIL smlark@oneimage.com	FAX 970-668-2037
WEBSITE www.toski.com/lark	

LOCATION   From Denver, take I-70 west to the Frisco Main Street exit, 201. Drive 0.75 mile down Main, turn right on First Avenue. The Lark is at First and Granite, one block off Main Street.

OPEN   All year

DESCRIPTION   A 1972 two-story log and timber inn with hand-carved lodgepole and piñon-pine interior.

NO. OF ROOMS   Three bedrooms with private bathrooms, four rooms with shared bathrooms.

RATES   Seasonal rates are $80-100 for low and regular seasons and $80-170 for holiday and prime seasons.

CREDIT CARDS	MasterCard, Visa
BREAKFAST	Full breakfast, served in the dining room or on the sun deck, includes a hot entrée with fresh fruit, cereals, yogurt, and fresh-baked item.
AMENITIES	Hot tub, robes, down comforters, mountain bikes for guests' use, rock gardens with native flowers, free transportation to all Summit County resorts.
RESTRICTIONS	No smoking, children over eight are welcome. Resident keeshond and "snow Frisbee" champ is Lexi Lopez.
MEMBER	Summit County Bed & Breakfast Association, Bed & Breakfast Innkeepers of Colorado, Colorado Hotel and Lodging Association, Professional Association of Innkeepers International
AWARDS	Won 1st Place in Frisco's 1995 Christmas Decorating Contest

MARDEI'S MOUNTAIN RETREAT

221 South 4th Avenue, Frisco, CO 80443   970-668-5337
Mike & Amy Wolach, Resident Owners   888-658-5337
EMAIL mardeis@colorado.net   WEBSITE www.mardeis.com

LOCATION	From I-70 exit 201, go west on Main Street; at the first four-way stop, turn south and go two blocks.
OPEN	All year
DESCRIPTION	A 1950 two-story mountain cabin host home with comfortable furniture.
NO. OF ROOMS	Three rooms with private bathrooms and three rooms share two bathrooms. Columbine is the best room.
RATES	Holiday (Christmas, Presidents' Day, Easter) rates are $90-120 for a double with a private bathroom, $70-90 for a single or double with a shared bathroom, and $35-45 for a bed in the dorm room. Ski-season rates are $70-90 for a double with a private bathroom, $50-60 for a single with a shared bathroom, and $25-35 for a bed in the dorm. Off-season rates are lower. There is a three-day minimum stay during holidays and two-week cancellation policy.
CREDIT CARDS	MasterCard, Visa
BREAKFAST	Full European breakfast is served in the dining room and includes granola, yogurt, cheeses, fresh-baked muffins, bagels, fresh fruit, and beverages.
AMENITIES	Fireplaces in common areas, one bedroom with private fireplace, hot tub on deck, cooking surprises, European down comforters and sinks in the rooms, TV and VCRs in rooms with private bathrooms, movie library, snowshoes available in the winter and horseshoes in summer.

RESTRICTIONS	No pets, no smoking. Children are welcome. The resident golden Lab is Sage.
REVIEWED	*Recommended Country Inns of the Rocky Mountain Region*
KUDOS/COMMENTS	"Excellent!" (1997) "Warm and cozy atmosphere, great fireplaces, centrally located to all Summit County ski areas." (1999)

OPEN BOX H BED & BREAKFAST

711 Belford Street, Frisco, CO 80443   *970-668-0661*
Chuck & Phyllis Hugins, Resident Owners   *FAX 970-668-0671*
Limited Spanish spoken
EMAIL *phugins@juno.com*
WEBSITE *www.home.att.net/~bear-denver/hugins*

LOCATION	From I-70 take exit 203. Go south on Summit Boulevard and continue through fourth stop light. Pass Main Street for a block and a half, turn right on 8th Avenue, right on Pitkin, left on 7th Avenue, and left into alley.
OPEN	All year except April 20 to May 20
DESCRIPTION	A 1988 three-level contemporary host home with contemporary furnishings and beautiful mountain views.
NO. OF ROOMS	Two rooms with private bathrooms and two suites share one bathroom. Try the Butterfly Room or Mountain View Suite.
RATES	December 15 to April 15, rates are $69-89 for a single or double with a private bathroom and $99 for a suite. May 20 to December 14, rates are $59-79 for a single or double with a private bathroom and $89 for a suite. There is no minimum stay and cancellation requires 30 days' notice
CREDIT CARDS	American Express, Discover, MasterCard, Visa
BREAKFAST	Full breakfast, served in the dining room, includes waffles, pancakes, eggs, corned-beef hash, French toast, meat, cereal, muffins, home-baked bread, yogurt, and beverages.
AMENITIES	Robes, deck and fireplace in Mountain View Suite; Jacuzzi in Butterfly Room's private bath; free shuttle to ski areas; TVs and recliners in rooms.
RESTRICTIONS	No smoking, no pets. Children of all ages are welcome.
REVIEWED	*Colorado Bed & Breakfast Cookbook, Discover the Rockies*
MEMBER	Summit County Bed & Breakfast Association

FRISCO   145

FRUITA

As its name practically insists, this lovely little town is surrounded by orchards. Is anyone surprised? Just north of Colorado National Monument and 10 miles west of Grand Junction on Highway 6.

STONEHAVEN BED & BREAKFAST

798 North Mesa Street, Fruita, CO 81521   970-858-0898
Debra Menger, Innkeeper   800-303-0898
EMAIL *stonehvn@gj.net*   FAX 970-858-7765
WEBSITE *www.gj.net/~stonehvn*

LOCATION	Take exit 19 off I-70 to Aspen Street. Turn right and pass the city market. Turn right at Circle Park and right again onto Mesa Street and go seven blocks.
OPEN	All year
DESCRIPTION	A 1908 two-and-a-half-story Georgia Victorian country inn with Victorian decor, listed on the National and State Historic Registers.
NO. OF ROOMS	Two bedrooms with private bathrooms and two rooms with two shared bathrooms. Try the Gray Room.
RATES	April through September, rates are $85-145 for a single or double with a private bathroom, $65-75 for a single or double with a shared bathroom, $110 for a suite, and $350 for the entire B&B. October through March, rates are $65-110 for a single or double with a private bathroom, $45-65 for a single or double with a shared bathroom, $85 for a suite, and $295 for the entire B&B. There is no minimum stay. Ask about a cancellation policy.
CREDIT CARDS	American Express, Discover, MasterCard, Visa
BREAKFAST	Full breakfast is served in the dining room or on the veranda and includes homemade breads and egg dishes made with fresh eggs from the resident hens. "There's so much homemade food, you won't need lunch."
AMENITIES	Hot tub under starry skies, one-and-a-half acres with playground equipment and farm animals ("kids' paradise"), space for weddings, kitchen available for guests' use.
RESTRICTIONS	No smoking inside, no pets, children are welcome. There are chickens on the property. Phil is the resident rooster.
MEMBER	Bed & Breakfast Innkeepers of Colorado, Professional Association of Innkeepers International

VALLEY VIEW BED & BREAKFAST

8880 21 Road, Fruita, CO 81501   970-858-9503
Lou & Jan, Resident Owners

GARDENER

Tucked into the fertile Huerfano River Valley just south of the Wet Mountain Valley and San Isabel National Forest, this beautiful, somewhat remote area remains a well-kept secret. Ranching and farming are pretty much what goes on around here, but there's action to be had in Westcliffe: the Rainbow Trail Round-Up Mountain Bike Race in July is one of the best of its kind; and in August, Jazz in the Sangres attracts multitudes. From Pueblo, south on I-25 to Walsenburg, then 27 miles northwest on Highway 69.

HEARTS' SONG BED & BREAKFAST

8055 County Road 570, Gardener, CO 81040   719-746-2412
Alan Mace & Dove Hibbert, Resident Owners
EMAIL dove8hibb@aol.com

GEORGETOWN

A remarkably well-restored Victorian mining town and National Historic District with more than 200 of the original buildings still standing. Don't miss the bighorn sheep viewing station next to Georgetown Lake. Close to Loveland Ski area. Major events include the Georgetown Christmas Market and Santa Lucia Celebration in early December. Check out the Georgetown Loop railroad or take a tour in a horse-drawn carriage. Fifty miles west of Denver on I-70.

ALPINE HIDEAWAY B&B

PO Box 788, Georgetown, CO 80444   303-569-2800
Dawn Janov, Innkeeper   800-490-9011
EMAIL aahideaway@aol.com
WEBSITE www.entertain.com/wedgwood/hide.html

LOCATION   From Denver, take I-70 west approximately 45 minutes to exit 228
                  at Georgetown.

OPEN	All year
DESCRIPTION	A 1993 two-story extended A-frame with traditional decor situated above Georgetown Lake with spectacular views of the valley and surrounding peaks.
NO. OF ROOMS	Three bedrooms with private bathrooms. Try the Mountain Contemporary Room.
RATES	June through August, rates are $145-165 for a single or double with a private bathroom. September through May, rates are $125-165 for a single or double with a private bathroom. There is no minimum stay and cancellation requires 14 days' notice.
CREDIT CARDS	MasterCard, Visa
BREAKFAST	Full gourmet breakfast is delivered to guestrooms and includes quiches, cremes, fresh fruit and cheese, coffee and tea, and other delectable foods.
AMENITIES	Each room has a fireplace; Jacuzzi tub; access to swings, ponds, and fountains; turndown service with chocolates; fresh flowers; key location to Colorado Rockies and within 15 to 45 minutes of eight major ski areas.
RESTRICTIONS	No smoking, no pets, no children
REVIEWED	*Quick Escapes, Off the Beaten Path, The Colorado Guide*
KUDOS/COMMENTS	"Wonderful romantic getaway. Beautiful rooms with Jacuzzi and fireplaces. Friendly hosts." (1999)

HARDY HOUSE

605 *Brownell Street, Georgetown, CO 80444*   303-569-3388
Carla & Mike Wagner, *Resident Owners*   800-490-4802
EMAIL *hhousebb@aol.com*
WEBSITE *www.entertain/wedgewood/hardy.html*

LOCATION	Fifty miles west of Denver on I-70. Take exit 228, and head south on Argentine, which turns into Brownell.
OPEN	All year
DESCRIPTION	An 1880 two-story Victorian Cape Cod with a white picket fence, a potbellied stove in the parlor, and Victorian decor, located in the Georgetown Historic District.
NO. OF ROOMS	Four rooms with private bathrooms. The Wagners recommend the Victoria Suite.
RATES	Year-round rates are $79-125 for a single or double with a private bathroom and $89-125 for a suite. There is no minimum stay and cancellation requires seven days' notice.
CREDIT CARDS	No

BREAKFAST	Full formal candlelight breakfast is served. Box lunches are available in the summer. Dinner is available with the romance package.
AMENITIES	All rooms have TV/VCR, phone for guests in the hallway, hot tub outside, afternoon tea and coffee with home-baked goodies. The inn is an easy walk to the Historic District, shops and restaurants. Romance and other packages are available.
RESTRICTIONS	No smoking, no pets, children over 12 are welcome. Frankie is the resident parrot and the schnauzer is Guss.
REVIEWED	*Recommended Country Inns of the Rocky Mountain Region*
MEMBER	Colorado Hotel and Lodging Association
KUDOS/COMMENTS	"Run by friendly owners." (1996) "Beautifully furnished 19th-century home. Nice people." (1999)

HILLSIDE HOUSE

1034 Main Street, Georgetown, CO 80444   303-569-0912
Ken & Marge Acker, Resident Owners   800-490-9012

LOCATION	Take exit 228 from I-70, go past the Total gas station, and turn right at the stop sign. Turn left at the first street (11th), go four short blocks to Main, and turn right. The inn is the second house on the left.
OPEN	All year
DESCRIPTION	An early 1900s-era Victorian with stained glass, planked floors, antiques, and a veranda that stretches across the front of the house.
NO. OF ROOMS	Two rooms with private bathrooms. Try the Columbine Room.
RATES	Year-round rates are $70-$95 for a double with a private bathroom. There is no minimum stay and cancellation requires one weeks' notice.
CREDIT CARDS	MasterCard, Visa
BREAKFAST	Full breakfast is served in the dining room and includes Belgian waffles with peaches or strawberries and cream, breads and cakes, juices, and fruit.
AMENITIES	Freestanding fireplace in Columbine Room; hot tub in beautiful backyard; very comfortable sitting room with TV, movies, books, puzzles, games; great doll and book collections; lots of handmade quilts; evening tea, hot chocolate with cookies.
RESTRICTIONS	No smoking, no pets. Mandy is the resident German shepherd. She stays in the owners' part of the house unless invited to see guests.
REVIEWED	*Georgetown Loop Railroad Guide*
KUDOS/COMMENTS	"Wonderful hosts and a comfy home." (1996)

GLACIER

At the eastern edge of Arapaho National Forest, St. Mary's Glacier lays claim to being the southern-most glacier in North America. Come prepared for a little summer skiing. Glacier is also a good starting point for exploring the area's numerous ghost towns.

ST. MARY'S GLACIER BED & BREAKFAST

336 Crest Drive, Glacier, CO 80452   303-567-4084
Ingrid Selby, Innkeeper   303-914-3324 *(Denver)*
EMAIL *stmg66@oneimage.com*   FAX *303-567-4084 (call first)*
WEBSITE *www.coloradovacation.com/bed/stmary/index.html*

LOCATION	From Denver, take I-70 west about 45 minutes to exit 238. Take Fall River Road north 9.5 miles until you reach Silver Lake. Go along the south side of the lake and bear left at the "T." Go about 50 feet and take the next right; continue 100 yards to the B&B.
OPEN	All year
DESCRIPTION	A 1993 three-story hand-hewn log inn with country furnishings surrounded by the snowcapped Continental Divide.
NO. OF ROOMS	Seven rooms with private bathrooms and a cabin. Try the Arapaho Room.
RATES	Year-round rates are $85-159 for a single or double with a private bathroom. There is no minimum stay, but there is a discount for stays of more than one night. Cancellation requires 14 days' notice.
CREDIT CARDS	American Express, Diners Club, Discover, MasterCard, Visa
BREAKFAST	Full breakfast is served in the dining room and includes eggs, meat, potatoes, bread, and fruit. Lunch and dinner are also available.
AMENITIES	River-rock fireplaces, hot tub, whirlpool tubs, private decks, brass beds with hand-sewn quilts, parlor and library, VCR/TV, hammock for two, facilities for weddings and seminars. "Because of our remote location," says Ingrid, "guests are invited to use our kitchen facilities to prepare an evening meal."
RESTRICTIONS	No smoking, no pets
MEMBER	Bed & Breakfast Innkeepers of Colorado
KUDOS/COMMENTS	"Wonderful, huge log home with fireplaces." "Built with guests in mind in a beautiful mountain setting." "Hosts are friendly, caring people." (1997)

GLEN HAVEN

INN AT GLEN HAVEN

7468 County Road 43, Glen Haven, CO 80532   970-586-3897

GLENWOOD SPRINGS

Known for, and named after, its wonderful hot springs, this community is also a hotspot for biking, rafting, kayaking, and hiking in and around Glenwood Canyon. Explore the Glenwood Caverns and Yampah Vapor Caves. Aspen and historic Redstone are both short drives from here. Eighty-nine miles east of Grand Junction and 157 miles west of Denver on I-70.

ADDUCCI'S INN BED & BREAKFAST

1023 Grand Avenue, Glenwood Springs, CO 81601   970-945-9341
Virginia Adducci, Resident Owner

LOCATION	Center of town, five blocks south of I-70 exit.
OPEN	All year
DESCRIPTION	A 1900 Victorian with antique furnishings.
NO. OF ROOMS	One room with a private bathroom, two rooms share a half-bathroom and shower, and two rooms share a full bathroom.
RATES	Year-round rates are $75 for a single or double with a private bathroom, $28-65 for a single or double with a shared bathroom, and $150 for a single or double with a private hot tub. There is a reservation/cancellation policy.
CREDIT CARDS	MasterCard, Visa
BREAKFAST	Full breakfast is available in the Adducci's restaurant.
AMENITIES	Hot tub during ski season, TV and radio in dining room, phone in parlor, complimentary refreshments, small meeting facilities.
RESTRICTIONS	No smoking, no pets
REVIEWED	*The Colorado Guide, Let's Go USA*

Back In Time Bed & Breakfast, Glenwood Springs

BACK IN TIME BED & BREAKFAST

927 Cooper Avenue, Glenwood Springs, CO 81601   970-945-6183
June & Ron Robinson, Resident Owners   888-854-7733
EMAIL *bitbnb@sprynet.com*   FAX 970-947-1324

LOCATION	Take exit 116 off I-70 (150 miles west of Denver). The B&B is near the train station and the center of town.
OPEN	All year
DESCRIPTION	A 1903 two-story Victorian inn filled with antiques, family quilts, and clocks.
NO. OF ROOMS	Three bedrooms with private bathrooms. Try the Olde Room.
RATES	May through October and December through March, rates are $50 for a single, $85 for a double with a private bathroom, and the entire B&B goes for $380 for two nights. November and April, rates are $45 for a single, $85 for a double with a private bathroom, and the entire B&B goes for $200 for one night. There is a minimum stay during weekends and cancellation requires 48 hours' notice.
CREDIT CARDS	American Express, Discover, MasterCard, Visa
BREAKFAST	Full breakfast is served in the dining room and includes fruit, yogurt, beverages, fresh breads, and a gourmet entrée such as to-die-for French toast.

AMENITIES	Turndown service with chocolate, air conditioning, down comforters, fridge for guests' use.
RESTRICTIONS	No smoking, no pets, children over 12 are welcome.
REVIEWED	*Non-Smokers Guide to B&Bs*
MEMBER	Bed & Breakfast Innkeepers of Colorado, Bed & Breakfast Innkeepers of Glenwood Springs
AWARDS	Bed & Breakfast Innkeepers of Colorado "Award of Excellence"
KUDOS/COMMENTS	"Warm, friendly innkeepers." (1997) "Comfortable. Hospitable. innkeepers; well informed about community and events." (1999)

"THE" BED & BREAKFAST ON MITCHELL CREEK

1686 Mitchell Creek Road, Glenwood Springs, CO 81601   970-945-4002
Carole & Stan Rachesky, Resident Owners   FAX 970-928-7842
Some Spanish spoken
EMAIL carole@rof.net   WEBSITE www.bbhost.com/mitchellcreekb&b

LOCATION	Take exit 114 from I-70, turn left (west) at the traffic light and go one long block, then turn right on Storm King Road. Turn left at the stop sign (Donagon Road), go 0.25 mile and turn right onto Mitchell Creek Road, continue up winding country road for 1.25 miles to the fish hatchery, drive through hatchery for 0.25 mile and follow the stream.
OPEN	All year
DESCRIPTION	A 1993 one-story contemporary log home with contemporary furnishings located on Mitchell Creek.
NO. OF ROOMS	One room with private bathroom and separate entrance.
RATES	Year-round rate is $90. There is a two-night minimum stay on weekends and a 10-day cancellation policy.
CREDIT CARDS	Credit cards to hold reservation only.
BREAKFAST	Full breakfast is served in the dining room and includes a bottomless glass of juice, coffee, tea, and entrées that feature hobohash, cinnabun French toast, fruit crepes, and whole-wheat oatmeal pancakes.
AMENITIES	Cookies, brownies, sodas, candy, fire pit adjacent to stream, hiking trails directly from property, accommodations for small weddings, small refrigerator, wet bar, board games, total privacy.
RESTRICTIONS	No smoking, no pets in suite, children of all ages welcome. The resident German shepherd is Abby, and Tigger is the tabby cat. Abby is also the resident tour guide on local hikes.
MEMBER	Bed & Breakfast Innkeepers of Colorado

Four Mile Creek Bed & Breakfast, Glenwood Springs

FOUR MILE CREEK BED & BREAKFAST

6471 County Road 117, Glenwood Springs, CO 81601   *970-945-4004*
Sharill & Jim Hawkins, Innkeepers   *FAX 970-945-2820*
Spanish spoken
EMAIL *hawk@rof.net*   WEBSITE *www.aspen.com/fourmile*

LOCATION	Six-and-a-half miles south of Glenwood Springs on the road to Sunlight ski area. Sunlight ski area is 10 miles south of Glenwood Springs on County Road 117 (also known as Four Mile Road).
OPEN	All year
DESCRIPTION	A 1926 two-story log ranch house and log cabin, decorated with western furnishings and folk art, located in a quiet valley with a trout pond and creek running through the five-and-a-half acre grounds. Listed on the National and State Historic Registers.
NO. OF ROOMS	One bedroom with private bathroom and two rooms with one shared bathroom. Sharill and Jim suggest the log cabin.
RATES	Year-round rates are $110 for the cabin and $85 for a single or double in the house. There is no minimum stay. The Hawkins recommend that you reserve early. There is no deposit required. "We trust people to come."
CREDIT CARDS	American Express, MasterCard, Visa
BREAKFAST	Full breakfast is served in the dining room and includes coffee, juice, tea, fresh fruit, usually two hot dishes such as stuffed French toast and shredded potatoes baked with fresh herbs, homemade orange scones and turkey sausage. Breakfast can be modified to fit dietary needs or desires.

AMENITIES	Hiking trails; secluded sitting areas; a picnic area and campfire ring; a stocked trout pond ("We feed them but don't catch them—they love Trout Chow"); a trout stream (for fishing); downhill skiing and cross-country skiing 3.5 miles away; historic big red barn; flower and herb gardens; robes and flowers in every room; the largest hot springs pool in the country is a 15-minute drive away.
RESTRICTIONS	No smoking, no pets, children are welcome. Oso ("bear" in Spanish) is a Bernese mountain dog, Max is the golden Lab, and Sophie is the cat. "We also have a llama named Muñeca, and a friend's llama named Antonio."
MEMBER	Bed & Breakfast Inns of Colorado
KUDOS/COMMENTS	"Beautiful country setting. Gracious and friendly innkeepers." (1999)

THE LAVENDER SWING

802 Palmer Avenue, Glenwood Springs, CO 81601   970-945-8289
Carolyn & Pat, Innkeepers   FAX 970-947-0379
EMAIL *lavenderswing@att.net*

LOCATION	Take exit 116 from I-70 into Glenwood Springs. At the base of the bridge, as you come into town, turn left onto 8th Street and drive four blocks east.
OPEN	All year
DESCRIPTION	A 1903 two-story modified Victorian host home situated above town with an interior of antiques and country furnishings.

The Lavender Swing, Glenwood Springs

NO. OF ROOMS	Three bedrooms with private bathrooms. Try the Foxy Lady Room.
RATES	May through October 15, rates are $85 for a single or double with a private bathroom and $229 for the entire B&B. October 16 through April, rates are $75 for a single or double with a private bathroom and $202 for the entire B&B. There is a two-night minimum stay during weekends and holidays and cancellation requires 14 days' notice less a $20 fee.
CREDIT CARDS	Discover, MasterCard, Visa
BREAKFAST	Full breakfast is served in the dining room and includes a baked entrée, seasonal fruit or baked fruit dishes in winter, baked muffins or rolls, juice, tea, and coffee.
AMENITIES	Hot tub; air conditioning; ceiling fans; wraparound porch with lavender swing; bikes and snowshoes; robes; towels for hot springs pool in town; fresh cookies, scones, and biscotti; wine and flowers for special occasions.
RESTRICTIONS	No smoking, no pets, children over 15 are welcome.
MEMBER	Glenwood Springs Chamber Resort Association, Bed & Breakfast Innkeepers of Colorado
AWARDS	1998 Award for Excellence, awarded by the Bed & Breakfast Innkeepers of Colorado

SUNLIGHT MOUNTAIN INN BED & BREAKFAST

10252 County Road 117, Glenwood Springs, CO 81601   *970-945-5225*
Grechenn and Pierre DuBois, Resident Owners   *800-733-4757*
EMAIL *gdb@aol.com*   *FAX 970-947-1900*

LOCATION	Twelve miles south of I-70 Glenwood Springs exit 116, at the base of Ski Sunlight.
OPEN	All year
DESCRIPTION	A 1968 mountain inn with a casual western decor.
NO. OF ROOMS	Twenty rooms with private bathrooms.
RATES	Summer rates are $60-125 for a single or double. Winter rates are flexible. Call for details.
CREDIT CARDS	American Express, Discover, MasterCard, Visa
BREAKFAST	Full hot-and-hearty breakfast is served in the dining room in the summer. On-site restaurant open during winter.
AMENITIES	Hot tub, fireplace in romance suite, meeting facilities, handicapped access, bar, ice rink in winter, horseback riding, skiing.
RESTRICTIONS	No pets. Children are welcome.
MEMBER	Professional Association of Innkeepers

GOLDEN

The state's former territorial capitol, Golden sits at the entrance to Lookout Mountain Park and Golden Gate Canyon State Park. The city is home to the Colorado School of Mines and Coors Brewery. Buffalo Bill Days in July and Oktoberfest in September are fun fests. Just west of Denver's metroplex via Highway 6.

ANTIQUE ROSE BED & BREAKFAST INN

1422 Washington Avenue, Golden, CO 80401   303-277-1893
                                                  FAX 303-278-9747

LOCATION	On the southern end of Golden's Historic District, near the Colorado School of Mines.
OPEN	All year
DESCRIPTION	An 1880s two-story Queen Anne Victorian with gables, dormers, and Victorian furnishings.
NO. OF ROOMS	Four rooms with private bathrooms. The Victoria Suite is the best room in the house.
RATES	Year-round rates are $75-95 for a single or double with a private bathroom and $115-128 for a suite. There is no minimum stay. Ask about a reservation/cancellation policy.
CREDIT CARDS	MasterCard, Visa
BREAKFAST	Full "American-style" breakfast is served in the dining room.
AMENITIES	Roses and candlelight dinner catered upon request, whirlpool tubs.
RESTRICTIONS	No smoking. Room occupancy limited to two people. The resident toy poodle is called Brandy.

ASHLEY HOUSE BED & BREAKFAST

30500 Highway 40, Golden, CO 80401   303-526-2411

CEDARIDGE LODGE

33247 Highway 72, Golden, CO 80403   303-642-7181

THE DOVE INN BED & BREAKFAST

711 14th Street, Golden, CO 80401
Tim & Connie Sheffield, Resident Owners
EMAIL *innkeep@ix.netcom.com*
WEBSITE *www.doveinn.com*

303-278-2209
888-278-2209
FAX 303-278-5272

LOCATION	From I-70, take exit 265 to Highway 58 and travel six miles to Washington Street, turn left (south) and go eight blocks to 14th, turn left half a block.
OPEN	All year
DESCRIPTION	An 1864 two-story Victorian inn. The outside is stucco over original golden brick; the interior is comfortable. The huge blue spruce in the front yard is over 100 years old.
NO. OF ROOMS	Seven rooms with private baths. Try the Bunkhouse Suite.
RATES	Year-round rates are $65-80 for a single with a private bathroom, $70-90 for a double with a private bathroom, and a suite is $90 for a double. There is a five-day cancellation policy.
CREDIT CARDS	American Express, Discover, MasterCard, Visa
BREAKFAST	Full breakfast, served in the dining room, includes a hot entrée, muffins, rolls, cereal, juice, fruit, coffee, and tea.
AMENITIES	Coffee, tea, cocoa; phones (with private extensions and voicemail), TVs and VCRs in rooms; VCR tape library.
RESTRICTIONS	No smoking, no pets
MEMBER	Colorado Hotel and Lodging Association, Professional Association of Innkeepers International
RATED	ABBA 1 Crown, Mobil 2 Stars

GRANBY

In the beautiful Fraser Valley, Granby is 20 miles from Winter Park, offering easy access to all of its amenities, plus those of Lake Granby, Grand Lake, and Rocky Mountain National Park. Silver Creek ski resort, on the doorstep of Granby, is very accommodating to beginning and intermediate skiers.

CIRCLE H LODGE

6732 US Highway 34, Granby, CO 80446

970-887-3955

SHADOW MOUNTAIN GUEST RANCH

5043 Highway 125, Granby, CO 80446   970-887-9524
Jim White, Innkeeper   800-647-4236
EMAIL thebest@coweblink.net   FAX 970-887-3059
WEBSITE www.coloradodirectory.com/shadowmtnranch

LOCATION	Take Highway 40 three miles west of Granby to Highway 125. Highway 125 only goes north. The ranch is on the left, 5.5 miles north of Highway 40.
OPEN	All year
DESCRIPTION	Cozy log cabins built in 1936 and decorated with western furnishings, set among aspen and pines.
NO. OF ROOMS	All bedrooms with private bathrooms.
RATES	Cabins start at $130; larger cabins are $195 for two plus $10 for each additional person over the age of seven. There is no minimum stay and cancellation requires 60 days' notice less 50% of the deposit unless the cabin is rebooked.
CREDIT CARDS	Discover, MasterCard, Visa
BREAKFAST	Full all-you-can-eat breakfast is served family style in the dining room at the lodge. Lunch and dinner are also available.
AMENITIES	The lodge is open to guests from 8:00 a.m. to 9:00 p.m.; each cabin has a kitchenette or full kitchen, barbecue grill, and picnic tables; large log building for group cookouts and games; large hot tub under the stars.
RESTRICTIONS	None. There are dogs, horses, and cattle on the property.

TRAIL MOUNTAIN BED & BREAKFAST

4850 County Road 41, Granby, CO 80446   970-887-3944

KUDOS/COMMENTS   "Exceptional service and awesome property, very high end." (1999)

GRAND JUNCTION

In the heart of Colorado's fledgling wine country, Grand Junction is home to a number of wineries and a wine festival. Explore Colorado National Monument, Grand Mesa (the world's largest flat-top mountain), and the dinosaur museum. Jump in a raft and head down the Colorado River, or don your ten-gallon cowboy hat and catch all the pickin' and grinnin' at Country Jam USA. Twenty-five miles from the Utah border, 246 miles from Denver off I-70.

THE HOUSE ON OURAY

760 Ouray Avenue, Grand Junction, CO 81501   970-245-8452
Marlene Johnsen, Innkeeper
EMAIL *webmaster@grandjunction.net*

LOCATION	One block off 7th and Grand in downtown Grand Junction.
OPEN	All year except Thanksgiving, Christmas Eve, and Christmas
DESCRIPTION	A 1905 two-story Victorian with antiques and Victorian furnishings.
NO. OF ROOMS	Three rooms with private bathrooms. The Molly Brown Room is the best.
RATES	Year-round rates are $50-65 for a single with a private bathroom, and $60-75 for a double with a private bathroom. There is no minimum stay and cancellation requires seven days' notice.
CREDIT CARDS	MasterCard, Visa
BREAKFAST	Full hot breakfast is served in the dining room and may include eggs and bacon, Palisade peaches and French toast. Lunch, dinner, and special meals are available with prior arrangement.
AMENITIES	TV, game room, coffee delivered to room on request, small gift shop with collectibles and items from around the world.
RESTRICTIONS	No smoking, no pets, children over 14 are welcome. Sam is the resident Alaskan snow dog.
MEMBER	Colorado Hotel and Lodging Association
KUDOS/COMMENTS	"Hosts were very warm and gracious. Rooms were spotless and in good taste. A very elegant feeling." (1997)

LOS ALTOS BED & BREAKFAST

375 Hillview Drive, Grand Junction, CO 81503   970-256-0964
Lee & Young-Ja, Innkeepers   888-774-0982
Fluent Korean spoken   FAX 970-256-0964 *(call first)*
EMAIL *losaltos@wic.net*   WEBSITE *www.colorado-bnb.com/losaltos*

Los Altos Bed & Breakfast, Grand Junction

LOCATION	From downtown Grand Junction, head west on Grand Avenue. Two miles after 1st Street, take a left onto Ridges Boulevard, the first right-hand turn onto Ridge Circle, a right onto Ridge View, and then a right onto Hillview Drive.
OPEN	All year
DESCRIPTION	A 1997 two-story Victorian inn on a high hill with panoramic views of Grand Mesa and Mount Garfield, with Victorian country decor and a wraparound deck.
NO. OF ROOMS	Seven bedrooms with private bathrooms.
RATES	May through October, rates are $80-150 for a single or double with a private bathroom, $90-150 for a suite, and $700 for the entire B&B. November through April, rates are $68-120 for a single or double with a private bathroom, $72-120 for a suite, and $560 for the entire B&B. There is no minimum stay and cancellation requires two weeks' notice for a full refund less a fee.
CREDIT CARDS	American Express, Discover, MasterCard, Visa
BREAKFAST	Full breakfast is served in the dining room and includes fresh-baked muffins, bread, and coffeecakes; fresh fruit; seafood strata; Dutch apple pancakes; tea, coffee, and juice. Special meals are also available.
AMENITIES	Free local calls, pick-up from the airport and train station, afternoon tea, conference room for up to 20, air conditioning, recreation room with antique pool table, observatory, sitting rooms with fireplaces.
RESTRICTIONS	No smoking, no pets, children over 12 are welcome. Toby is the resident rottie. Toby is "very loving and gentle—loves attention and on invitation accompanies guests on short hikes."
REVIEWED	*Quick Escapes, Hidden Colorado*
MEMBER	Professional Association of Innkeepers International, Bed & Breakfast Innkeepers of Colorado
RATED	AAA 3 Diamonds

MT. GARFIELD B&B

3355 F Road, Grand Junction, CO 81520   970-434-8120
Todd & Carrie McKay, Innkeepers   800-547-9108
German spoken   FAX 970-434-1250
EMAIL *mckayinn@gj.net*   WEBSITE *www.gj.net/mckayinn/*

LOCATION
From the northeast or northwest, take exit 37 off I-70 to the first stoplight, F Road (also called Patterson Road), and turn left. Drive approximately one mile east over overpass. At the bottom of the overpass turn right at the Y in the road and the B&B is the first place on the right. From the south, take Highway 50 north to Highway 141 (to Clifton) and turn right, taking Highway 141 into Clifton where it meets Highway 6. Turn right onto Highway 6 (Business 70) and at the next stoplight turn right onto F Road and follow the above directions.

OPEN
All year

DESCRIPTION
A 1992 one-and-a-half-story country farmhouse on seven acres surrounded by peach orchards in Colorado's wine country. Separate owners' quarters are attached to the inn.

NO. OF ROOMS
Five bedrooms with private bathrooms. Try the Grand Mesa Room.

RATES
April through October, rates are $61-125 for a single or double with a private bathroom, $95-125 for a suite, and $400 for the entire B&B. Regular rates are $48-100 for a single or double with a private bathroom, $76-100 for a suite, and $370 for the entire B&B. There is no minimum stay and cancellation requires one weeks' notice with a $10 fee.

CREDIT CARDS
American Express, Discover, MasterCard, Visa

BREAKFAST
Full breakfast is served in the dining room or the guestrooms and includes buttermilk Belgian waffles, pancakes, or French toast; fresh fruit; farm-fresh egg dishes; buffalo sausage or bacon; fresh breads; homemade peach preserves (also for sale); and juice, coffee, tea, hot chocolate, or milk.

AMENITIES
Afternoon refreshments and snacks; air conditioning and cable TV in rooms; robes and outdoor hot tub; in-room Jacuzzi tubs; private sunken living room with TV and VCR, 125-gallon freshwater aquarium; piano; loft area with dinette, refrigerator, and furniture; use of kitchen/breakfast room; a do-not-disturb attitude toward guests; private patio overlooking the back orchard.

RESTRICTIONS
No smoking, no pets, children over six are welcome on certain weekends only. Sally is the resident dalmatian, Hamms is the shepherd/Chesapeake mix, and the cats are Spice, Mattie, and Hamm's Cat. All the animals are kept out of the Bed & Breakfast area unless guests want to see them. You will also find two buffalo, a horse, and 18 chickens on the property.

MEMBER	Bed & Breakfast Innkeepers of Colorado
RATED	AAA 3 Diamonds
AWARDS	Finalist in the 1997 "Inn of the Year Contest" held by Bed & Breakfast Innkeepers of Colorado
KUDOS/COMMENTS	"Great hosts, truly dedicated to guests' happiness."

GRAND LAKE

At the west entrance to Rocky Mountain National Park on the shores of the state's largest natural lake (from which it takes its name), Grand Lake overflows with tremendous recreational opportunities. Fun times to be had here include the Western Weekend Buffalo BBQ and Lighted Boat Parade in mid-July, the Annual Lipton Cup Regatta (hosted by the nation's highest chartered yacht club) in early August, and the Olde Fashioned Christmas celebration. The summer-long Fishing Derby for tagged trout is challenging, as is the local 18-hole golf course. In winter, zillions of snowmobilers descend on the area. About 100 miles northwest of Denver via Highways 40 and 34.

B&B LAKEVIEW

164 Lakeview Lane, Grand Lake, CO 80447   970-627-1200

HUMMINGBIRD BED & BREAKFAST

132 Lakeview Drive, Grand Lake, CO 80447   970-627-3417
Dave & Judy Case, Resident Owners
WEBSITE *www.grandlakecolorado.com*

LOCATION	Two miles south of Grand Lake off County Road 465.
OPEN	All year
DESCRIPTION	A 1992 two-story contemporary host home with a covered outside deck and country furnishings.
NO. OF ROOMS	Two rooms with private bathrooms. Try the Ruby Suite.
RATES	Year-round rates are $75-95 for a double with a private bathroom.
CREDIT CARDS	No
BREAKFAST	Full breakfast, served in the dining room, includes a hot entrée with breakfast meats, homemade breads, muffins, fruit, and beverages.
AMENITIES	Wildflowers in the rooms, roses for special occasions, VCR/TV,

private entrance, lake view, special accommodations for quilt and sewing retreats, refreshments offered on arrival or in the evening, and the innkeepers will make dinner reservations for guests.

RESTRICTIONS	No smoking, no pets, children over five are welcome.

OLDE GRAND LAKE CABINS BED & BREAKFAST

325 Vine Street, Grand Lake, CO 80447　　　　　970-627-9393
Benji & Janet Bendixen, Resident Owners

LOCATION	Half block north of Main Street in Grand Lake Village.
OPEN	All year
DESCRIPTION	A 1930s two-story peeled-log home with cabins and eclectic furnishings.
NO. OF ROOMS	Two rooms share one bathroom. Inquire about cabins.
RATES	Year-round rates are $75 for a single or double with a shared bathroom. There is a reservation/cancellation policy.
CREDIT CARDS	MasterCard, Visa
BREAKFAST	Continental breakfast is served in the kitchen, sun porch, or den.
AMENITIES	Robes, TV, books, laundry room, outdoor grill and complimentary coffee and tea.
RESTRICTIONS	No pets, due in part to the resident goat.

ONAHU LODGE

2096 County Road 491, Grand Lake, CO 80447　　　　970-627-8523
Donna Lyons, Resident Owner

LOCATION	Five miles north of Grand Lake Village, at the west entrance of Rocky Mountain National Park.
OPEN	All year
DESCRIPTION	A 1969 hand-hewn log host home with comfortable antique and rustic furnishings.
NO. OF ROOMS	One room with private bathroom and one room shares a bathroom.
RATES	Year-round rates are $75 for a double with a private bathroom and $125 for three or four persons with a shared bath. There is a two-night minimum stay with some exceptions, and a reservation/cancellation policy.
CREDIT CARDS	No

BREAKFAST	Continental plus is served in the dining room. Lunch for hikers and skiers with prior notice.
AMENITIES	Seclusion; views of the Never Summer Range; Colorado River and Rocky Mountain National Park; skiing out the backdoor; wildlife walk through the yard in the summer; special rates for artists or writers who need quiet, bright studio space; overnight boarding for horses.
RESTRICTIONS	No smoking inside lodge, no pets. Children over five are welcome.
KUDOS/COMMENTS	"Best location for wildlife viewing; borders Rocky Mountain National Park." (1997)

SPIRIT MOUNTAIN RANCH BED & BREAKFAST

3863 County Road 41, Grand Lake, CO 80447   970-887-3551
Beth Wamer & Sandy Wilson, Innkeepers   FAX 970-887-3551 *(call first)*
EMAIL *spiritmtn@rkymtnhi.com*   WEBSITE *www.fcinet.com/spirit*

LOCATION	Exit I-70 onto Highway 40 and go through Granby. Take Highway 34 east to Grand Lake and Rocky Mountain National Park. Turn left on County Road 41. Drive 3.9 miles; the ranch is on the left.
OPEN	All year
DESCRIPTION	A 1995 two-story timber-framed inn with cedar exterior and mission-style interior with numerous antiques. Located on 72 private acres.
NO. OF ROOMS	Four rooms with private bathrooms.
RATES	Year-round rates are $115-125 for a single or double with a private bathroom. There is no minimum stay. Ask about a cancellation policy.
CREDIT CARDS	Discover, MasterCard, Visa
BREAKFAST	Full breakfast is served in the dining room and includes homemade breads, scones, or muffins followed by an entrée such as blue-corn waffles with seasonal fruit and cream, frittatas with fresh herbs, homefries, or ranch biscuits and bacon, plus coffee, tea, and juice.
AMENITIES	Hot tub in aspen grove, robes in guestrooms, afternoon refreshments, hiking and snowshoe trails, wildlife viewing on 72 mountain acres, horse boarding, moss-rock fireplaces, sun-drenched decks, and handicapped access.
RESTRICTIONS	No smoking, no pets (except horses), and children over eight are welcome. Resident pets include two black Labs named Lakota and Blue; a schnauzer named Tao, two thoroughbreds named Traveler and Red (Traveler enjoys a nice slice of watermelon on hot afternoons); and several llamas.
REVIEWED	*The Colorado Guide*

MEMBER   Bed & Breakfast Innkeepers of Colorado

KUDOS/COMMENTS   "Exceptional service, great decor, and unbridled hospitality." (1999)

TERRACE INN

813 Grand Avenue, Grand Lake, CO 80447   970-627-3000
David Lawrence, Innkeeper
Spanish spoken

LOCATION	At the west end of main street (Grand Avenue) on the north side of Grand Lake.
OPEN	June through October. The rest of the year, open on weekends only.
DESCRIPTION	A 1905 three-story wood-frame Victorian-style inn with hardwood floors, rock walls, and newly remodeled bathrooms.
NO. OF ROOMS	Four bedrooms with private bathrooms.
RATES	Year-round rates are $65-120 for a single or double. There is a two-night minimum stay during weekends from July through September 10. Ask about a cancellation policy.
CREDIT CARDS	MasterCard, Visa
BREAKFAST	Continental breakfast is served in the dining room and includes juice, muffins, granola, and cereal.
AMENITIES	Two lovely patios, soaps and shampoo, sodas and nightly beer on the upper terrace, great views, full-service restaurant 50 feet away.
RESTRICTIONS	No smoking, no pets, children over six are welcome.

GREELEY

New York Tribune publisher Horace Greeley, Nathan Meeker, and the Union Colonists founded this agricultural community—and James Michener immortalized it in *Centennial*. Greeley is home to the University of Northern Colorado. From Denver, 54 miles northeast via I-25 and Highway 34.

GERMAN HOUSE BED & BREAKFAST

1305 6th Street, Greeley, CO 80631   970-356-1353
Detlef & Celia Scholl, Innkeepers
German and Spanish spoken
EMAIL *germanhaus@ctos.com*
                            WEBSITE *www.greeleycvb.com/gh*

LOCATION	Five blocks west of 8th Avenue on the corner of 13th Avenue and 6th Street.
OPEN	All year
DESCRIPTION	An 1885 three-story brick Queen Anne Victorian on one landscaped acre, decorated with turn-of-the-century European antiques.
NO. OF ROOMS	Three bedrooms with private bathrooms and one room with one shared bathroom. Detlef and Celia suggest the Kaiser Wilhelm Room.
RATES	April through October, rates are $59-84 for a single or double with a private bathroom and $55-80 for a single or double with a shared bathroom. Rates are 10% less from November through March. There is no minimum stay and cancellation requires 14 days' notice with a $15 charge.
CREDIT CARDS	No
BREAKFAST	Full German-style breakfast is served in the dining room or out on the deck or gazebo and includes European coffee and gourmet teas, home-baked breads and delicacies, fresh fruit, German-style eggs, sliced meats and cheeses, juice, and condiments.
AMENITIES	Hot tub and pool house with bar; outdoor pool; robes; tea, refreshments, and pecan tarts upon arrival; cable TV; European bedding, duvets, and down bedding; German antiques; hosts share personal experiences and relate the history of Germany before and after the fall of the Berlin Wall.
RESTRICTIONS	No smoking, no pets, well-behaved children over three are welcome. No handicapped access to bedrooms—all bedrooms on the second floor. Jäger and Missy are the resident German shepherd/beagle mixes.
REVIEWED	*Inn for a Night*
MEMBER	Northern Colorado Bed & Breakfast Innkeepers Association

GREELEY GUEST HOUSE

5401 9th Street, Greeley, CO 80634   970-353-9373

GREEN MOUNTAIN FALLS

A small, pretty community in the Ute Pass area. The centerpiece lake and gazebo are busy summer and winter, and the annual Christmas Yule Log Hunt is a major event. Handy to Pikes Peak toll road, about 18 miles west of Colorado Springs on Highway 24.

LAKEVIEW TERRACE HOTEL

10580 Foster Avenue, Green Mountain Falls, CO 80819   *719-684-9119*
Marc & Victoria Marelich, Resident Owners   *FAX 719-684-8313*
Spanish spoken

OPEN	All year
NO. OF ROOMS	Two rooms with private bathrooms.
RATES	$60 for one room: $100 for the whole house.
CREDIT CARDS	No
BREAKFAST	Continental breakfast is served in the dining room.

GROVER

Pawnee National Grasslands and Pawnee Buttes are great locations for bird watching. About 20 miles south of the Wyoming border.

PLOVER INN

223 Chatoga Avenue, Grover, CO 80729   *970-895-2275*
Joyce Held, Innkeeper

LOCATION	From Denver, take I-25 north to Fort Collins. Exit to Highway 14 east, go 16 miles to Ault, and continue for 23 miles on Highway 14 to Briggsdale. Turn left (north) on Highway 77 and go 17 miles to the Grover signs. Turn right (east) for six miles. The inn is on the main street, the second block on the left.
OPEN	May through October
DESCRIPTION	A 1908 two-story brick inn with original stained-glass windows, decorated with antiques and paintings. Listed on the State Historic Register.
NO. OF ROOMS	Three suites with private bathrooms and two rooms with one shared bathroom. Try the Prairie Falcon Suite.

RATES	Rates are $70-90 for a single or double with a private bathroom and $50 for a single or double with a shared bathroom. There is no minimum stay and cancellation requires 14 days' notice.
CREDIT CARDS	No
BREAKFAST	Full breakfast is served in the dining room and includes fruit and yogurt, quiche, bread or rice pudding, and homemade muffins or cinnamon rolls.
AMENITIES	Flowers throughout inn; robes in rooms with shared bath; homemade cakes or cookies on arrival; library.
RESTRICTIONS	No smoking, no pets
REVIEWED	A Birder's Guide to Colorado; Colorado Bed & Breakfast Cookbook
AWARDS	"Best Bird-Watching Bed & Breakfast," 1997, Westword

WEST PAWNEE RANCH

29451 WCR 130, Grover, CO 80729   970-895-2482
Paul & Louanne Timm, Resident Owners   FAX 970-895-2482
WEBSITE www.bbonline.com/co/pawnee/

LOCATION	From Greeley, take Highway 85 to Road 122 (twelve miles beyond Nunn) until it dead-ends, then turn north on Road 55 and drive to dead end; turn east on Road 126 and go to dead end, turn north on Road 57 and drive two miles to Road 130. Take Road 130 to the ranch.
OPEN	All year
DESCRIPTION	A 1917 and 1965 one-story host home with western and southwestern decor, on a working ranch. The Prairie House, built in 1997, is adjacent to the ranch house.
NO. OF ROOMS	Three rooms with private bathrooms.
RATES	Year-round rates are $50-90 for a single or double. Minimum stay required during the last full week of July and cancellation requires 10 days' notice.
CREDIT CARDS	No
BREAKFAST	Full rancher's breakfast is served in the dining room and includes a hot entrée such as pancakes and bacon or the West Pawnee Ranch frittata, plus homemade jelly, fruit, and hot beverages. Lunch and dinner are also served, including steaks from the rancher's own cattle.
AMENITIES	Flowers in rooms, queen-size beds, common area with picture window overlooking the prairie, refreshments served every afternoon, pictures taken of guests at the ranch and sent to them.

RESTRICTIONS	No smoking, no pets. Children are always welcome. Pebbles, the resident dog, loves kids and women. There are also numerous barn cats, four quarter horses, several other horses, and loads of cattle.
REVIEWED	*America's Wonderful Little Hotels & Inns*
MEMBER	Bed & Breakfast Innkeepers of Colorado
KUDOS/COMMENTS	"A wonderful 'old west' ranch experience in an unspoiled environment. A great getaway, especially for a family." (1997)

GUNNISON

This totally western town is a main artery to such wonders as Gunnison National Forest, Black Canyon of the Gunnison, Blue Mesa and Taylor Park Reservoirs, and Curecanti National Recreation Area (bird watchers: don't miss Neversink Trail at the eastern tip). The Upper Gunnison runs directly through town. Looking for something to do in July? Cattlemen's Day is a major event here in Gunnison. For skiing, Crested Butte is a mere 30 miles away. From Denver, 196 miles southwest via Highways 285 and 50 over Monarch Pass.

GOLD CREEK INN

8506 County Road 76, Gunnison, CO 81237   970-641-2086
Joe Benge, Resident Owner

LOCATION	Approximately 20 miles east/northeast of Gunnison. Call for directions.
OPEN	May 1 through October 15
DESCRIPTION	An 1890 log host home on Gold Creek with log and wainscoting interior.
NO. OF ROOMS	Two rooms share one bathroom.
RATES	Seasonal rates are $50 for a single with a shared bathroom and $70 for a double with a shared bathroom. There is no minimum stay and cancellation requires two weeks' notice.
CREDIT CARDS	MasterCard, Visa
BREAKFAST	Continental plus is served in the lounge area.
RESTRICTIONS	No smoking, no pets, children over 12 are welcome.
REVIEWED	*Recommended Country Inns of the Rocky Mountain Region*

THE MARY LAWRENCE INN

601 North Taylor, Gunnison, CO 81230   970-641-3343
Doug & Beth Parker, Resident Owners
EMAIL marylinn@gunnison.com

LOCATION	From Highway 50, turn north on Highway 135, go five blocks to Ruby Street, turn right, and go two blocks. On corner of Ruby and Taylor.
OPEN	All year
DESCRIPTION	An 1886 two-story Italianate Victorian Inn, restored in 1988, and furnished with antiques, hand-stenciled walls, and colorful artwork.
NO. OF ROOMS	Five rooms with private baths. Two rooms are two-room suites. Beth's favorite is Kokopelli's Mountain Hideaway.
RATES	Summer rates are $75-129 for a single or double. Winter rates are $69-115 for a single or double. An additional $15-25 is charged for each person over two in the suites. There is a reservation/cancellation policy.
CREDIT CARDS	MasterCard, Visa
BREAKFAST	Full breakfast, served in the dining room, includes a main dish, meat, seasonal fruit, coffee, juices.
AMENITIES	Enclosed sun porch and large deck, robes and handmade quilts in the rooms, TV in the suites, interesting books and magazines, local interest material available, maps of the area and knowledge of interesting places to see.
RESTRICTIONS	No smoking, no pets, children are welcome.
REVIEWED	America's Wonderful Little Hotels & Inns; B&Bs, Guesthouses & Inns of America; Bed & Breakfast U.S.A.; The Colorado Guide; Non-Smokers Guide to Bed & Breakfasts
MEMBER	Bed & Breakfast Innkeepers of Colorado, Colorado Hotel and Lodging Association
RATED	AAA 3 Diamond
KUDOS/COMMENTS	"A wonderful experience." "Gourmet food and very hospitable hosts!" (1996)

HAHN'S PEAK
(STEAMBOAT SPRINGS)

In Hahn's Mining District on pristine Steamboat Lake in the splendid wilderness of the Routt National Forest, Hahn's Peak is 25 miles north of Steamboat Springs on County Road 129, just south of the Wyoming border.

THE COUNTRY INN AT STEAMBOAT LAKE

61027 County Road 129, Hahn's Peak, CO 80428   970-879-3906
Tom & Stephanie Berry, Resident Owners   800-934-7829

LOCATION	On Steamboat Lake, 25 miles north of Steamboat Springs at Hahn's Peak in the Routt National Forest.
OPEN	All year
DESCRIPTION	A two-story log lodge with restaurant and bar.
NO. OF ROOMS	Eight rooms with private bathrooms.
RATES	Seasonal rates change according to length of stay and time of year. Please call for details.
CREDIT CARDS	MasterCard, Visa
BREAKFAST	Full breakfast is served in the dining room.
AMENITIES	Hot tub, guest lounge with satellite TV, wood-burning stove, complimentary refreshments, full-service bar, handicapped access, and meeting and conference facilities.
RESTRICTIONS	None

HEENEY

GREEN MOUNTAIN INN

7101 Summit County Road 30, Heeney, CO 80498   970-724-3812
Scott & Jeanette Astaldi, Resident Owners

HESPERUS

LA PLATA VISTA RANCH

13400 County Road 120, Hesperus, CO 81326   970-247-9062
Kathy & John, Resident Owners   FAX 970-247-5056

HOT SULPHUR SPRINGS

This small town, perched at an elevation of 7,600 feet in the Arapahoe National
Forest, provides access to tourist favorites like Lake Granby, Grand Lake, and
Rocky Mountain National Park. Skiing is 20 miles away at Silver Creek.

STAGECOACH COUNTRY INN

412 Nevava, Hot Sulphur Springs, CO 80451   970-725-3910
Lou & Kathy Bridges, Innkeepers   800-725-3919
EMAIL stagecoach@rkymtnhi.com   FAX 970-725-0141

LOCATION	Three blocks north of Highway 40 on the corner of Aspen Street and Nevava Street.
OPEN	All year
DESCRIPTION	An 1874 two-story western Victorian inn with contemporary and turn-of-the-century furnishings on two private acres along the bank of the Colorado River. Some famous people who stayed at this former stagecoach stop are Teddy Roosevelt, William Taft, Woodrow Wilson, Wyatt Earp, and Doc Holiday.
NO. OF ROOMS	Five bedrooms with private bathrooms and nine rooms with four shared bathrooms. The Bridges recommend room 4.
RATES	June through September, rates are $64-74 for a single or double with a private bathroom and $59 for a single or double with a shared bathroom. October through May, rates are $59-69 for a single or double with a private bathroom and $59 for a single or double with a shared bathroom. There is no minimum stay and cancellation requires 48 hours' notice for a full refund.
CREDIT CARDS	MasterCard, Visa
BREAKFAST	Full, home-cooked country breakfast is served in the dining room.
AMENITIES	Hot tub on deck, excellent facilities for workshops and family retreats, fishing and hunting information about local hotspots.
RESTRICTIONS	No smoking, no pets, children are welcome.

HOWARD

A small mountain town on the Arkansas River. From here, the scenery is awesome in any direction you care to look, and scenic byways branch out in all directions. Twelve miles southwest of Salida.

WIT'S END BED & BREAKFAST

9100 Highway 50, Howard, CO 81233   719-942-4176
Todd & Joe Witlock, Resident Owners   877-942-4176
EMAIL *witsend@rmi.net*   WEBSITE *www.bbonline.com/co/witsend*

LOCATION	Twelve miles east of Salida and 80 miles west of Pueblo and Colorado Springs on Highway 50.
OPEN	All year
DESCRIPTION	A 1972 traditional country home with country furnishings set on two acres of land.
NO. OF ROOMS	Two rooms with private bathrooms and two suites share one bathroom. The best room is the Shavano Room.
RATES	Year-round rates are $57-95 for a double with a private bath and $75-$85 for a suite. Cancellation requires seven days' notice.
CREDIT CARDS	Discover, MasterCard, Visa
BREAKFAST	Full breakfast is served in the dining room. Special meals are available on request.
AMENITIES	Spa on covered patio, fruit orchard and gardens, books, relaxation tapes, microwave and refrigerator available, fresh flowers.
RESTRICTIONS	No smoking, no pets, children over 12 are welcome. The resident dog is Shadow.
MEMBER	Bed & Breakfast Innkeepers of Colorado

HUGO

LINCOLN MANOR

521 2nd Avenue, Hugo, CO 80821   719-743-2173

IDAHO SPRINGS

A half-hour west of Denver off I-70, Idaho Springs features tours of working mines. Enjoy a nostalgic look at the past during Gold Rush Days, ride the historic Georgetown Loop Railroad, and soak yourself in the Indian Hot Springs.

CLEAR CREEK BED & BREAKFAST

2717 County Road 308, Idaho Springs, CO 80452   303-567-2117
Dan & Gayle Burtt, Innkeepers   800-757-2117
EMAIL clearcreekbb@juno.com   FAX 303-567-9198
WEBSITE www.entertain.com/wedgwood/clearol.html

LOCATION	Three miles east of Georgetown. From Denver, take I-70 west to exit 232. Take the first right off the ramp, which is the access to the frontage road. Go east on the frontage road for 0.33 mile.
OPEN	All year
DESCRIPTION	A 1940s ranch house with elegant, modern decor.
NO. OF ROOMS	Five bedrooms with private bathrooms. Try the Master Suite.
RATES	Year-round rates are $65-85 for a single or double with a private bathroom, $125 for a suite, and $425 for the entire B&B. There is no minimum stay and cancellation requires three to 10 days' notice.
CREDIT CARDS	American Express, Discover, MasterCard, Visa
BREAKFAST	Full breakfast is served in the dining room and includes blintzes, eggs Benedict, and dilled potatoes. Lunch, dinner, and special meals (including packages for hunters) are also available.
AMENITIES	Enclosed hot tub; complimentary minibar and snack bar; coffee-makers in rooms; cable TV (with HBO); master suite has a private fireplace, hot tub, and robes.
RESTRICTIONS	No smoking, no pets, well-behaved children are welcome. Ashley is the resident blue heeler.

MINERS PICK BED & BREAKFAST

1639 Colorado Boulevard, Idaho Springs, CO 80452   303-567-2975
Deb & Ty Davies, Innkeepers   800-567-2975
EMAIL minerspik@bewellnet.com   FAX 303-567-2975

LOCATION	Take I-70 to exit 240 and go north for three blocks to Colorado Boulevard. Turn right (east) and go four blocks to 17th Avenue.
OPEN	All year

DESCRIPTION	A restored 1895 two-story Victorian inn decorated with Victorian, country, and southwestern furnishings, with wrought-iron fence and quaint gardens, located downtown in a small mining town in the mountains.
NO. OF ROOMS	Three bedrooms with private bathrooms. Deb and Ty suggest the Prospector Room.
RATES	Year-round rates are $76-86 for a single or double with a private bathroom. There is no minimum stay and cancellation requires seven days' notice.
CREDIT CARDS	Discover, MasterCard, Visa
BREAKFAST	Full gourmet breakfast is served in the dining room.
AMENITIES	Fresh flowers from the garden; snacks and beverages; fireplace in dining room; sitting room with large-screen TV; air conditioning in Prospector Room; walking distance to shops and restaurants.
RESTRICTIONS	No smoking, no pets, children over 10 are welcome. Meeker is the resident Lab mix and Husky is the tabby. Both are sweet animals who stay in owners' living quarters and will only be seen if requested.
REVIEWED	*Complete Guide to Bed & Breakfasts, Inns, and Guesthouses in the United States, Canada, and Worldwide; The Colorado Guide*
MEMBER	Bed & Breakfast Innkeepers of Colorado
KUDOS/COMMENTS	"Very clean, nicely decorated, and always busy." (1999)

THE RIVERSIDE BED & BREAKFAST

2130 Riverside Drive, Idaho Springs, CO 80452   *303-567-9032*
Theresa Gonzales, Resident Owner

LOCATION	From I-70 going west, take exit 241A into Idaho Springs, staying to the right (past the Safeway and park). Take the 21st Street bridge across Clear Creek. Turn left on Riverside Drive. The B&B is west of the Argo gold mill.
OPEN	Weekends only, all year
DESCRIPTION	A 1910 three-story country guesthouse with country and antique furnishings. The rooms are named after local attractions.
NO. OF ROOMS	One room with a private bathroom and three rooms share two bathrooms. If the small room is not taken, then each room has its own bathroom. Theresa Gonzales recommends the Hot Springs Room.
RATES	Year-round rates are $74 for a single or double with a private or shared bathroom. There is no minimum stay.
CREDIT CARDS	MasterCard, Visa

BREAKFAST	Full breakfast, served in the dining room, includes muffins, cinnamon rolls, egg dishes, French toast, meat, coffee, and juice.
AMENITIES	Hot tub by a spring, robes, teas and cookies, movies.
RESTRICTIONS	No smoking, no pets, and children over 10 are welcome.
REVIEWED	*Recommended Country Inns*

INDIAN HILLS

Just west of the sprawling Denver metroplex, and a few minutes west of Golden, Indian Hills offers access to the happenings in both cities, while hanging on to a little small-town charm all its own.

MOUNTAIN VIEW BED & BREAKFAST

4754 Picutis Road, Indian Hills, CO 80454   *303-697-6896*
Graham & Ortrud Richardson, Innkeepers   *800-690-0434*
German spoken   *FAX 303-697-7771*
EMAIL *mtnviewbandb@juno.com*
WEBSITE *www.virtualcities.com/co/mountainviewbandb.htm*

LOCATION	Five miles from Evergreen. Take I-70 west from Denver and exit to C-470 (exit 260). Go east on C-470 to Highway 285 and head south to Indian Hills. Take the second exit. Turn right onto Parmalee Gulch, go 2.5 miles, and turn right onto Picutis Road.
OPEN	All year
DESCRIPTION	A 1920 two-story mountain home on two-and-a-half acres with European and antique decorations, and one cottage furnished in southwestern style.
NO. OF ROOMS	Four bedrooms with private bathrooms. Try the Lavender Suite.
RATES	Year-round rates are $70-80 for a single or double with a private bathroom, $115 for a suite, and $160 for the cottage. There is no minimum stay and cancellation requires seven days' notice, 24 hours' notice for business travelers.
CREDIT CARDS	American Express, Diners Club, MasterCard, Visa
BREAKFAST	Full breakfast is served in the dining room, cabin, suite, or on the deck. Breakfast includes juice, hot beverages, fresh fruit, homemade muffins or coffeecake, and a hot entrée such as eggs Benedict with smoked salmon, dilled hollandaise sauce, and caviar; or cheese-filled, crusty French toast with warm banana compote, whipped cream, and toasted almonds. Breakfast by candlelight is also available.
AMENITIES	Afternoon tea; fresh flowers for special occasions; fresh-baked

cookies at night; hot and cold beverages available at all times; books, magazines, videos, games; close to beautiful mountain parks.

RESTRICTIONS	No smoking, no pets
MEMBER	Bed & Breakfast Innkeepers of Colorado
KUDOS/COMMENTS	"The best gourmet breakfast in the Rockies." (1996)

KEYSTONE

SKI TIP LODGE

0764 Montezuma Road , Keystone, CO 80435   970-468-4202
Angela Cartwright, Resident Innkeeper

LA JUNTA

At the spot where the Sante Fe and Navajo trails once converged, La Junta ("the junction") was once a major trading center along the Arkansas River. Don't miss seeing Bent's Old Fort, a massive adobe structure and National Historic Site. Other points of interest inlcude the Koshare and Otero County museums and Comanche National Grassland. About an hour east of Pueblo on Highway 50.

JANE ELLIN INN

722 Colorado Avenue, La Junta, CO 81050   719-384-8445
Jane & Ron Nordin, Innkeepers   800-743-2108
EMAIL janellin@rmi.com   .

LOCATION	Take Highway 50 to La Junta. Turn south onto Colorado Avenue at the stoplight across from the train station. The inn is on the northwest corner of 8th and Colorado.
OPEN	All year
DESCRIPTION	A 1907 two-story Salt Box Victorian hotel with turn-of-the-century decor, including a deacon's bench, leaded-glass china closet, and intricate oak parquet wall.
NO. OF ROOMS	One bedroom with a private bathroom and two rooms with one shared bathroom. Try the Columbine Room.
RATES	Year-round rates are $55-60 for a single or double with a private bathroom and $50-55 for a single or double with a shared

bathroom. There is no minimum stay and cancellation requires
seven days' notice.

CREDIT CARDS	MasterCard, Visa
BREAKFAST	Full breakfast, served in the dining room, may include sourdough waffles, berries and cream, sweet roll, bacon, coffee and tea.
AMENITIES	Robes in room; coffee, soda, and tea bar.
RESTRICTIONS	No smoking, no pets, children over four are welcome.

LA VETA

This quiet little town at the north end of the beautiful Cuchara Valley is alive with art,
artists, and theatrical productions. The annual Huerfano County Rodeo on July Fourth is a
big draw. Adjacent to town is a championship 18-hole gold course. From Walsenburg, 14
miles southwest via Highways 160 and 12.

HUNTER HOUSE BED & BREAKFAST

115 West Grand Avenue, La Veta, CO 81055   719-742-5577
Bill & Wanda Hunter, Resident Owners
WEBSITE www.flash.net/~hunterhs

LOCATION	At the five-mile marker on Highway 12 out of La Veta.
OPEN	All year
DESCRIPTION	A 1906 gabled adobe home furnished with antiques and collectibles.
NO. OF ROOMS	Three rooms share one bathroom. Choose the Collins Room with 1865 furnishings.
RATES	Year-round rates are $65-95 for a double with a shared bathroom. There is no minimum stay.
CREDIT CARDS	No
BREAKFAST	Full breakfast, served in the dining room, includes biscuits and gravy, country ham, scrambled eggs, hashbrowns or grits, and beverages. Lunch, dinner, and special meals are available with advance notice.
AMENITIES	Fifty-two inch TV in living room, library in the den, private sitting room, robes, afternoon and evening snacks and beverages, patio with outdoor fireplace, fruit orchard, homemade jelly.
RESTRICTIONS	No smoking, no pets (owners are allergic to animals and smoke), children are welcome.
KUDOS/COMMENTS	"Comfortable, gracious, nice hosts from Texas." (1995) "Huge breakfast, nice gift shop." (1996)

INN AT SPANISH PEAKS

PO Box 207, La Veta, CO 81055   719-742-5313
Bill Stark & Tracy Webb

KUDOS/COMMENTS   "A beautiful new Southwestern B&B with spacious rooms, amiable
                 hosts and private balconies and baths." (1999)

POSADA DE SOL Y SOMBRA

113 West Virginia, La Veta, CO 81055   719-742-3159
Carroll & Betty Elwell, Resident Owners

LOCATION	Take Fourth Street south from railroad off Main Street.
OPEN	January through October
DESCRIPTION	A two-story restored brick farmhouse built around 1895 with Victorian interior. A vintage woodcraft porch was added in the 1920s.
NO. OF ROOMS	Two rooms share one bathroom.
RATES	Year-round rates for a single or double with a shared bathroom are $40-50. There is a two-night minimum stay on certain holidays, a 50% deposit reserves a room, and cancellation requires five days' notice.
CREDIT CARDS	No
BREAKFAST	Full breakfast, served in the dining room or on the terrace, includes fruit, choice of bread, eggs, and condiments. Special meals on request. "We specialize in the use of fresh herbs."
AMENITIES	Robes; art gallery of local artists' work; close to golf course and shopping; excellent hiking, biking, and fishing; TV/VCR; games; library; two sitting rooms; large yard; patio.
RESTRICTIONS	No smoking, no pets. Resident cat is named . . . Cat. Limited facilities for children.
REVIEWED	*Recommended Inns*
KUDOS/COMMENTS	"Great cook! Lovely gardens." (1996) "Well decorated; nice, relaxed hosts." (1997) "A fantastic couple runs this home-style B&B with great breakfasts." (1999)

LAKE CITY

Located on the Alpine Loop National Backcountry Byway and the Silver Thread National Scenic Byway, Lake City is the site of the infamous 1874 Alferd Packer Massacre. Less macabre claims to fame include local musical and theatrical productions, a summer chamber music series in the four historic churches, and the Arts and Crafts Festival during the third Tuesday in July. Take the historic walking tour.

ALPINE LOOP B&B

Henson Creek Road, Lake City, CO 81235　　　　970-944-2944
Dolly & Kelly Perryman, Resident Managers　　　FAX 505-525-2065

LOCATION	On the Alpine Loop Backcountry Byway, nine miles west of Lake City on the Henson Creek Road toward Engineer Pass in the abandoned mining townsite of Capitol City.
OPEN	All year
DESCRIPTION	A 1987 three-story modern host home with saltillo tile kitchen and living areas, Native American pottery, and country decor.
NO. OF ROOMS	One room with private bathroom and two rooms share two bathrooms. The managers' favorite is the Matterhorn Room.
RATES	Rates vary from $67-117 depending on season, call for details. There is no minimum stay requirement. Holidays and special events require 30 days' cancellation notice. Otherwise, cancellation requires eight days' notice for a refund less a $15 charge.
CREDIT CARDS	MasterCard, Visa
BREAKFAST	Full breakfast, served family style in the dining room with the innkeepers, includes ham, bacon, or sausage; eggs; breakfast casseroles; homemade breads or muffins; fresh fruit; and beverages. Lunch and dinner are also available.
AMENITIES	Home-baked delights, fireplace in living room, robes, large wraparound deck, bright stars, and crisp Rocky Mountain spring water.
RESTRICTIONS	No pets, smoking permitted on outside deck
MEMBER	Bed & Breakfast Innkeepers of Colorado
RATED	1995 Spectacular Location Award (Bed & Breakfast Innkeepers of Colorado)

CINNAMON INN BED & BREAKFAST

426 Gunnison Avenue, Lake City, CO 81235   970-944-2641
Larry Washburn & Kathie Steele, Resident Owners   800-337-2335
Spanish and German spoken   FAX 970-944-2641 *(call first)*
WEBSITE *www.hinsdale-county.com*

LOCATION	In the village of Lake City on the southeast corner of 5th and Gunnison Avenue (Highway 149).
OPEN	All year
DESCRIPTION	An 1878 two-story Victorian inn with front and back porches, a white picket fence, large shade trees, flower gardens, a fountain, and decorated with simple Victorian furnishings with American and international accents. Listed on both the National and State Historic Registers.
NO. OF ROOMS	Four rooms with private bathrooms. Try the Kitty Eastman Suite with a whirlpool tub, fireplace, and private balcony.
RATES	Year-round rates are $90-125 for a double with a private bathroom. The entire B&B rents for $420-500. There is a minimum stay during July 4th weekend.
CREDIT CARDS	MasterCard, Visa
BREAKFAST	Full country breakfast, served in the family kitchen, includes fresh-roasted coffee, tea, fruit bowl and homemade yogurt sauce, bacon or sausage, and a hot entrée such as quiche, fritatta, Dutch baby, a variety of French toasts or multigrain pancakes, served on plates decorated with edible flowers and veggies. Special meals may be arranged.
AMENITIES	Fresh flowers in the rooms during the summer, Kathie's silk-flower arrangements, suite with whirlpool tub and fireplace, Larry (a professional jazz pianist) performs "java jazz" at breakfast, robes in rooms, common room for reading or watching TV, snowshoes available. Arrangements can be made for horseback riding, Jeep tours, and bike and snowmobile rentals.
RESTRICTIONS	No smoking, no pets, supervised children over five are welcome.
REVIEWED	*Lonely Planet, Recommended Country Inns, 22 Days in the West*
MEMBER	Bed & Breakfast Innkeepers of Colorado
RATED	Mobil 1 Star
KUDOS/COMMENTS	"Larry is a professional pianist: he loves 'Java Jazz'; Kathie is a gourmet cook." (1997)

OLD CARSON INN

8401 County Road 30, Lake City, CO 81235
Don & Judy Berry, Resident Owners

970-944-2511
800-294-0608
FAX 970-944-2742

LOCATION	Go south of Lake City on Highway 149, turn on County Road 30 (look for Lake San Cristobal Recreation Area sign), the inn is 8.5 miles on CR 30.
OPEN	All year
DESCRIPTION	A 1990 three-story log inn filled with antiques, murals, and southwestern art, located in the shadow of two fourteeners.
NO. OF ROOMS	Seven rooms with private bathrooms. Judy suggests the Big Indian Mine.
RATES	Year-round rates are $69-110 for a single or double with a private bathroom. There is no minimum stay. Ask about a cancellation policy.
CREDIT CARDS	American Express, Discover, MasterCard, Visa
BREAKFAST	Full breakfast, served in the dining room, is a "very large" mountain breakfast with a hearty egg dish, meat, fruit, two kinds of homemade breads, and beverages. Lunch and dinner are available.
AMENITIES	Outdoor hot tub, satellite TV, VCR, film library, books and games in large common area with wood-burning stove, beverages available anytime.
RESTRICTIONS	No smoking, no pets
REVIEWED	*Recommended Inns of the Rocky Mountains, Best Places to Stay in the Rocky Mountains*
MEMBER	Bed & Breakfast Innkeepers of Colorado

STUART HOUSE

120 Broken Arrow Path, Lake George, CO 80827

719-748-1100

UTE TRAIL RIVER RANCH

21446 County Road 77, Lake George, CO 80827
Debra Baxter & Jim Fagerstrom, Resident Owners

719-748-3015

The Apple Blossom Inn, Leadville

LEADVILLE

This historic mining town was once the epitome of boom town wealth. Indeed, Leadville's history is as heady as its altitude—10,188 feet. The ghosts of H.A.W. Tabor, Baby Doe, and others of the Matchless Mine still fill the town. Situated in the spectacular Arkansas Valley in the shadow of Colorado's two highest peaks, Mount Elbert and Mount Massive (a name not intended to be ironic), Leadville is the home of the Leadville 100, a fairly serious ultra-marathon. From Denver, 103 miles to Copper Mountain, then south 24 miles on Highway 91.

THE APPLE BLOSSOM INN

120 West 4th Street, Leadville, CO 80461   719-486-2141
Maggie Senn & Family, Innkeepers   800-982-9279
EMAIL *applebb@rmi.net*   FAX 719-486-0994
WEBSITE *www.colorado-bnb.com/abi*

LOCATION	Entering Leadville from the north, take Poplar Street, which turns right at 9th Street and then becomes Harrison Avenue, and take a right onto West 4th Street. The inn is a half block on the right side.
OPEN	All year
DESCRIPTION	An 1879 two-story Victorian inn with Victorian decor, stained glass, crystal and brass chandeliers, hardwood floors, and ornate woodwork. Full of 19th-century charm and 20th-century comforts,

the Apple Blossom Inn is listed on the National and State Historic Registers.

NO. OF ROOMS: Five rooms with private bathrooms. The Library is Maggie's favorite room.

RATES: Year-round rates are $79-89 for a single or double with a private bathroom, suites rent for $128, and the entire inn rents for $495. There is a minimum stay during holidays and special events. One night (or 50%) deposit is due at the time of booking and cancellation requires 14 days' notice.

CREDIT CARDS: American Express, Diners Club, Discover, MasterCard, Visa

BREAKFAST: Full breakfast is served in the dining room and includes bacon, sausage, homefried potatoes, an egg dish, home-baked goods like cinnamon rolls or muffins, fresh fruit, yogurt, hot or cold cereal, milk, juice, coffee, and tea.

AMENITIES: Robes, bubble bath, amenity basket, afternoon snacks including home-baked fudge brownies, assorted hot and cold beverages.

RESTRICTIONS: No smoking, no pets

REVIEWED: *Recommended Country Inns of the Rocky Mountain Region*

MEMBER: Bed & Breakfast Innkeepers of Colorado, Professional Association of Innkeepers International, Colorado Hotel and Lodging Association

KUDOS/COMMENTS: "Maggie is a wonderful hostess with beautiful rooms. She really goes out of her way to make you feel at home." "Wonderful food." (1996)

DELAWARE HOTEL

700 Harrison Avenue, Leadville, CO 80461   719-486-1418
Scott & Susan Brackett, Resident Owners   800-748-2004
                                                   FAX 719-486-2214

LOCATION: On Harrison Avenue (main street) and the corner of 7th Street in the heart of greater Leadville's Historic District.

OPEN: All year

DESCRIPTION: An 1886 three-story French Mansard Victorian with Second Empire elements on the roof. The hotel has been renovated with oak paneling, crystal chandeliers, and period antiques and is listed on the National and State Historic Registers.

NO. OF ROOMS: Thirty-six rooms with private bathrooms. The Bracketts like room 2.

RATES: Year-round rates are $65-70 for a single or double with a private bath and $115-135 for a suite. There is no minimum stay and

---

	cancellation requires 72 hours' notice, two weeks' notice during holidays.
CREDIT CARDS	American Express, Diners Club, Discover, MasterCard, Visa
BREAKFAST	Breakfast choices are continental, which includes hot or cold cereal, fresh fruit, and a variety of breads, or a full hot breakfast that changes each morning. Special meals are available for functions with 25 persons or more.
AMENITIES	Weekend entertainment in the lobby, hot tub, lobby bar, special theme weekends (murder mystery, medieval, etc.), meeting facilities for up to 35, banquet facilities for up to 100, full-service on-site restaurant.
RESTRICTIONS	No smoking in restaurant (OK in rooms), no pets. Bruno is the resident Maine coon cat. He's popular with the guests and is known as the CEO.
REVIEWED	*The Best Bed & Breakfasts and Country Inns: West; American and Canadian Bed & Breakfasts; Recommended Country Inns of the Rocky Mountain Region*
MEMBER	Association of Historic Hotels of the Rocky Mountain West, American Bed & Breakfast Association, Professional Association of Innkeepers International, Colorado Hotel and Lodging Association, Leadville Lodging Association
RATED	AAA 2 Diamonds, ABBA 2 Crowns, Mobil 2 Stars
AWARDS	Colorado Historical Society, Stephen Hart Award for Outstanding Historic Preservation, 1993

THE ICE PALACE INN BED & BREAKFAST

813 Spruce Street, Leadville, CO 80461   719-486-8272
Giles & Kami Kolakowski, Resident Owners   800-754-2840
EMAIL *ipalace@sni.net*   FAX 719-486-0345
WEBSITE *www.colorado-bnb.com/icepalace*

LOCATION	From I-70, take exit 195. Take Highway 91 south to Leadville. Highway 91 becomes Leadville's main street. The first right is West 8th, and the next right is Spruce.
OPEN	All year
DESCRIPTION	An 1899 three-story Victorian inn decorated with antiques and built with lumber taken from Leadville's famous Ice Palace.
NO. OF ROOMS	Six rooms with private bathrooms. Try the Grand Ballroom Suite.
RATES	High-season (all months except April, May, October, and November) rates are $79-99 for a single or double with a private

bathroom and $109-119 for a suite. Low-season rates are $59-79 for a single or double with a private bathroom and $89-99 for a suite. There is no minimum stay and cancellation requires 30 days' notice less $25 fee (less than 14 days' notice results in 50% of deposit returned if room is rebooked).

CREDIT CARDS	American Express, Discover, MasterCard, Visa
BREAKFAST	Full gourmet breakfast is served in the dining room and includes juice, coffee, or tea; fresh fruit; homemade bread; and a main course of stuffed French toast, German apple pancakes, Belgian waffles, or quiche, followed by a fresh fruit smoothie in a champagne glass.
AMENITIES	Feather beds, garden hot tub, afternoon teas and goodies, turndown service, ceiling fans, champagne for honeymoons and anniversaries, coffee and tea station in each room.
RESTRICTIONS	No smoking, no pets
REVIEWED	*America's Favorite Inns, B&Bs and Small Hotels*

THE LEADVILLE COUNTRY INN

127 East 8th Street, Leadville, CO 80461   719-486-2354
Judy & Sid Clemmer, Resident Owners   800-748-2354
WEBSITE *www.leadvillebednbreakfast.com*   FAX 719-486-0300

LOCATION	Half a block off Harrison Avenue, third house on the right.
OPEN	All year
DESCRIPTION	An 1893 Queen Anne Victorian with country Victorian furnishings.
NO. OF ROOMS	Nine rooms with private bathrooms.
RATES	Year-round rates are $57-139 for a single or double with a private bathroom. Rooms having more than two guests add $15 per person. There is a minimum stay during high season and a reservation/cancellation policy.
CREDIT CARDS	American Express, Diners Club, Discover, MasterCard, Visa
BREAKFAST	Full gourmet breakfast is served in the dining area. Ask about special packages. Candlelight dinners with carriage or sleigh rides are available at extra cost.
AMENITIES	Jacuzzi in gazebo, robes in some rooms, TV, radio in all rooms and phone in some rooms, bicycles, complimentary fresh-baked goods, wedding and meeting facilities, limited handicapped access.
RESTRICTIONS	No smoking, no pets, children over three are welcome.
REVIEWED	*America's Wonderful Little Hotels & Inns, The Colorado Guide, Inn Places for Bed & Breakfasts*

MEMBER	Bed & Breakfast Innkeepers of Colorado, Distinctive Inns of Colorado
KUDOS/COMMENTS	"A truly elegant country inn." "A top-notch inn that is professionally run but still warm and friendly." "Afternoon snacks were elegant. The best waffles I ever tasted." (1997)

PERI & ED'S MOUNTAIN HIDEAWAY

201 West 8th Street, Leadville, CO 80461   719-486-0716
Peri & Ed Solder, Resident Owners   800-933-3715
EMAIL *solder@sni.net*   FAX *719-486-2181*
WEBSITE *www.mountainhideaway.com*

LOCATION	Follow Highway 91 to Leadville, to Harrison Avenue (main street), take the first right on 8th, the inn is one block on the left.
OPEN	All year
DESCRIPTION	An 1879 three-story Victorian inn with Victorian and western decor, "where you can put up your feet and feel at home."
NO. OF ROOMS	Eight rooms with private bathrooms. Two guesthouses. Peri recommends the Tabor Suite.
RATES	Year-round rates are $45-90 for a single or double, $65-90 for a suite, $100 for two in the guesthouse, and $650 for the entire B&B. There is a 10-day cancellation policy.
CREDIT CARDS	American Express, Discover, MasterCard, Visa
BREAKFAST	Full breakfast is served in the dining room and includes a hot dish with meat, yogurt, granola, and plenty of juice and coffee. Special meals are available.
AMENITIES	Robes, telephones available in some rooms, hot tub on deck, kitchen for guest use, TV and VCR in parlor, musical instruments, games, and books.
RESTRICTIONS	No smoking, no pets (Brendan, the resident cocker, loves kids). Children of all ages are welcome.
KUDOS/COMMENTS	"Peri, Ed, and family love to share their home and lifestyle . . . a real breath of fresh air." (1994) "Recent renovations are wonderful." (1996)

WOOD HAVEN MANOR BED & BREAKFAST

809 Spruce, Leadville, CO 80461
Jolene & Bobby Wood, Innkeepers
WEBSITE www.colorado-bnb.com/woodhavn

719-486-0109
800-748-2570
FAX 719-486-0210

LOCATION	From Harrison Street (Leadville's main street), turn west on 8th Street and go two blocks, then turn right on Spruce.
OPEN	All year
DESCRIPTION	A restored 1898 three-story Victorian inn on Banker's Row decorated with period antiques, lace curtains, and designer decor.
NO. OF ROOMS	Four rooms with private bathrooms. Jolene suggests the Secret Garden Suite.
RATES	June through September and December through March, rates are $69-129 for a single or double with a private bathroom, $119-129 for a suite, and $400 for the entire B&B. April through May and October through November, rates are $49-99 for a single or double with a private bathroom, $89-99 for a suite, and $300 for the entire B&B. There is a minimum stay during holidays and special events, and cancellation requires 10 days' notice.
CREDIT CARDS	American Express, Discover, MasterCard, Visa
BREAKFAST	Full breakfast, served in the dining room, includes coffee, juice, hot tea, hot chocolate, fresh fruit, homemade breads and muffins, bacon or sausage, and an entrée such as an egg dish or waffles. Lunch and weekend dinners are available by reservation.
AMENITIES	Afternoon snacks, coffee and tea anytime, fireplace in Garden Suite, whirlpool in Garden and Tabor Suites, piano and fireplace in living room, TV/VCR in Garden Suite and common room, 150 videos, robes, breakfast in bed on request, picnic lunches available, ski lift and recreation packages, fruit baskets and wine for special occasions on request.
RESTRICTIONS	No smoking, no pets, children over five are welcome.
REVIEWED	*Non-Smokers Guide to Bed & Breakfasts*
MEMBER	Colorado Hotel and Lodging Association, Bed & Breakfast Innkeepers of Colorado, Professional Association of Innkeepers International
RATED	Mobil 1 Star
KUDOS/COMMENTS	"Bobby and Jolene make everyone feel like they've just come home." (1997)

LONGMONT

This agricultural center in Boulder County was started as the Chicago-Colorado Colony. It retains much of its midwestern flavor, with beautiful old homes and wide streets surrounded by subdivisions. Longmont provides excellent access to Boulder, Denver, and Estes Park. From Denver, 30 miles north on I-25 and five miles west on Highway 119.

ELLEN'S BED & BREAKFAST

700 Kimbark Street, Longmont, CO 80501   303-776-1676
Baldwin "Baldy" & Ellen Ranson, Resident Owners
Spanish, French, and Bulgarian spoken   FAX 303-776-1676 *(call first)*
EMAIL *b_eranson@compuserve.com*

LOCATION	In Longmont go one block east of Main Street and four blocks north of Third Avenue.
OPEN	All year
DESCRIPTION	A 1910 two-story Victorian with eclectic furnishings that reflect the owners' worldwide travels.
NO. OF ROOMS	One room with a private bathroom and one room with a shared bathroom. Ask for the largest room with the poster bed.
RATES	Year-round rate is $75 per couple and $25 per each additional guest (children). Cancellation requires 24 hours' notice.
CREDIT CARDS	No
BREAKFAST	Full hearty breakfast, served in the sunny dining room on Bulgarian china and heirloom silver, includes stuffed croissants, fresh-fruit scones, or Santa Fe quiche.
AMENITIES	Flowers, private outdoor hot tub, imported chocolate, beverage on arrival, rubber duck and Gary Larson cartoons in the bathroom, and conversation with well-traveled hosts.
RESTRICTIONS	None. Children are welcome, and there are two miniature schnauzers, Rufus and Rosie, whom "our guests keep wanting to take home."
AWARDS	Award for redevelopment, "Architecture and Design Excellence," City of Longmont Planning Commission.

LOVELAND

At the mouth of the Big Thompson Canyon lies America's "Sweetheart City." Valentines from around the country (and world) are sent here to be remailed with Loveland's postmark and special cachet. Named for railroad pioneer W.A.H. Loveland, not romance, this important agricultural and recreational area features Boyd Lake State Recreational Area and three public golf courses. Some of the finest bronze sculpture in the country is showcased at the Loveland Sculpture Park and during the International Sculpture Show every August. Estes Park, Rocky Mountain National Park, and Fort Collins are within easy access. Fifty miles north of Denver on I-25 and Highway 34.

APPLE AVENUE BED & BREAKFAST

3321 Apple Avenue, Loveland, CO 80538　　　　　970-667-2665
Tom & Ann Harroun, Resident Owners　　*FAX 970-667-2665 (call first)*
Bits and pieces of French and Spanish spoken
EMAIL *ktvh@aol.com*　　　　　WEBSITE *www.bbonline.com/co/apple/*

LOCATION	From Highway 34 go north on Taft Avenue 1.3 miles, right on Beech, second left on Apple, third driveway on left.
OPEN	All year
DESCRIPTION	An airy 1973 contemporary ranch home with traditional and early American decor.
NO. OF ROOMS	Two rooms share one-and-a-half bathrooms. Ann recommends the Green Room.
RATES	February through November, rates are $60-68 for a single or double with a shared bathroom. December and January, rates are $50-58. There is a minimum stay during the sculpture shows in August, and cancellation requires seven days' notice.
CREDIT CARDS	American Express, Discover, MasterCard, Visa
BREAKFAST	Full breakfast is served in the dining room and may include blueberry pancakes, orange French toast, veggie-filled omelets, or eggs Benedict with bacon, ham, or sausage, and fresh-baked muffins. Pure Vermont maple syrup is served. Restricted diets are accommodated and afternoon tea is available by arrangement.
AMENITIES	Air conditioning; ceiling fans; robes; fresh flowers in season; laundry facilities; clock radios in bedrooms; living room with TV, books, and games; three decks; gas grill; fax and copier; portacrib, highchair, toys; flexible mealtimes and menus.
RESTRICTIONS	No smoking, no pets. Children are welcome.
MEMBER	Bed & Breakfast Innkeepers of Colorado, Northern Colorado Bed & Breakfast Association

Cattail Creek Inn Bed & Breakfast, Loveland

CATTAIL CREEK INN BED & BREAKFAST

2665 Abarr Drive, Loveland, CO 80538　　　　　970-667-7600
Sue & Harold Buchman, Resident Owners　　　　　800-572-2466
　　　　　　　　　　　　　　　　　　　　　　　FAX 970-667-8968

LOCATION	From I-25, take Highway 34 west five miles to Taft. Turn right on Taft and go one mile. Turn left on 28th, go half a block, and turn left on Abarr Drive. The Inn is on the right side of the street.
OPEN	All year
DESCRIPTION	A 1995 two-story Mediterranean inn with finely crafted cherry woodwork and vaulted ceilings.
NO. OF ROOMS	Eight bedrooms with private bathrooms. The innkeepers recommend the Coal Creek Room.
RATES	Year-round rates are $95-155 for a single or double with a private bathroom. There is no minimum stay and cancellation requires seven days' notice.
CREDIT CARDS	American Express, Discover, MasterCard, Visa
BREAKFAST	Full breakfast, served in the dining room, includes sherried eggs, sautéed apples with vanilla sauce, assorted scones, juices, coffee, tea, and milk.
AMENITIES	Air conditioning, handicapped access, hair dryers, iron and ironing board, robes, wine, seasonal afternoon refreshments, art gallery tours, foundry tours, golf packages, and a guest refrigerator.
RESTRICTIONS	No smoking, no pets, and children over 14 are welcome.
REVIEWED	*Recommended Country Inns*
MEMBER	Distinctive Inns of Colorado, Professional Association of

Innkeepers International, Northern Colorado Innkeepers
Association

RATED   Mobil 3 Stars

KUDOS/COMMENTS   "Great view of the mountains, perfectly set on the edge of a golf
                        course." "Close to the Sculpture Gardens and Lake Loveland,
                        excellent wine cellar, good conversation." (1997) "Outstanding new
                        construction, faces a park, knowledgeable concierges, very friendly
                        couple." "Elegant. Good location." (1999)

DERBY HILL INN BED & BREAKFAST

2502 Courtney Drive, Loveland, CO 80537   970-667-3193
Dale & Bev McCue, Resident Owners   800-498-8086
Limited German spoken   FAX 970-667-3193 (call first)
EMAIL dmccue31@aol.com   WEBSITE www.questinns.com/derbyhill

LOCATION   In a neighborhood on the south side of Loveland about one mile
                        from the center of town. Fifty miles from Denver, 5.5 miles from
                        I-25, and 30 miles from Rocky Mountain National Park.

OPEN   All year

DESCRIPTION   A 1975 four-story traditional host home with stylish traditional
                        decor, artwork, and antiques in a quiet neighborhood.

NO. OF ROOMS   Two rooms with private bathrooms.

RATES   Year-round rates for a single or double with a private bathroom are
                        $70-85. There is a minimum stay during Colorado State University
                        graduation in May and the sculpture show in August. Cancellation
                        requires seven days' notice.

CREDIT CARDS   American Express, Diners Club, MasterCard, Visa

BREAKFAST   Full breakfast, served on antique china in the dining room or on
                        the deck in the summer, includes a choice of two entrées, fresh
                        fruit, homemade muffins and specialty breads, juice, and gourmet
                        coffee and tea.

AMENITIES   Fresh flowers, chocolates, early morning coffee, robes,
                        complimentary snacks and soft drinks, air conditioning, in-room
                        phone and TV, computer, and fax machine.

RESTRICTIONS   No smoking, no pets, children over 12 are welcome.

REVIEWED   *Inn for the Night*

MEMBER   Bed & Breakfast Innkeepers of Colorado, Professional Association
                        of Innkeepers International

AWARDS   1997 Inn of the Year, in the New, Small Inn category, awarded by
                        the Bed & Breakfast Innkeepers of Colorado

JEFFERSON HOUSE

342 East Third Street, Loveland, CO 80537   970-669-6220
Art & Jeanne Myers, Resident Owners

LOCATION	One block from downtown and two blocks west of the Loveland Civic Center, on the southwest corner of Third and Jefferson.
OPEN	All year
DESCRIPTION	An 1897 three-story brick Victorian, filled with paintings and sculptures by Art Myers, located in the heart of Loveland's art community. Highlights include the original woodwork and transoms above all doors.
NO. OF ROOMS	Three rooms share one bathroom. The Myers' favorite room is the Queen Room.
RATES	A single with a shared bath is $40 and a double is $50. There is no minimum stay and a one-week cancellation policy.
CREDIT CARDS	No
BREAKFAST	Continental breakfast is served in the dining room and includes muffins, croissants, juice, fruit, coffee, tea, and hot chocolate.
RESTRICTIONS	No smoking, no pets, children over 10 are welcome.

THE LOVELANDER BED & BREAKFAST INN

217 West 4th Street, Loveland CO 80537   970-669-0798
Lauren & Gary Smith, Innkeepers   800-459-6694
EMAIL *love@ezlink.com*   FAX 970-669-0797
WEBSITE *www.bbonline.com/co/lovelander*

LOCATION	Center of town just east of Garfield Avenue.
OPEN	All year
DESCRIPTION	A 1902 two-story Victorian inn with Victorian decor that combines historic charm with contemporary convenience.
NO. OF ROOMS	Eleven bedrooms with private bathrooms. Try the Namaqua Room.
RATES	Year-round rates are $100-150 for a single or double with a private bathroom. There is no minimum stay and cancellation requires seven days' notice.
CREDIT CARDS	American Express, Discover, MasterCard, Visa
BREAKFAST	Full gourmet breakfast is served in the dining room.
AMENITIES	Evening dessert and beverages; separate meeting facilities and special events center; phones in rooms; rooms with fireplace,

whirlpool, steam shower and/or balcony deck. "We guarantee a memorable stay or next stay is on us," Lauren and Gary promise.

RESTRICTIONS	No smoking, no pets, children over 10 are welcome.
MEMBER	Independent Innkeepers Association, Distinctive Inns of Colorado, Professional Association of Innkeepers International
RATED	AAA 3 Diamonds, Mobil 3 Stars
KUDOS/COMMENTS	"Very hospitable innkeepers; cozy retreat from everyday life." "Very comfortable beds and delicious breakfast." (1997) "Very nice. Good location." (1999)

SYLVAN DALE GUEST RANCH

2939 North County Road 31D, Loveland, CO 80537   970-667-3915
Susan Jessup, Resident Owner
WEBSITE www.sylvandale.com

WILD LANE BED & BREAKFAST INN

5445 Wild Lane, Loveland, CO 80538   970-669-0303
Steven Wild, Resident Owner   800-204-3320
WEBSITE www.bbonline.com/co/wildlane

LOCATION	Take Highway 34 west through Loveland and turn right on Wild Lane.
OPEN	All year
DESCRIPTION	A 1905 two-story Victorian country inn with Victorian interior on a landscaped 200-acre estate. This historic family home is listed on the National and State Historic Registers.
NO. OF ROOMS	Five rooms with private bathrooms. The owner recommends the Blue Rose Room.
RATES	Year-round rates are $89-109 for a single or double with a private bathroom. Rates may go up, call for details. No minimum stay is required and cancellation requires five days' notice.
CREDIT CARDS	American Express, Discover, MasterCard, Visa
BREAKFAST	Full breakfast with "herbal flair" is served in the dining room, guestrooms, or on the sun porch. Lunch and dinner are available with advance notice and a minimum number of guests is required.
AMENITIES	Three fireplaces, parlor, library, enclosed sun porch, landscaped grounds, herb farm, and gift shop.

LYONS

A picturesque western town and designated National Historic District (for its 15 sandstone buildings), Lyons features great antiquing and, during the summer, some of the best square dancing in Colorado. Forty-five miles northwest of Denver on Highway 36.

INN AT ROCK 'N RIVER BED & BREAKFAST AND TROUT POND FISHING

16858 North Saint Vrain Drive, Lyons, CO 80540   *303-823-5011*
Richard & Marylou Gibson, Resident Owners   *800-448-4611*
EMAIL *rocknriver@estes-park.com*
WEBSITE *www.estes-park.com/rocknriver*

LOCATION	Three miles west of Lyons on Highway 36.
OPEN	From April 1 through October 31
DESCRIPTION	A 1965 frame country inn with pine furnishings — a trout farm, on 18 acres along the Saint Vrain River.
NO. OF ROOMS	Nine rooms with private bathrooms. Try the Carriage House.
RATES	Seasonal rates are $95-125 for a single and $140-155 for a double. There is a two-night minimum stay on holiday weekends and a cancellation policy.
CREDIT CARDS	American Express, Discover, MasterCard, Visa
BREAKFAST	Full breakfast, served in the dining room, features a choice of nine different entrées. Lunch, dinner, and special meals for groups are available.
AMENITIES	Full kitchens in rooms, catch 10-to-28-inch Rainbow trout in stocked ponds (the innkeepers will cook them for you or trade for smoked trout at a small charge), hiking nearby.
RESTRICTIONS	No smoking in rooms, no pets. Children of all ages are welcome.
RATED	AAA 2 Diamonds

MANCOS

The eastern gateway to Mesa Verde National Park, one of the nation's major archaeological preserves. This small rural town at the north end of Mancos River Canyon is a great place to start exploring Mancos State Park. Between Cortez and Durango on Scenic Highway 160.

BAUER HOUSE

100 Bauer, Mancos, CO 81328　　　　　　　　*970-533-9707*
Bobbi Black, Resident Innkeeper　　　　　　　*800-733-9707*
EMAIL bauerhouse@fone.net　　　　　　　*FAX 970-533-7022*
WEBSITE www.bauer.house.com

LOCATION	Located half a block south of Highway 160 at the junction of Highways 160 and 184.
OPEN	April 15th through November 15th (or earlier, depending on the weather)
DESCRIPTION	An 1890 three-story Victorian Italianate host home decorated with classic antiques.
NO. OF ROOMS	Four rooms with private bathrooms.
RATES	Year-round rates are $75-125 for a single or double with a private bathroom and $125 for a suite. A two-night minimum stay is required during holidays and is preferred at other times. Cancellation requires 14 days' notice.

Bauer House, Mancos

CREDIT CARDS	Discover, MasterCard, Visa
BREAKFAST	Full breakfast is served in the dining room or on the patio. Lunch, dinner, and special meals are available upon request.
AMENITIES	Fresh flowers and robes; wine and hors d'oeuvres at reception; barbecue; phone, fax, and computer use; one-way transportation for narrow-gauge railroad trips (if time allows); family reunions; July 4th celebration; historic tours of home and town.
RESTRICTIONS	No smoking inside, no pets
REVIEWED	*America's Favorite Inns, B&Bs and Small Hotels*

FLAGSTONE MEADOWS RANCH B&B

PO Box 1137, Mancos, CO 81328   *970-533-9838*

GINGERBREAD INN BED & BREAKFAST

41478 Highway 184, Mancos, CO 81328   *970-533-7892*
                                                          800-617-2479

RIVERSBEND BED & BREAKFAST

42505 Highway 160, Mancos, CO 81328   *970-533-7353*
Gaye & Jack Curran, Innkeepers   *800-699-8994*
EMAIL *riversbn@fone.net*   FAX *970-533-1221*
WEBSITE *www.riversbend.com*

LOCATION	On Highway 160 on the east side of Mancos as you cross the Mancos River bridge.
OPEN	All year
DESCRIPTION	A 1995 two-story log cabin inn furnished with antiques and with the sounds of the river in the background.
NO. OF ROOMS	Five bedrooms with private bathrooms.
RATES	Year-round rates are $75-125 for a single or double with a private bathroom. There is no minimum stay and cancellation requires 15 days' notice.
CREDIT CARDS	American Express, Discover, MasterCard, Visa

BREAKFAST	Full breakfast is served in the dining room and includes homebaked breads, fruits, coffee, tea, and a hot entrée such as caramel nut French toast served with fresh peaches and cream.
AMENITIES	Fluffy terry robes, hot tub off the back porch, afternoon refreshments.
RESTRICTIONS	No smoking, no pets, children over 12 are welcome.
REVIEWED	*Lanier's Guide to Bed & Breakfasts*
MEMBER	Bed & Breakfast Inns of Colorado, Professional Association of Innkeepers International, North American Association of Bed & Breakfasts
RATED	AAA 3 Diamonds

MANITOU SPRINGS

The natural mineral waters once made this spot a gathering place for the Ute and Arapahoe Indians. Now one of America's largest National Historic Districts, this small town with art colony overtones is built on steep hillsides against the foothills of Pikes Peak. Manitou Springs features the Lilac Festival in May, the Emma Crawford Memorial Coffin Races in October, and the Fruitcake Toss in January. Check out the Iron Springs Chateau Melodrama Theatre, Miramont Castle, and Cave of the Winds. The Pikes Peak Cog Railway is a good way to get to the top of the mountain. About six miles west of Colorado Springs.

BLUE SKIES INN

402 Manitou Avenue, Manitou Springs, CO 80829   719-685-3899
Sally Thurston, Innkeeper   800-398-7949
EMAIL *sally@blueskiesbb.com*   FAX 719-685-3099
WEBSITE *www.blueskiesbb.com*

LOCATION	Take the Manitou Avenue exit off Highway 24 and go 0.4 mile west; look for the 40-foot Gothic arch.
OPEN	All year
DESCRIPTION	Three 1996 two-story Gothic Revival buildings with eclectic decor located on the wooded, streamside estate of Manitou's founder.
NO. OF ROOMS	Twelve bedrooms with private bathrooms. Try the Blue Skies Suite.
RATES	Year-round rates are $120-220 for a suite. There is no minimum stay and cancellation requires two weeks' notice (30 days during holidays) with a $25 charge unless the room is rebooked.
CREDIT CARDS	American Express, Discover, MasterCard, Visa

BREAKFAST	Continental plus is served in the dining room or guestrooms and includes fresh fruit, coffee or tea, juice, pastries, and an egg dish.
AMENITIES	Meeting facilities for up to 225, banquet facilities for 125, commercial kitchen for caterers, handicapped access, air conditioning in all areas, outdoor structures for weddings and family reunion parties.
RESTRICTIONS	No smoking, no pets, children are welcome. There are deer and wild birds on the property.
MEMBER	Bed & Breakfasts of the Pikes Peak Region, Bed & Breakfast Innkeepers of Colorado

FRONTIER'S REST

341 Ruxton Avenue, Manitou Springs, CO 80829   719-685-0588
Jeanne Vrobel, Resident Owner   800-455-0588
WEBSITE www.bbonline.com/co/frontier/

LOCATION	From Colorado Springs, take I-25 to Highway 24 west (exit 141). Go four miles to Manitou Avenue and turn west. Go to Ruxton Avenue and turn left. Go three blocks.
OPEN	All year
DESCRIPTION	An 1890 one-and-a-half-story Victorian folk home and cottage with "old west" Victorian furniture and antique-filled theme rooms, located in the Manitou Historic District at the foot of Pikes Peak.
NO. OF ROOMS	Four rooms with private bathrooms.
RATES	May 15 through October, rates are $85-115 for a room with a private bathroom. November through mid-May, rates are $65-100. The entire B&B rents for $425 during high season and $360 during low season. Minimum stays are required during holiday weekends or during high season weekends. Cancellation requires seven days' notice.
CREDIT CARDS	American Express, Discover, MasterCard, Visa
BREAKFAST	Full breakfast is served in the dining room and includes any one of 12 theme breakfasts, like southwestern, Scandinavian immigrant, or Native American. Special meals are also available. A food list is given to guests at check-in.
AMENITIES	Fresh-baked cookies, "Manitou" lemonade, nightly homemade desserts, rocking chairs, full guest kitchen, laundry facilities, 24-hour beverage bar, Olde Fashioned Christmas and Murder Mystery weekends, and small meeting facilities.
RESTRICTIONS	No smoking, children with well-behaved adults are welcome. "Due to stairs, the inn is probably not suitable for people who have difficulty walking."

GRAY'S AVENUE HOTEL

711 Manitou Avenue, Manitou Springs, CO 80829   *719-685-1277*
Tom & Lee Gray, Resident Owners   *800-294-1277*
EMAIL *mackeson/@aol.com*   *FAX 719-685-1847*
WEBSITE *www.spectroweb.com/graysb&b.htm*

LOCATION	From I-25, take exit 141 to Highway 24 and go west four miles. Take first Manitou exit to Manitou Avenue and go 1.2 miles west.
OPEN	All year
DESCRIPTION	An 1886 three-story shingled Queen Anne Victorian decorated with antiques and family mementos. "A large, old-fashioned front porch and lots of stairs offer built-in aerobics."
NO. OF ROOMS	Seven rooms with private bathrooms. The Grays suggest the General's Room.
RATES	Year-round rates are $60-75 for a double with a private bathroom and $15 for each additional guest. There is a two-night minimum stay during holiday weekends.
CREDIT CARDS	American Express, Discover, MasterCard, Visa
BREAKFAST	Full breakfast, usually served buffet style in the dining room or on the front porch, includes a main course (waffles, pancakes, casserole, etc.), plus bacon or ham, fresh fruit, juice, and muffins.
AMENITIES	Some clawfoot tubs, outdoor hot tub, extensive video library, afternoon refreshments, fireplace in library, piano, fax available, and small meeting room.
RESTRICTIONS	No smoking, no pets, children over 10 are welcome. The resident dogs are a German shepherd named Mackeson, who "loves to play soccer with his toys," a golden Lab called Cody, and an Australian cattle dog named Kaya, who loves playing Frisbee.
REVIEWED	*The Colorado Guide, Country Inns of the Rocky Mountain Region, Non-Smokers Guide to Bed & Breakfasts*
AWARDS	1986 City of Manitou Spring Design Award, presented by the Historic Preservation Commission.

ONALEDGE BED & BREAKFAST

336 El Paso Boulevard, Manitou Springs, CO 80829   719-685-4265
Adam Kevil, Resident Owner   800-530-8253
EMAIL onledgebb@aol.com   WEBSITE www.bbonline.com

LOCATION	From Manitou Avenue, two blocks west to Mayfair Street, right to El Paso Boulevard, top of the hill.
OPEN	All year
DESCRIPTION	A 1912 three-story English Tudor with Victorian furnishings.
NO. OF ROOMS	Three rooms with private bathrooms, three suites with private bathrooms and hot tubs.
RATES	Year-round rates are $75-150 for a single or double with a private bathroom. There is a reservation/cancellation policy.
CREDIT CARDS	American Express, Discover, MasterCard, Visa
BREAKFAST	Full gourmet breakfast is served in the dining room or on the patio.
AMENITIES	TV and air-conditioning in rooms, fireplace in one suite, hot tubs in three rooms, complimentary refreshments.
RESTRICTIONS	Smoking limited, no pets. Children 12 and over are welcome.
REVIEWED	*Recommended Country Inns of the Rocky Mountain Region*
MEMBER	Bed & Breakfast Innkeepers of Colorado
KUDOS/COMMENTS	"The antiques, potbellied stoves, storybook setting, along with the stories the innkeepers tell, make us hate to leave." (1996)

RED CRAGS BED & BREAKFAST INN

302 El Paso Boulevard, Manitou Springs, CO 80829   719-685-1910
Howard & Lynda Lerner, Innkeepers   800-721-2248
EMAIL info@redcrags.com   FAX 719-685-1073
WEBSITE www.redcrags.com

LOCATION	From I-25, take exit 141 and go west four miles to Manitou Avenue. Exit and stay in the right-hand lane. Turn right on Garden of the Gods Place, go one block to El Paso Boulevard, and turn left. Go one block to Rockledge and turn right.
OPEN	All year
DESCRIPTION	An 1870s four-story Victorian mansion decorated with period antiques on two acres with views of Pikes Peak and Garden of the Gods.

Red Crags Bed & Breakfast Inn, Manitou Springs

NO. OF ROOMS	Eight rooms with private bathrooms. The Lerners suggest the Streamside Suite in the Carriage House.
RATES	Year-round rates are $80-180 for a single or double with a private bathroom. The entire B&B rents for $1115 (up to 18 people). There is a two-night minimum stay during holidays and special events, and cancellation requires 10 days' notice, 30 days during holidays and special events.
CREDIT CARDS	American Express, Discover, MasterCard, Visa
BREAKFAST	Full gourmet breakfast is served in the dining room or the solarium and may include spinach mushroom quiche or peach French toast served with fresh homemade breads and a fruit course. Special dietary needs are accommodated upon request.
AMENITIES	Rooms have robes, feather beds with down comforters, fireplaces, phones, and TVs upon request; outdoor spa with herb and flower gardens for guests to wander through; 24-hour beverage service with fresh-baked goods to nibble on; complimentary sherry, wine, and port in the evenings; two suites have jetted tubs for two; three suites are air-conditioned.
RESTRICTIONS	No smoking, no pets, children over 10 are welcome. Jackson is the resident English springer spaniel, and the mallard ducks are Wilma, Fred, Manny, and Moe. Jackson sings and is a loveable dog who protects the patches of sunlight on the carpets. The ducks march into their duckhouse at night so wild animals don't get them.
REVIEWED	*Recommended Country Inns; Complete Guide to Bed & Breakfasts, Inns and Guesthouses; American Historic Inns*

Bed & Breakfast Innkeepers of Colorado, Professional Association of Innkeepers International

RATED
AAA 3 Diamonds, Mobil 2 Stars

KUDOS/COMMENTS
"Elegant but very comfortable." "Wonderful grounds, excellent hosts." (1997) "Exceptional property and home. Best in the area. Wonderful hosts and excellent food." (1999)

RED EAGLE MOUNTAIN B&B INN

616 Ruxton Avenue, Manitou Springs, CO 80829　　　719-685-4541
Stacie & Don LeVack, Resident Owners　　　　　　　800-686-8801
EMAIL *redeagle@pcisys.net*
　　　　　　　　　　　　　　　　WEBSITE *www.redeaglemtn.com*

LOCATION
From I-25 take exit 141 and go west on Highway 24. Take the Manitou Avenue exit, continue west to Ruxton Avenue, turn left on Ruxton, we are two blocks past the Cog Railway on the right side of the road.

OPEN
All year

DESCRIPTION
An 1894 two-story Queen Ann with Victorian furnishings and spectacular views.

NO. OF ROOMS
Five rooms with private bathrooms. Try the Red Eagle Suite.

RATES
Year-round rates are $80-125 for a single or double with a private bathroom. There is a two-night minimum stay from May through September and cancellation requires seven days' notice or forfeit 50% of the deposit. For children under 12, there is an extra $5 charge.

CREDIT CARDS
American Express, Discover, MasterCard, Visa

BREAKFAST
Full gourmet breakfast, served in the dining room or in guestrooms, includes such things as strata or quiche, fresh breads, and fruit. Homemade snacks are always available, as are special meals.

AMENITIES
Homemade cookies and cakes, one room with private sauna, hot tub outdoors, fresh flowers, robes and slippers, TV, and bomb shelter.... just in case.

RESTRICTIONS
No smoking, pets negotiable. The resident cocker is called Dreyfus. Children are welcome.

MEMBER
Bed & Breakfast Innkeepers of Colorado

RED STONE CASTLE BED & BREAKFAST

Red Stone Castle, Manitou Springs, CO 80829
Cavan Daly McGrew, Resident Owner

719-685-5070
FAX 719-685-5665

LOCATION	Four blocks from downtown, take Manitou Avenue to Pawnee, go left to South Side Road, then left to castle gate.
OPEN	All year
DESCRIPTION	An 1892 small Victorian castle on 20 acres. Listed on the National Historic Register and furnished with antiques.
NO. OF ROOMS	One luxury suite called Inspiration.
RATES	A single with a private bathroom is $110 and a double is $140. Additional guests are $25 per person. There is no minimum stay and there is a reservation/cancellation policy.
CREDIT CARDS	No
BREAKFAST	Full breakfast is served in the dining room or on the patio in the summer.
AMENITIES	Fresh and dried flowers, coffee and tea at the wet bar, telephone, robes, small reception and outdoor wedding facilities.
RESTRICTIONS	No smoking, no pets. Sara and Duke are the resident dogs.

TWO SISTERS INN—A BED & BREAKFAST

Ten Otoe Place, Manitou Springs, CO 80829
Sharon Smith & Wendy Goldstein, Resident Owners
WEBSITE www.twosis.inn.com

719-685-9684
800-274-7466

LOCATION	Exit 141 on I-25 in Colorado Springs. Go four miles west on Highway 24 to Manitou Avenue, then one mile west on Manitou. Left at town clock onto Otoe Place, and the inn is on the right.
OPEN	All year
DESCRIPTION	A 1919 two-story Victorian bungalow with Victorian furnishings and a garden cottage with a fireplace and skylight shower.
NO. OF ROOMS	Three rooms with private bathrooms and two rooms share one bathroom. Sharon and Wendy suggest the Honeymoon Cottage.
RATES	Year-round rates are $85 for a single or double with a private bathroom, $69 for a single or double with a shared bathroom, and $105 for the cottage. The entire B&B rents for $413. There is a minimum stay during weekends, holidays, and high season, and a seven-day cancellation policy with a $15 fee. Nonrefundable advance payment for holidays and special events.

CREDIT CARDS	Discover, MasterCard, Visa
BREAKFAST	Full "creative gourmet" breakfast, prepared by resident, schooled chefs using herbs and flowers from the inn's garden, is served in the dining room.
AMENITIES	Fresh flowers and home-baked treats in the rooms, beverages including Manitou's natural sparkling water lemonade, antique piano and games in the parlor, books and maps of local points of interest, on-site parking.
RESTRICTIONS	No smoking, no pets, children over 10 are welcome.
REVIEWED	*America's Wonderful Little Hotels & Inns, Frommer's Guide to Colorado, The Colorado Guide, Recommended Country Inns*
MEMBER	Bed & Breakfast Innkeepers of Colorado, Professional Association of Innkeepers International, Tourist House Association of America, Colorado Hotel and Lodging Association, Colorado Travel and Tourism Authority
RATED	Mobil 3 Stars
AWARDS	Manitou Springs Historic Preservation Commission, Historic Renovation Award, 1990
KUDOS/COMMENTS	"Small B&B with cozy rooms and very hospitable hosts." (1994) "A warm and friendly inn with caring owners and wonderful food." "Their place is great; the Honeymoon Cottage is exquisite." "Gourmet breakfasts, Sharon and Wendy are the perfect hosts." (1997) "Beautifully appointed, great innkeepers and breakfasts." (1999)

VICTORIA'S KEEP: A BED & BREAKFAST INN

202 Ruxton Avenue, Manitou Springs, CO 80829   719-685-5354
Victoria & Marvin Keith, Owners   800-905-5337
FAX 719-685-5913

LOCATION	West from Colorado Springs on Highway 24 to Manitou Springs business exit, continue west through town then take a left on Ruxton, then two blocks down on the right, directly in front of the Miramont Castle.
OPEN	All year
DESCRIPTION	A restored 1891 two-story Queen Anne Victorian with wraparound porch and antique furnishings.
NO. OF ROOMS	Six rooms with private baths and fireplaces. The Keith's favorite room is the Parlor Suite.
RATES	Year-round rates are $90 for a single or double with a private bath and $150-180 for a suite with a private bath. There is no minimum

	stay. Cancellation requires seven days' notice or forfeit deposit for one night.
CREDIT CARDS	American Express, Discover, MasterCard, Visa
BREAKFAST	Full breakfast, served just about anywhere in the house, might be crabmeat and eggs, frittatas, or biscuits and gravy. Lunch and picnic baskets are available.
AMENITIES	Spa, mountain bikes, 24-hour beverages, TV/VCR and video library, phone, air conditioning, flowers, candles, fireplaces, wine and cheese tasting, breakfast in bed, and candy dish.
RESTRICTIONS	No smoking
REVIEWED	*National Trust's Guide to Historic B&Bs, Inns and Small Hotels*
MEMBER	Professional Association of Innkeepers International, Bed & Breakfast Innkeepers of Colorado
KUDOS/COMMENTS	"Cozy Victorian home with spacious rooms and great breakfasts." "Romantic getaway to die for! Personal welcome note and turndown service were special touches." "Marvin is a marvelous gourmet chef." "Wine and cheese tasting a definite plus." (1996)

MARBLE

The famous Yule marble quarry is open again, and the town's two digit population is on the rebound. Summer do's: the Marble Art Fair and Sculptors Symposium along the Crystal River in July. The view of Crystal Mill is worth the hike, and the fishin's good in town at Beaver Lake. Down the road from Redstone, and about 60 miles southwest of Aspen via Highway 133 and County Road 3.

THE INN AT RASPBERRY RIDGE

5580 County Road 3, Marble, CO 81623   *970-963-3025*
Gary & Patsy Wagner, Resident Owners

LOCATION	On the edge of town as you enter Marble. You can't miss us.
OPEN	All year except for the weeks of Thanksgiving, Christmas, and New Year's.
DESCRIPTION	A 1960 log ranch/country inn located in a town with 55 year-round residents.
NO. OF ROOMS	Four rooms with private bathrooms. The Brass Room is the best.
RATES	Summer (April through October) rates are $70-80 for a double with a private bath and off-season rates are $50 for a double. There is a reservation/cancellation policy.
CREDIT CARDS	No
BREAKFAST	Full breakfast, served in the dining room or on the deck, includes

egg dishes, fresh-baked coffeecake, and fresh fruit. Lunches are packed on request.

AMENITIES	Snacks always available, very helpful innkeepers.
RESTRICTIONS	No smoking, no pets, and children over 12 are welcome.
MEMBER	Bed & Breakfast Innkeepers of Colorado
KUDOS/COMMENTS	"Great hospitality and terrific breakfast in one of Colorado's most fascinating and historic mountain communities." "Great breakfast, beautifully presented." "Tastefully decorated, not cutesy." "Great setting, great hosts." (1996)

MEREDITH

Don't blink or you'll miss this village in the White River National Forest. Follow along the Frying Pan River for 20 miles or so east of Basalt.

DOUBLE DIAMOND RANCH BED & BREAKFAST

23000 Frying Pan River Road, Meredith, CO 81642   970-927-3404
Jack & Joan Wheeler, Resident Owners   FAX 970-927-3404

LOCATION	Take Frying Pan River Road 23 miles from Main Street in Basalt to Ruedi Reservoir. The driveway and ranch gate is 0.25 mile past the end of the reservoir on the right.
OPEN	All year
DESCRIPTION	A 1987 log ranch house and cabins with upscale, traditional old west furnishings, antiques, and western memorabilia.
NO. OF ROOMS	Two rooms in the ranch house with private bathrooms and two cabins. Pick the Rose Room.
RATES	Year-round rates are $85 per room in the ranch house with a private bathroom, $195 for the two-bedroom cabin, and $125 for the wilderness cabin. There is no minimum stay and cancellation requires 30 days' notice.
CREDIT CARDS	No
BREAKFAST	Full breakfast, served in the dining room, includes an egg dish, seasonal fruit, homemade biscuits, muffins, breads and jams, and beverages. Lunch and dinner are available with prior notice.
AMENITIES	Fresh flowers in the guestrooms, hot tub in meadow, horseback trips, wilderness horseback rides, hiking and cross-country ski trails, guided fly-fishing in gold medal water and on high country lakes.
RESTRICTIONS	No smoking, children are welcome. There are 18 horses, five mules, an Australian shepherd named Max, and a Border collie named Ty.
KUDOS/COMMENTS	"Delightful farmhouse and cabin . . . Try their dinners!" (1996)

Eagle River Inn, Minturn

MINTURN

Brought to life over 100 years ago by the Rio Grande Railroad, this small, pretty village has a couple of great, reasonably priced restaurants and is handy to Vail and the Holy Cross and Eagle's Nest Wilderness Areas. Seven miles west of Vail via I-70 exit 171.

EAGLE RIVER INN

145 North Main Street, Minturn, CO 81645   970-827-5761
Patty Bidez, Innkeeper   800-344-1750
Some Spanish spoken   FAX 970-827-4020

LOCATION	Between Vail and Beaver Creek ski resorts. Take the Minturn exit off I-70 and go south two miles on Highway 24. Take the first left as you enter town.
OPEN	All year except for late April and most of May
DESCRIPTION	An 1894 three-story adobe inn, totally remodeled with southwestern interior, earth-red adobe walls, and a riverside deck overlooking the Eagle River.
NO. OF ROOMS	Twelve rooms with private bathrooms.
RATES	Winter rates, December through April, are $125-215 for a single or double with a private bathroom. Off-season rates, May through November, are $75-105 for a single or double with a private

bathroom. There is a two-day minimum stay during holidays and Saturday stays. Cancellation requires 14 days' notice—30 days at Christmas.

CREDIT CARDS	American Express, Discover, MasterCard, Visa
BREAKFAST	Full breakfast, served in the dining room, includes a fresh fruit course, muffins or bread; homemade granola; yogurt; and a hot entrée such as peaches-and-cream French toast or green-chile quiche.
AMENITIES	Wine and hors d'oeuvres each evening; fresh flowers; hot tub on the wraparound deck; meeting room; six mountain bikes, a tandem bike, and five pairs of snowshoes are lent to guests.
RESTRICTIONS	No smoking, no pets, children over 11 are welcome.
REVIEWED	*Fodor's, Frommer's, America's Wonderful Little Hotels & Inns, The Colorado Guide, Recommended Country Inns of the Rocky Mountain Region, American Historic Inns*
MEMBER	Professional Association of Innkeepers International, Bed & Breakfast Innkeepers of Colorado, American Bed & Breakfast Association
RATED	AAA 3 Diamonds, ABBA 3 Crowns, Mobil 3 Stars

THE MINTURN INN

442 Main Street, Minturn, CO 81645   970-827-9647
Tom & Cathy Sullivan & Mick Kelly, Resident Owners   800-646-8876
                                      FAX 970-827-5590

LOCATION	From I-70, take exit 171, turn right, and go two miles to the town of Minturn. The inn is four blocks down on the left.
OPEN	All year
DESCRIPTION	A 1915 three-story refurbished hewn-log home with an elegant rustic atmosphere that features custom-made log beds, antler chandeliers, hardwood floors, and a river-rock fireplace.
NO. OF ROOMS	Eight rooms with private bathrooms and two rooms share one bathroom. The Camphale Room has a river-rock fireplace and Jacuzzi.
RATES	Winter rates, mid-November through April, are $89-209 for a single or double with a private bathroom and $79-129 for a single or double with a shared bathroom. Summer rates are $75-125 for a single or double with a private bathroom and $65 for a single or double with a shared bathroom. There is a two-night minimum stay if one night is a Saturday. Cancellation requires 14 days' notice.

CREDIT CARDS	American Express, Diners Club, Discover, MasterCard, Visa
BREAKFAST	Full homestyle breakfast is served in the dining room and includes omelets, French toast, banana pancakes, and more. "We try to give our guests a good start for an active day in the mountains," says Tom.
AMENITIES	Two large river-rock fireplaces, sauna, snowshoes available, handcrafted log beds, down comforters and quilts, wine and cheese après-ski in the winter, and cookies and lemonade in the summer.
RESTRICTIONS	No smoking, no pets, children over 12 are welcome. The resident dog is called Chasis.
REVIEWED	*Fodor's, Travel & Leisure, New York Times*
MEMBER	Bed & Breakfast Innkeepers of Colorado

MONARCH PASS

About 20 miles west of Salida along Highway 50, perched at a dizzying 11,312 feet, Monarch Pass offers exceptional mountain vistas that include several fourteeners.

OLD MINE—MOUNT SHAVANO BED & BREAKFAST

16780 Highway 50 West, Monarch Pass, CO 81201   719-539-4640
M. Robins, Resident Owner

OPEN	All year
DESCRIPTION	A log B&B shaped like an old mine.
NO. OF ROOMS	Three rooms with shared two bathrooms.
RATES	Year-round rate is $50 for a single or double with shared bath.
CREDIT CARDS	MasterCard, Visa
BREAKFAST	Full breakfast is served in the dining room.
RESTRICTIONS	No smoking in house, no pets.

MONTE VISTA

This is the agricultural trade center for the San Luis Valley. Don't miss the Monte Vista National Wildlife Refuge for migratory birds. They are in abundant flurry between October and April. The cowboys arrive in late July for the Ski-Hi Stampede and Rodeo. From Alamosa, 17 miles west via Highways 285 and 160, within close proximity to the Rio Grande National Recreation Area.

THE WINDMILL BED & BREAKFAST

4340 West Highway 160, Monte Vista, CO 81144   719-852-0438
Sharon & Dennis Kay, Resident Owners   800-467-3441

LOCATION	Four miles west of Highway 285 on Highway 160.
OPEN	All year
DESCRIPTION	A 1950 one-story Spanish-style ranch home with early southwestern and antique furnishings.
NO. OF ROOMS	Four rooms with private bathrooms. The owners' favorite is the Frontier Room.
RATES	Year-round rates are $65-99 for a single or double with a private bathroom. There is no minimum stay requirement. Ask about the reservation/cancellation policy.
CREDIT CARDS	MasterCard, Visa
BREAKFAST	Full breakfast, served in the dining room, includes natural-grown meats, grains and pastries, egg dishes, and San Luis potatoes.
AMENITIES	Hot tub under the windmill, wildlife viewing, afternoon refreshments, fresh flowers, telephones in all rooms, TV and VCR in common area, view of the San Luis Valley and surrounding mountains, hiking, bird-watching.
RESTRICTIONS	No smoking, no pets, children of well-behaved parents are welcome. Granny Rags, the resident cat, patrols the premises. Watch for antelope on property.
MEMBER	Professional Association of Innkeepers International

Montezuma

Six miles and about 100 years from Keystone resort. From Highway 6, go right onto Montezuma Road, take an immediate left (still on Montezuma Road), and follow for 5.5 miles.

Granny's B&B

5435 Montezuma Road, Montezuma, CO 80435   970-468-9297
Donna Hellyer, Resident Owner
WEBSITE *www.colorada-bnb.com/grannys*

LOCATION	The B&B is at the end of town on the left.
OPEN	All year except for Christmas Day
DESCRIPTION	A log home with antique mining- and cabin-era furnishings. A high-mountain hideaway surrounded by grand mountain peaks, towering pines, and postcard views of historic Montezuma.
NO. OF ROOMS	Three rooms share one bathroom. One cabin sleeps up to three adults, or a family of four. Donna Hellyer calls her best room Columbine.
RATES	Year-round rates are $50 for a single with a shared bath and $70 for a double. The cabin is $85 for two. The cancellation policy is 20 days for a full refund.
CREDIT CARDS	MasterCard, Visa
BREAKFAST	Full breakfast is served in the dining room and includes sausage, ham, hashbrowns, sourdough pancakes, eggs, fruit, juices, and coffee.
AMENITIES	Après-ski or hot soup and granny's sourdough. Dinner sleigh rides in the winter available at extra charge.
RESTRICTIONS	No smoking, no pets (resident outside dogs, cats, horses, and burro), no children.
MEMBER	Summit County Bed & Breakfasts
KUDOS/COMMENTS	"Old mining atmosphere and small town, mountain setting; antiques, sleigh rides, excellent food, full breakfast and other meals." (1996)

MONTROSE

Situated between Grand Junction and Durango at the junction of Highways 550 and 50. Local events and nearby attractions include the Ute Indian museum, Ouray hot springs pool, the July 4th Lighter than Aire Balloon Affaire, Black Canyon of the Gunnison, Grand Mesa, the San Juan Mountains, Curecanti National Recreation Area, and the Tabeguache Mountain Bike Trail.

ANNIE'S ORCHARD: A HISTORIC B&B

Spring Creek & 63.00 Road, Montrose, CO 81401   970-249-0298
Mary Needham, Innkeeper
Elementary German spoken
EMAIL *mneedham@montrose.net*   WEBSITE *www.bbonline.com/co/annies*

LOCATION	Two miles west from the downtown intersection of Highways 50 (Main Street) and 550 (Townsend Avenue). The Inn is situated at the corner of Spring Creek Road and Highway 90 at the hilltop.
OPEN	All year
DESCRIPTION	A 1909 two-story country Tudor inn decorated with antiques on a two-acre estate surrounded by trees.
NO. OF ROOMS	Three rooms with private bathrooms.
RATES	May through October, rates are $55-80 for a single or double with a private bathroom. November through April, rates are $50-65 for a single or double with a private bathroom. There is a minimum stay during July 4th and Christmas, and cancellation requires 14 days' notice for refund less a $10 service charge—refund with less notice if room is rebooked.
CREDIT CARDS	American Express, Discover, MasterCard, Visa
BREAKFAST	Full breakfast is served in the formal dining room and includes a hot dish such as puffed peach pancakes (during summer), fresh fruit, homemade breads or muffins, and beverages.
AMENITIES	Afternoon refreshments; robes; hot tub under the stars; feather beds; down comforters in deluxe rooms during cooler months; in-room air conditioners during summer; fireplace in parlor; sun room/game room; inn-to-inn bicycling packages; space for weddings; plush baths; sitting areas; romantic fireplace suite; easy access to scenic sites of western Colorado.
RESTRICTIONS	No smoking indoors, no pets, children over nine are welcome. Rex is the resident Siamese cat, Harriet is the domestic cat, and Nala is the Norwegian elkhound. The pets love attention. There are also two geese roaming around the fruit trees.
MEMBER	Bed & Breakfast Innkeepers of Colorado, Professional Association of Innkeepers International

TRAVELER'S B&B INN

502 South 1st Street, Montrose, CO 81401   970-249-3472
Lois Straughn, Resident Owner

UNCOMPAHGRE BED & BREAKFAST

21049 Uncompahgre Road, Montrose, CO 81401   800-318-8127
Barbara & Richard Helm, Innkeepers   FAX 970-249-6546
EMAIL rhelm@gwe.net   WEBSITE www.travelguides.com/bb/uncompahgre

LOCATION	In downtown Montrose, 7.8 miles south of Routes 50 and 550 at Uncompahgre Road. From Ridgway, go north on Route 550 for 18 miles to Uncompahgre Road and east about 100 yards.
OPEN	All year
DESCRIPTION	A 1914 two-story brick schoolhouse with a penthouse and little bell tower on scenic byway to the San Juans.
NO. OF ROOMS	Eight rooms with private bathrooms. Barbara recommends the French Country Room.
RATES	May 15 through October 31, rates are $75 for a single or double with a private bathroom. November through May 14, rates are $55 for a single or double with a private bathroom. There is no minimum stay and cancellation requires 72 hours during high season, 24 hours during low.
CREDIT CARDS	American Express, Diners Club, Discover, MasterCard, Novus, Visa
BREAKFAST	Full breakfast is served in the dining room.
AMENITIES	Meeting facilities, handicapped accessible, evening treks to Uncompahgre River, hot teas and cookies, piano-organ, day-trip plans and recommendations.
RESTRICTIONS	No smoking. Tara is the resident Lab mix. "She is a doggie doorbell," says Barbara, "anxious to meet and play with guest dogs."
REVIEWED	*Official Colorado Vacation Guide*
MEMBER	Colorado Bed & Breakfast Innkeepers
RATED	AAA 2 Diamonds

MONUMENT

The area around Monument is a pastoral, country quilt of horse ranches, wide green acres, and impressive homes. From here it's a straight shot to the Renaissance Festival in Larkspur and the outlet shops at Castle Rock. Twenty miles north of Colorado Springs via I-25.

CROSS KEYS INN B&B

20450 Beacon Lite Road, Monument, CO 80132
Rick & Suzanne Laidlaw, Resident Owners
EMAIL *innkeep@crosskeys.net*
WEBSITE *www.crosskeys.net*

719-481-2772
800-250-5397
FAX 719-481-8992

LOCATION	Three-hundred yards west of I-25 at Monument exit 163.
OPEN	All year
DESCRIPTION	A 1984 two-story log host home with rustic/antique furnishings on 5 acres.
NO. OF ROOMS	Three rooms with private bathrooms.
RATES	Year-round rates for a single or double are $85-120. There is no minimum stay; ask about a cancellation policy.
CREDIT CARDS	American Express, Diners Club, Discover, MasterCard, Visa
BREAKFAST	Full breakfast, served in the dining room, includes an egg dish or pancakes/waffles, bread, fruit, and beverages.
AMENITIES	Solarium with hot tub; fireplace in living room; TV/VCR and videos; hiking, biking, and horseback trails close by.
RESTRICTIONS	No smoking, no pets, children over 12 are welcome.
MEMBER	Bed & Breakfast Innkeepers of Colorado, Professional Association of Innkeepers International
KUDOS/COMMENTS	"Mountain views and gourmet breakfasts." (1997)

MORRISON

This delightful National Historic District is a terrific stay-over spot from which to explore the amazing sandstone formations in the 640-acre Red Rocks Park. Easter Sunrise Services and summer concerts at Red Rocks Amphitheater are also worth trying. About 15 miles west of Denver via I-70 and State Road 74.

CLIFF HOUSE LODGE B&B INN & COTTAGES

121 Stone Street, Morrison, CO 80465   *303-697-9732*
Peggy Hahn, Resident Owner   *FAX 303-697-0113*
French and Spanish spoken

LOCATION	From I-70, take exit 259 south along the hogback past Red Rocks Park. The inn is the first building on the right as you enter the village of Morrison. Turn right under the archway.
OPEN	All year
DESCRIPTION	An 1873 two-story French sandstone lodge and country cottages decorated with antiques, listed on the National and State Historic Registers.
NO. OF ROOMS	Ten rooms with private bathrooms.
RATES	Year-round rates are $149 and up. There is no minimum stay and cancellation requires two weeks' notice.
CREDIT CARDS	MasterCard, Visa
BREAKFAST	Continental breakfast is included. A full candlelight, champagne breakfast for two is also available.
AMENITIES	Fireplaces, robes, cable TV/VCR, free movies, stereo in rooms. Private hot tubs in all rooms, romance packages, air conditioning.
RESTRICTIONS	No pets, restricted smoking. The cottage accommodates a maximum of two people.
REVIEWED	*Recommended Country Inns Rocky Mountain Region, A Treasury of Bed & Breakfasts*
MEMBER	Bed & Breakfast Innkeepers of Colorado
KUDOS/COMMENTS	"Romantic and private." (1997)

HORTON HOUSE BED & BREAKFAST

105 Canon Street, Morrison, CO 80465   *303-697-8526*

MOSCA

Mosca is situated at the foot of the Sangre de Cristos, near the Great Sand Dunes, the tallest dunes in North America, rising some 700 feet from the desert floor. Zapata Falls offers panoramic views of the valley. Fifteen miles north of Alamosa on Highway 17.

INN AT ZAPATA RANCH

5303 Highway 150, Mosca, CO 81146
Angela Moses, Innkeeper
EMAIL *zapatainn@greatsanddunes.com*
WEBSITE *www.greatsanddunes.com*

719-378-2806
800-284-9213
FAX *719-378-2428*

LOCATION	Guests coming from east and west, take Highway 160 to Highway 150. Turn north and drive 12 miles. Those coming from north and south, take Highway 7 to County Road 6, turn east and drive 16 miles to Highway 150, then turn south and drive one mile.
OPEN	Closed October 31 through mid-March
DESCRIPTION	Rough-hewn log buildings of late-1800s construction, renovated in 1989 with western decor, listed on the National Historic Register.
NO. OF ROOMS	Fifteen rooms with private bathrooms. Innkeeper recommends room 9.
RATES	High-season rates are $150-225; off-season rates are $112-168. There is no minimum stay.
CREDIT CARDS	American Express, Diners Club, Discover, MasterCard, Visa
BREAKFAST	Full breakfast, offered in spring and summer, includes homemade pastries, fruit, cheese, juice, and granola. Lunch and dinner are also available. On Sundays during high season, there's a barbecue and music.
AMENITIES	Outdoor pool and hot tub, sauna, exercise room, massage by appointment, hayrides, horseback riding, tours of largest bison ranch in America, 18-hole championship golf course.
RESTRICTIONS	No smoking. The resident bison is Amelia.
REVIEWED	*Frommer's Colorado, Association of Historic Hotels, Distinctive Inns of Colorado, Colorado Restaurants & Recipes*
MEMBER	Association of Historic Hotels, Independent Innkeepers Association, Distinctive Inns of Colorado, Colorado Hotel & Motel Association
KUDOS/COMMENTS	"Wonderful, relaxed atmosphere; exquisite dining; tour and history of the ranch was excellent, as was the hospitality." (1997)

Streamside Bed & Breakfast, Nathrop

NATHROP

This town offers major access to the incredible Collegiate Peaks. Pick your peak and head for the summit, forge the Arkansas River, or soak it up in the Mount Princeton Hot Springs. Adjacent to Buena Vista, 93 miles west of Colorado Springs on Highway 24.

STREAMSIDE BED & BREAKFAST

18820 County Road 162, Nathrop, CO 81236   719-395-2553
Denny & Kathy Claveau, Resident Owners
WEBSITE *www.southwesterninns.com/strmside.htm*

LOCATION	On Chalk Creek in Chalk Creek Canyon. From Buena Vista, take Highway 285 to Nathrop. Go west from Nathrop on County Road 162 for eight miles to our driveway on the left.
OPEN	All year except December 24 through 26
DESCRIPTION	A 1975 rustic mountain home and two-story cottage with country/traditional furnishings. "A mountain paradise" located within San Isabel National Forest.
NO. OF ROOMS	Three rooms with private bathrooms.
RATES	May 16 through October 14, rates are $71-76 for a single or double. October 15 through May 15, rates are $64-69 for a single or double. There is a minimum stay on holiday weekends and a ten-day cancellation policy.

CREDIT CARDS	No
BREAKFAST	Full breakfast is served in the dining room.
AMENITIES	No phones, no TV, but lots of solitude; close to hot springs; picnic table, lounge chairs, and fire pit streamside; endless hiking and exploring opportunities; cross-country skiing, snowshoeing, and alpine skiing 45 minutes away at Monarch (where Denny is a ski instructor).
RESTRICTIONS	No smoking, no pets, children over six are welcome on a limited basis.
MEMBER	Bed & Breakfast Innkeepers of Colorado
AWARDS	Finalist, 1997 Inn of the Year contest, judged by Bed & Breakfast Innkeepers of Colorado
KUDOS/COMMENTS	"Friendly hosts; away from town." (1997)

NORWOOD

Thirty miles northeast of Telluride, this small town features Pioneer Day and the San Miguel Fair, plus local rodeos.

ANNIE'S COUNTRY BED & BREAKFAST

551 County Road 44ZN, Norwood, CO 81423   970-327-4331
Anne Shaffer, Resident Owner
EMAIL annes@independence.net
WEBSITE www.telluridemm.com/norwood/annies.html

LOCATION	Take Highway 145 to County Road 44ZN (between mileposts 99 and 100) and go 0.5 mile north, make a right-hand turn across the cattle guard onto the ranch lane, and go another 0.25 mile.
OPEN	All year
DESCRIPTION	A 1917 western homestead with tin roof and low ceilings, constructed during the lean years of World War I, "where plumbing, electricity, and central heating are the amenities."
NO. OF ROOMS	One room with a private bathroom and four rooms share two bathrooms.
RATES	Year-round rates are $45-55 for a single or double with a private bathroom and $35-40 for a single or double with a shared bathroom. There is no minimum stay. Ask about a cancellation policy.
CREDIT CARDS	No

BREAKFAST	Full ranch-style breakfast is served family style in the kitchen and includes eggs, bacon, ham, sausage, sourdough pancakes, muffins, biscuits, and "real" coffee. Dinner is also available on request.
AMENITIES	"Peace, quiet, and sourdough," and if that's not enough . . . line-dried linens, piano, board games, and "absolutely no TV."
RESTRICTIONS	No smoking, no pets. Children are welcome. The resident dog is Katie, Robie is the horse, and the 37-year-old burro is Ouno. "This is a working ranch, with cattle and sheep—but not the petting kind."
REVIEWED	*Cabins, Lodges and Country B&Bs*

LONE CONE RANCH BED & BREAKFAST

42 Z Road, Norwood, CO 81423   970-327-4300
Bob & Sharon Hardman, Resident Owners   800-355-7624
EMAIL *elkranch@independence.com*
WEBSITE *www.telluridemm.com/norwood/elkranch.html*

LOCATION	One mile west of Norwood on Z Road.
OPEN	All year
DESCRIPTION	A 1970 two-story rustic home decorated with antiques on a working cattle and elk ranch.
NO. OF ROOMS	Four rooms share two bathrooms.
RATES	Year-round rates are $35 for a single and $45 for a double. There is no minimum stay; ask about a cancellation policy.
CREDIT CARDS	No
BREAKFAST	Full breakfast, served in the dining room, includes fruit; blueberry or buttermilk pancakes; French toast; eggs, bacon, or sausage; and orange juice. Dinner and special meals are also available.
AMENITIES	Ranch living, horse boarding, hiking, elk watching, fishing, hunting elk, deer, bear, and lion.
RESTRICTIONS	No smoking. Resident pets include a cow dog named Spud and various barn cats. In October, listen to the elk bugle and watch them lock horns. Pets OK, children OK.

OAK CREEK

A little hamlet tucked between the White River and Route National Forests, Oak Creek is situated 20 miles southwest of Steamboat Springs via Highway 40 and Highway 131.

HIGH MEADOWS RANCH

20505 Rural County Road 16, Oak Creek, CO 80467   970-736-8416
Jan & Dennis Stamp, Resident Owners   800-457-4453
EMAIL *highmeadows@sprynet.com*   FAX 970-736-8416

LOCATION	From Steamboat Springs, go one mile on Highway 40 east, turn right on Highway 131 and go 6.3 miles, then turn left on County Road 14 and go 7.2 miles. Turn left at the bridge onto County Road 16. After 1.5 miles turn left, staying on County Road 16; the ranch has a large log entry on the right.
OPEN	All year
DESCRIPTION	A 1991 guest ranch with Victorian main lodge, log chalets, and western decor. Located on 140 acres in a quiet mountain valley surrounded by meadows and National Forest.
NO. OF ROOMS	Five rooms with private bathrooms. The best room is the front bedroom in the Elk Lodge.
RATES	Year-round rates for a single or double are $110-125. There is a two-night minimum stay and cancellation requires 30 days' notice.
CREDIT CARDS	MasterCard, Visa
BREAKFAST	Full breakfast is served in the dining room and includes Belgian waffles with fresh fruit, coffee, and juice. Lunch and dinner, along with a special "Barbecue at the Barn," are also available.
AMENITIES	Cabins are furnished with complete kitchens, living areas with woodburning stoves, laundry facilities, robes and toiletries, hot tub, and skis and snowshoes.
RESTRICTIONS	No smoking. Resident yellow Lab is called Jake, and he adopts all people as family. The calico is called Cassidy, and there are 17 quarter horses on the property.
REVIEWED	*Cross-Country Ski Vacation*

OURAY

Named after the famous chief of the Ute Indian tribe, Ouray is perched at an elevation of 7,700 feet. Its high and dry alpine climate makes it perfect for pursuing mountain activities. Take a Jeep tour into the majestic San Juan Mountains, explore the Box Canyon Falls, relax in the Ouray's natural hot springs pool.

CHINA CLIPPER BED & BREAKFAST INN

525 Second Street, Ouray, CO 81427   970-325-0565
Elaine & Earl Yarbrough, Resident Owners   800-315-0565
WEBSITE *www.colorado-bnb.com/clipper*   FAX 970-325-4190

LOCATION	Enter Ouray on Highway 550 (the main street through town), turn west on Sixth Avenue, go one block, and turn left onto Second Street. The inn is next to the Matterhorn Motel parking lot.
OPEN	All year
DESCRIPTION	A three-story southern traditional inn with English period and reproduction furniture.
NO. OF ROOMS	Eleven rooms with private bathrooms. Pick the Honeymoon Room.
RATES	June through October and Christmas, rates are $85 to $160 for a single or double. Winter rates for a single or double are $65-160. There is a minimum stay during holidays and cancellation requires 30 days' notice with a $15 fee.
CREDIT CARDS	MasterCard, Visa
BREAKFAST	Full breakfast is served in the dining room and may include homefries, potatoes O'Brien, eggs, pancakes or quiche, Belgian waffles, fresh fruit in season, juices, homemade bread, coffee, and tea.
AMENITIES	Honeymooners and two-night guests receive a full bottle of champagne; wedding facilities for up to 40; robes; handicapped access; ceiling fans and decks in all rooms; fireplaces and views; afternoon wine, beer, and spreads.
RESTRICTIONS	No smoking, no pets, no children. Lacy, the resident dog, is discreet. "She doesn't go into the living room, dining room, or guestrooms. Loves everyone, but waits for encouragement."
MEMBER	Distinctive Inns of Colorado, Bed & Breakfast Innkeepers of Colorado, Professional Association of Innkeepers International
RATED	AAA 3 Diamonds
KUDOS/COMMENTS	"Beautifully constructed new property with the feel of the past; tastefully decorated." "Nice location just off the main street; Elaine is charming." (1996) "Beautiful inn and setting." (1999)

COLUMBUS HOUSE BED & BREAKFAST

746 Main Street, Ouray, CO 81427   970-325-4551
Jim Ludington, Resident Owner   FAX 970-325-7388

LOCATION	On Main Street at the north end of town above the Silver Nugget Café.
OPEN	Open from May 27 to September 30
DESCRIPTION	An 1898 red-brick Victorian with Victorian furnishings.
NO. OF ROOMS	Six rooms share one bathroom. Try room 7.
RATES	Year-round rates are $59-69 for a single or double.
CREDIT CARDS	Discover, MasterCard, Visa
BREAKFAST	Full breakfast, served downstairs at the Silver Nugget Café, is included in the room price.
AMENITIES	Robes, sitting room, and TV room.
RESTRICTIONS	No smoking, no pets, children over 12 are welcome.

THE DAMN YANKEE COUNTRY INN

100 Sixth Avenue, Ouray, CO 81427   970-325-4219
Mike & Marj Manley, Resident Owners   800-845-7512
WEBSITE *www.montrose.net/users/damnyank*   FAX 970-325-4339

LOCATION	Two blocks downhill from the center of town (Sixth Avenue and Main), next to the river.
OPEN	All year
DESCRIPTION	A 1991 two-story English cottage with slate roof and Victorian and English country furnishings.
NO. OF ROOMS	Ten rooms with private bathrooms. Mike Manley suggests room 10.
RATES	June through September, rates are $102-185 for a single or double. Winter rates, October through May, are $68-150. There is no minimum stay, and cancellation requires one weeks' notice.
CREDIT CARDS	Discover, MasterCard, Visa
BREAKFAST	Full "giant gourmet" breakfast may include eggs Benedict, potatoes O'Brien, fresh fruits, Danish, juice and coffee, with "doggie bags." Dinner is available in the winter.
AMENITIES	Private entrances, phones and TV, hot tub, barbecue grills and picnic tables by the river, piano in the parlor.
RESTRICTIONS	No smoking, no pets, children over 12 are welcome.

MEMBER   Bed & Breakfast Innkeepers of Colorado

RATED   AAA 3 Diamonds, Mobil 3 Stars

THE EVERGREEN BED & BREAKFAST

430 Fourth Avenue, Ouray, CO 81427   970-325-7318
Thad & Marti Harris, Resident Owners

LOCATION   On Fourth Avenue (not 4th Street!), one-and-a-half blocks east of
                  Highway 550, which is the north-south main street through the
                  middle of town.

OPEN   All year

DESCRIPTION   An 1898 Victorian with Victorian furnishings.

NO. OF ROOMS   One room with a private bathroom.

RATES   Year-round rate is $65 plus tax for a single or double. There is a
               special rate of seven nights for the price of six, and senior discounts
               are available. Cancellation requires seven days' notice.

CREDIT CARDS   No

BREAKFAST   Full breakfast, served in the dining room or kitchen, includes eggs,
                   bacon, toast, pancakes, and beverages.

AMENITIES   Portable phone available; lounge with TV, music, piano, and books;
                   handicapped access.

RESTRICTIONS   No smoking, no pets, one child over 12 is OK (there is a foldout
                      bed). The three cats are Peaches, Picayune, and Tara. They are not
                      allowed in the guest room.

MEMBER   Ouray Chamber Resort Association

HISTORIC WESTERN HOTEL

210 7th Avenue, Ouray, CO 81427   303-325-4645
Gregg & Rosemarie Pieper, Resident Owners   888-624-8403
Dutch spoken   FAX 970-325-0773
WEBSITE *www.ouraycolorado.com-histwest.html*

LOCATION   Half a block west of Main Street.

OPEN   All year

DESCRIPTION   An 1891 three-story Victorian Italianate hotel with period-
                     preserved rooms and furnishings, listed on the State Historic
                     Register.

The Manor, Ouray

NO. OF ROOMS	Two rooms with private bathrooms and 12 rooms share four bathrooms. Pick room 1.
RATES	July through Labor Day, rates for a single or double with a private bathroom are $85-95, a single or double with a shared bathroom is $45-55. Off-season rates are $75 for a single or double with a private bathroom and $35 for a single or double with a shared bathroom. There is a multiple-day discount and no minimum stay is required. Cancellation requires 48 hours' notice.
CREDIT CARDS	Discover, MasterCard, Visa
BREAKFAST	Continental breakfast is served. Dinner is also available, and special meals are negotiable.
RESTRICTIONS	No smoking, no pets
MEMBER	Colorado Hotel & Motel Association
KUDOS/COMMENTS	"Very authentic." (1997)

THE MANOR

317 2nd Street, Ouray, CO 81427   970-325-4574
John & Kay Gowins, Innkeepers   800-628-6946
WEBSITE www.ouraycolorado.com/manor.html

LOCATION	On 2nd Street, one block west of Main Street between 3rd and 4th Avenues.

OPEN	All year
DESCRIPTION	An 1890 three-story Georgian/Victorian inn with Victorian and antique furnishings, listed on both the National and State Historic Registers.
NO. OF ROOMS	Seven rooms with private bathrooms.
RATES	Late May through early October, rates are $85-95 for a single or double. Mid-October through early June, rates are $55-65 for a single or double. There is a minimum stay during July 4th weekend and cancellation requires seven days' notice.
CREDIT CARDS	MasterCard, Visa
BREAKFAST	Continental plus is served in the dining room and includes homemade pastries, cereals, yogurt, juice, coffee, and tea. Hot dishes are served during the winter season. Boxed lunches are also available.
AMENITIES	Afternoon coffee and tea, sitting parlor, fireplace, down comforters, feather beds in winter, small library, fresh flowers (in season), half-price lift tickets to Telluride, hot tub in the backyard, three porches, perennial flower garden, daily maid service, robes.
RESTRICTIONS	No smoking, no pets, no alcohol, children over five are welcome.
REVIEWED	*Recommended Country Inns Rocky Mountain Region*
MEMBER	Bed & Breakfast Innkeepers of Colorado, American Bed & Breakfast Association
RATED	ABBA 3 Crowns

OURAY 1898 HOUSE

322 Main Street, Ouray, CO 81427   970-325-4871
Lee & Kathy Bates, Resident Owners
EMAIL *bates@netzone.com*   WEBSITE *www.colorado-bnb.com/mainst*

LOCATION	On Main Street at the south end of Ouray.
OPEN	May 25 through September 25
DESCRIPTION	An 1898 renovated Victorian host home with decks and antique furnishings.
NO. OF ROOMS	Four rooms with private bathrooms. The Bates recommend the Lilac Room, which has a large private deck.
RATES	Summer rates, July through September, are $68-95 for a single or double. Off-season rates, May through June, are $10 less. There is no minimum stay except for holidays, and cancellation requires seven days' notice.
CREDIT CARDS	American Express, MasterCard, Visa

BREAKFAST	Full breakfast is served in the dining room and includes "variety for every appetite." Special diets are accommodated.
AMENITIES	Cable TV in each room; candy and nuts by each bed; coffee, tea, and hot chocolate available at all times; and guests can relax in the spa "under the stars."
RESTRICTIONS	No smoking except on the decks; no pets. Children of all ages are welcome.
REVIEWED	*The Colorado Guide*
MEMBER	Bed & Breakfast Innkeepers of Colorado

Plain Jane Sack & Snack

3 *Munn Park, Ouray, CO 81427*   970-325-7313
Kit & Hank Skelding, Resident Owners   FAX 970-325-7250
Spanish, German, and French spoken
WEBSITE *www.colorado-bnb.plainjane*

LOCATION	From Main Street, go west on 6th Avenue to the bottom (end), then go right on Munn Court. Look for the yellow house—can't miss it.
OPEN	All year except December 22 through December 27
DESCRIPTION	A 1982 two-story host home with theme rooms that explore world cultures and the area's mining history. Plain Jane caters to families with children.
NO. OF ROOMS	Four rooms share three bathrooms. The Asian and Women in Mining Rooms have an adjoining door to accommodate families.
RATES	Year-round rates are $40 for a single, $55 for a double, and $95 for groups of four (each additional guest is $10 more). Stays longer than one day are discounted $5. There is a cancellation policy.
CREDIT CARDS	MasterCard, Visa
BREAKFAST	Continental plus is served in the dining room or guestrooms and includes fresh-baked bread and muffins, fresh fruit salad with a special sauce, cereal, freshly ground coffee, and a selection of teas and juice. Please advise the Skeldings of any dietary restrictions.
AMENITIES	Playground and park next to the river feature sandbox, teeter-totter, and play area; barbecue, picnic tables, and peaceful deck overlooking the river; half-price tickets to Telluride ski area in winter.
RESTRICTIONS	No smoking, no pets, no drinking. Dammit, the family cat, "will do her best to make guests feel welcome," says Kit, "but she doesn't do the same for other animals." Kit asks that guests respect the owners' policy of an alcohol- and tobacco-free environment. Children of all ages are welcome.

KUDOS/COMMENTS "Friendly hosts, beautiful town location." (1997)

St. Elmo Hotel

426 Main Street, Ouray, CO 81427 970-325-4951
Dan & Sandy Lingenfelter, Resident Owners FAX 970-325-0348
EMAIL *steh@rmi.net*

LOCATION	In town on the west side of Main Street.
OPEN	All year
DESCRIPTION	A restored 1898 two-story Victorian hotel with antique furnishings and restaurant, listed on the National Historic Register.
NO. OF ROOMS	Nine rooms with private bathrooms. Ask for room 2 or 3.
RATES	Summer rates, June through October, are $92-102 for a single, double, or suite. Off-season rates are $65-94 for a single, double, or suite. There is a minimum stay on certain holidays and cancellation requires seven days' notice.
CREDIT CARDS	American Express, Discover, MasterCard, Visa
BREAKFAST	Full breakfast buffet, served in the dining room, includes a daily entrée. Dinner and Sunday brunch are also available.
AMENITIES	Hot tub, sauna, social hour with wine and cheese, equipped to handle small meetings and catered parties.
RESTRICTIONS	No smoking, no pets
REVIEWED	*Country Inns of the Southwest, Country Inns of the West and Southwest, Recommended Country Inns Rocky Mountain Region*
MEMBER	Bed & Breakfast Innkeepers of Colorado
RATED	Mobil 3 Stars
KUDOS/COMMENTS	"The St. Elmo was a real treat." (1995) "Very Victorian and authentic, oldest lodging establishment in town, historic, attractive, and unique in that it also houses the finest restaurant in town. More of a hotel atmosphere than a B&B." (1997)

The Victorian Rose

637 5th Street, Ouray, CO 81427 970-325-4176
Jerry & Julia Klein, Resident Owners
French and Spanish spoken

LOCATION	Greater downtown Ouray, the "Switzerland of the Rockies."

OPEN	Summer only
DESCRIPTION	An 1883/1993 Queen Anne Victorian with Victorian furnishings, listed on the Colorado Historic Register.
NO. OF ROOMS	Two rooms with private bathrooms. The best room: Raseberry Pares Room.
RATES	Rate is $97 for a single or double.
CREDIT CARDS	No
BREAKFAST	Full breakfast is served in the parlor.
AMENITIES	Hot tub, private parlor and deck, common area, TV, telephone.
RESTRICTIONS	No smoking, no pets. Nicklas, the resident dog, is not allowed into the guest area.

PAGOSA SPRINGS

The word "Pagosah" means "land of healing waters." Beneath this quiet, beautiful community is a hotbed of geothermal activity. At 153 degrees, the waters are used to heat some of the town's buildings. So soak it up at Pagosah or Rainbow Hot Springs. The Anasazi's mountain home at Chimney Rock Archeological Area is definitely worth a tour, and don't miss the powder at Wolf Creek ski area. From Durango, 60 miles east on Highway 160.

BE OUR GUEST, A BED & BREAKFAST

19 Swiss Village Drive, Pagosa Springs, CO 81147   *970-264-6814*
Pam Schoemig, Resident Owner

DAVIDSON'S COUNTRY INN BED & BREAKFAST

2763 Highway 160 East, Pagosa Springs, CO 81147   *970-264-5863*
Gilbert Davidson, Resident Owner   *FAX 970-264-9276*
WEBSITE www.coloradolodging.com/davidsons.htm

LOCATION	Two miles east of Pagosa Springs on Highway 160.
OPEN	All year
DESCRIPTION	A 1980 three-story log country inn with knotty pine interior, antique furnishings, covered porch, and gazebo, sitting on 32 acres with a view of the Continental Divide.
NO. OF ROOMS	Three rooms with private bathrooms and five rooms share two bathrooms. Gilbert recommends the Ponderosa Suite.

RATES	Year-round rates range from $59-85. The cabin rents for $400 per week. Cancellation requires one weeks' notice.
CREDIT CARDS	American Express, Discover, MasterCard, Visa
BREAKFAST	Full country-style breakfast is served in the dining room.
AMENITIES	Books, table games, and a special indoor children's play corner. The game room includes a pool table and Ping-Pong table.
RESTRICTIONS	No smoking, children of all ages are welcome. The resident pets are a dog named Bear and two cats, Puff and Cally.
REVIEWED	*The Colorado Guide*
MEMBER	Bed & Breakfast Innkeepers of Colorado, Colorado Hotel & Motel Association

ECHO MANOR INN

3366 Highway 84, Pagosa Springs, CO 81147   970-264-5646
Maureen & John Widmer, Resident Owners   FAX 970-264-4617
German and French spoken
EMAIL *widmer@frontier.net*   WEBSITE *stationlink.com/echo-manor*

LOCATION	Three-and-a-half miles south of Pagosa Springs on Highway 84.
OPEN	All year
DESCRIPTION	A 1960s three-story Queen Anne Dutch country inn with a timber and plaster contemporary Tudor interior and a large art collection.
NO. OF ROOMS	Ten rooms with private bathrooms. The best room in the house is the Royal Suite.
RATES	Year-round rates for a single or double are $65-110 and suites are $160-280. There is no minimum stay and cancellation requires 14 days' notice or 30 days' notice for holidays.
CREDIT CARDS	American Express, Discover, MasterCard, Visa
BREAKFAST	Full breakfast is served in the breakfast room.
AMENITIES	Hot tub, satellite TV, wood-burning stoves, fireplace, meeting facilities, and horse boarding.
RESTRICTIONS	No smoking, no pets; children over 10 are welcome upstairs; children under 10 are welcome in the suite downstairs. Thomas and Abby are the resident cats, Phoebe is the Japanese chin, and Candy is the quarter horse.
REVIEWED	*Recommended Country Inns Rocky Mountain Region, America's Wonderful Little Hotels & Inns*
RATED	ABBA 3 Crowns

ENDABA WILDERNESS RETREAT

1197 Perry Drive A, Pagosa Springs, CO 81147　　　　970-731-4310
WEBSITE www.bbonline.com/co/endaba

PALISADE

Wine country in Colorado? You betcha. With tours and tastings. Still, down here in Colorado's "fruit belt," apples and peaches reign—so after sampling a few Colorado reds, don't forget to try the fresh-squeezed apple juice. Excellent year-round recreation can be found at Island Acres State Park, 10 miles east of town. From Grand Junction, 15 miles east via I-70.

THE GARDEN HOUSE BED & BREAKFAST

3587 G Road, Palisade, CO 81526　　　　970-464-4686
Bill & Joyce Haas, Innkeepers　　　　800-305-4686
WEBSITE www.bbinternet.com/gardenhouse

LOCATION	From I-70, take exit 42 and go to the four-way stop at G4 Road and Elberta Avenue. Turn right onto G4 Road and follow it as far as possible, until you must turn left. Continue south until you reach G Road. Turn right and go about 0.25 mile.
OPEN	All year
DESCRIPTION	A 1960 tri-level country manor in the heart of Colorado's fruit and wine country, with oak floors, bay windows, French country furnishings, and stenciling.
NO. OF ROOMS	Four bedrooms with private bathrooms. Bill and Joyce suggest the Secret Garden Suite, with a king-size four-poster bed and a whirlpool tub for two.
RATES	Year-round rates are $53-89 for a single, $65-109 for a double, and $67-109 for a suite. There is a minimum stay during holidays and festival weekends.
CREDIT CARDS	Discover, MasterCard, Visa
BREAKFAST	Full gourmet breakfast is served in the dining room and includes home-baked pastries, breads, and muffins; fresh fruit; and hot entrées such as eggs Florentine, Grande Mesa quiche, and baked pecan French toast. Dinner is also available with 48 hours' notice.
AMENITIES	Morning beverage tray delivered to guestrooms; afternoon snacks; soft drinks, coffee, and tea available throughout the day; evening turndown service; meeting facility; covered deck near fruit orchard.

RESTRICTIONS No smoking, no pets, children over 12 are welcome. Angel is the resident golden Lab mix and Scruffy is the calico. "Both animals adopted us shortly after we moved here."

REVIEWED *America's Favorite Inns, B&Bs and Small Hotels; Romantic Southwest*

MEMBER Professional Association of Innkeepers International, Bed & Breakfast Innkeepers of Colorado

AWARDS Bed & Breakfast Innkeepers of Colorado Award of Excellence, 1998

THE ORCHARD HOUSE BED & BREAKFAST INN

3573 East 1/2 Road, Palisade, CO 81526 970-464-0529
Stephanie Schmid, Resident Owners FAX 970-464-0681
WEBSITE *www.orchardhouse.com*

LOCATION Southwest of town on East Orchard Mesa.

OPEN All year

DESCRIPTION A 1983 country farmhouse with a large porch and contemporary country furnishings.

NO. OF ROOMS Three rooms with private bathrooms, one with shared bath. The best room is the deluxe suite—"Sorry, no cute names."

RATES Year-round rates are $60-125 for a double. There is a 14-day cancellation policy and no minimum stay.

CREDIT CARDS MasterCard, Visa

BREAKFAST Full breakfast, served in the dining room, is "guests' choice" with local fruit in season. Dinner and special meals are also available.

AMENITIES Fresh flowers, local Colorado wines and hors d'oeuvres, pick-your-own peaches in season, winery tours, weddings, family reunions and meeting facility for small groups.

RESTRICTIONS No smoking, no pets; call regarding children.

REVIEWED *The Colorado Guide, Frommer's Colorado*

PEACH ORCHARD

3684 G 7/10 Road, Palisade, CO 81526 970-464-0324

PAONIA

This small town in southwestern Colorado is a fine starting point for excursions to Black Canyon of the Gunnison and the Grand Mesa and Gunnison National Forests. About 30 miles east of Delta.

MINNESOTA CREEK BED & BREAKFAST

4175 O 50 Lane, Paonia, CO 81428   *970-527-4414*
Lynn Mattingly, Innkeeper

LOCATION	Turn off Highway 133 into Paonia. From the corner of 3rd and Grand, go south one block to 2nd and Grand. Turn east on 2nd and go one mile to its end. Take a right onto Paonia Street, go 0.2 mile, and turn left onto the dirt lane.
OPEN	All year
DESCRIPTION	A 1910 two-story Four Square farmhouse decorated with period furnishings on four acres of lawn, rose gardens, streams, and pastures.
NO. OF ROOMS	One bedroom with a private bathroom and six rooms with two shared bathrooms. Lynn suggests the Rose Room.
RATES	Year-round rates are $70-80 for a single or double with a private bathroom and $50-70 for a single or double with a shared bathroom. There is no minimum stay. Ask about a cancellation policy.
CREDIT CARDS	No
BREAKFAST	Full breakfast is served in the dining room and includes coffee or tea, juice, fruit, fresh biscuits, omelets, and sausage.
AMENITIES	Afternoon refreshments of iced tea or lemonade and cookies; generous lawn with hammock, croquet, and badminton; information for local hikes, cross-country skiing, antiquing.
RESTRICTIONS	No smoking inside, no pets. Tuxedo and Kita are the resident cats.
REVIEWED	*Colorado Cabins, Lodges & Country B&Bs*

PEACE & PLENTY BED & BREAKFAST

206 Rio Grande, Paonia, CO 81428   *970-527-7722*
Eames & Margit Yates, Resident Owners   *FAX 970-527-7722 (call first)*

PARSHALL

CASA MILAGRO BED & BREAKFAST

13628 County Road 3, Parshall, CO 80468　　　　　　970-725-3640

PINE

A very small and very beautiful wooded community in the Pike National Forest, southwest of Denver via Highway 185.

CRYSTAL LAKE RESORT—BED & BREAKFAST

29200 Crystal Lake Road, Pine, CO 80470　　　　　　303-838-5253

MEADOW CREEK BED & BREAKFAST INN

13438 Highway 285, Pine, CO 80470　　　　　　303-838-4167
Pat & Dennis Carnahan, Innkeepers

LOCATION	From the traffic light in Conifer (by Safeway Center), continue on Highway 285 for 5.3 miles. Exit left on 285—Frontage Road. Pass the school, turn left at Douglass Ranch Drive (into Douglass Ranch), follow the paved road around to the first right at Berry Hill Lane, then continue up lane to the inn.
OPEN	All year
DESCRIPTION	A 1929 two-story stone and wood country inn with mixed antique, country, and contemporary furnishings on 35 acres, listed on the State Historic Register.
NO. OF ROOMS	Seven rooms with private bathrooms.
RATES	Year-round rates are $95-180 for a single or double, $140-180 for a suite. There is a minimum stay on weekends and holidays and cancellation requires seven days' notice, 30 days if more than three rooms are booked.
CREDIT CARDS	American Express, MasterCard, Visa
BREAKFAST	Full breakfast, served in the dining room or buffet on the weekends, includes eggs or casserole, bacon or sausage, homemade

pastries, fruit, and beverages. Dinner is available Friday and Saturday with a three-day reservation.

AMENITIES	Outdoor hot tub; all rooms have tape or CD player and candlelight; sauna room; two large decks; hammock; gazebo; three rooms have private hot tubs, king beds and fireplaces; all rooms have robes; homemade chocolate "turtles" at bedside; fresh flowers in season; cookies, snacks, and beverages available anytime; and candlelit five-course dinners available Friday and Saturday nights.
RESTRICTIONS	No smoking, no pets, no children. The resident Shih Tzu is called Bear and the barn cats are called Mr. Meadow and Mr. Creek.
REVIEWED	*Recommended Country Inns Rocky Mountain Region*
MEMBER	Bed & Breakfast Innkeepers of Colorado, Colorado Hotel and Lodging Association
KUDOS/COMMENTS	"A romantic inn where your every need will be catered to. Warm, delightful innkeepers." (1994) "Great food! Secluded setting. Exceptional hosts. This place is perfect—the owners have remembered all the little things like homemade cookies, tissues on both sides of the bed, etc." "Never wanted to leave." (1997)

POWDERHORN

Along the Cebolla River in the Gunnison Valley between Gunnison National Forest and Uncompahgre National Forest, Powderhorn offers access to Curecanti National Recreation Area and Black Canyon of the Gunnison.

ALICE'S BED & BREAKFAST

18769 Highway 149, Powderhorn, CO 81243   *970-641-2080*
Alice Wilson, Resident Owner

OPEN	All year
DESCRIPTION	A 1900 log-and-frame ranch house with ranch-style interior.
NO. OF ROOMS	Two bedrooms share one bathroom.
RATES	Year-round rates are $20 for a single and $40 for a double. There is no minimum stay and cancellation requires two weeks' notice.
CREDIT CARDS	No
BREAKFAST	Full breakfast is served in the kitchen and includes "anything the guest desires—within reason." Dinner is also available.
RESTRICTIONS	No pets. Cub and Sandy are the resident dogs.

PUEBLO

The state's third largest city is at the transition zone between mountains and plains, at the confluence of Fountain Creek and the Arkansas River. Check out the Union Avenue National Historic District, the Sangre de Cristo Arts and Conference Center, and the Raptor Rehabilitation and Nature Centers. Pueblo Reservoir is the place to be for water sports. Interesting summer events include the annual Governor's Cup Regatta and Cinco de Mayo in (you guessed it) May; the National High School Rodeo Finals in July; and the State and County Fairs in August. Forty-two miles south of Colorado Springs on I-25.

ABRIENDO INN

300 West Abriendo Avenue, Pueblo, CO 81004   719-544-2703
Kerrelyn Trent, Resident Owner   FAX 719-542-6544
EMAIL abriendo@rmi.net

LOCATION	Take I-25 exit 97B and go west one mile.
OPEN	All year
DESCRIPTION	A 1906 three-story Four Square classical manor furnished with antiques and period reproductions on parklike grounds. Listed on the National Historic Register.
NO. OF ROOMS	Ten rooms with private bathrooms. Kerrelyn recommends the Blake Room.
RATES	Year-round rates are $55-110 for a single, $60-120 for a double, $80-85 for a suite, and $835 for the entire B&B. There is a minimum stay during special events and a reservation/cancellation policy.
CREDIT CARDS	American Express, Diners Club, MasterCard, Visa
BREAKFAST	Full breakfast, served in the dining room, includes an entrée such as a green-chile and chorizo egg bake, blueberry streusel coffeecake, almond and polenta coffeecake, Abriendo Inn toast, strawberry and banana fruit cup, and beverages.
AMENITIES	Fresh flowers and candy, air conditioning, modem hookups, telephones and TVs in all rooms; fresh fruit basket and homemade cookies; 24-hour snacks and beverages; off-street parking.
RESTRICTIONS	No smoking, no pets, children over seven are welcome. Old Michelle, the outside dog, "just lays around watching the coming and going of everyone."
REVIEWED	*The Colorado Guide, Official Guide to American Historic Inns, America's Wonderful Little Hotels & Inns*
MEMBER	Independent Innkeepers Association, Distinctive Inns of Colorado, Bed & Breakfast Innkeepers of Colorado, Professional Association of Innkeepers International.

RATED   AAA 3 Diamonds, Mobil 3 Stars

KUDOS/COMMENTS   "Beautiful and comfortable, warm and hospitable, Kerrelyn has done everything right." "The house is dressed to perfection, wonderful antiques." (1997) "Well-kept, enchanting historic home." (1999)

BAXTER INN BED & BREAKFAST

325 West 15th, Pueblo, CO 81003   719-542-7002
Lois & David Jones, Resident Owners   FAX 719-583-1560
EMAIL *baxtrinn@rmi.net*   WEBSITE *www.puebloonline.com/baxterinn*

LOCATION   Take exit 99B (Sante Fe/13th Street) off I-25 in Pueblo. Turn right (north) and drive two blocks to 15th. Take a left and go three blocks.

OPEN   All year

DESCRIPTION   An 1892 three-story Victorian inn with red, rusticated sandstone construction, extensive golden oak, stained-glass windows, and a wraparound veranda.

NO. OF ROOMS   Five rooms with private bathrooms. Lois recommends the Charles Kretschmer Room.

RATES   High-season rates are $85-120 for a single or double and $195 for a suite. Low-season rates are $75-110 for a single or double and $170 for a suite. There is no minimum stay and cancellation requires seven days' notice.

CREDIT CARDS   American Express, Diners Club, MasterCard, Visa

BREAKFAST   Full breakfast begins with coffee/tea and pastries outside the guestrooms, followed by two formal courses in the dining room.

AMENITIES   Fresh flowers in rooms, robes, double whirlpool tubs in some rooms, private phones, cable TV, turndown service, sitting areas/desks, antique furnishings, complimentary beverages, afternoon refreshments, library, music room with baby grand piano, parlor, expanded grounds with gazebo.

RESTRICTIONS   No smoking, no pets

MEMBER   Professional Association of Innkeepers International, Bed & Breakfast Innkeepers of Colorado

RED CLIFF

This little mining town is well known for its prime location at the base of Shrine Pass and for its view of Mount of the Holy Cross. Red Cliff is also the trailhead for the Tenth Mountain Trail Hut System. From Vail, seven miles west on I-70 to Minturn exit 171, then eight miles south via Highway 24.

PLUM HOUSE BED & BREAKFAST

236 Eagle Street, Red Cliff, CO 81649   970-827-5881
Sydney Summers, Resident Owner

LOCATION	Come into Red Cliff at the turnoff before the big bridge on Highway 24. Continue into town on a narrow road for about 0.5 mile. Half a block after crossing the small creek look for the plum-colored house with sunflowers on the garage.
OPEN	All year
DESCRIPTION	Secluded 1930s-era two-story semi-Victorian inn with comfortable, eclectic furnishings, located in the heart of the oldest town in Eagle County, high in the Rockies.
NO. OF ROOMS	One room shares a bathroom.
RATES	Year-round rates are $50 for a single and $60 for a double. There is no minimum stay and cancellation requires seven days' notice.
CREDIT CARDS	No
BREAKFAST	Full breakfast is served in the kitchen and is customized to meet guests' preferences. Breakfasts range from vegetarian to full breakfast with meats. Sydney consults with guests and plans breakfasts the night before. Dinner is available with three days' notice.
AMENITIES	Indoor hot tub; stereo/CD system/satellite TV; gas fireplace and stove in living room; flower-filled backyard; next to Shrine Pass for biking, hiking, and snowshoeing; world-class skiing nearby.
RESTRICTIONS	No smoking, no pets, no children

RED FEATHER LAKES

SUNDANCE TRAIL GUEST RANCH

17931 Red Feather Lakes Road   970-224-1222
Red Feather Lakes, CO 80545

REDSTONE

Also known as the "Ruby of the Rockies," Redstone boasts a population that hovers right around 100, and unique shops line the boulevard of this lovely small town.

CRYSTAL DREAMS BED & BREAKFAST

0475 Redstone Boulevard, Redstone, CO 81623   970-963-8240
Lisa & Steve Wagner, Resident Owners
EMAIL *redstone@rof.net*   WEBSITE *www.net-unlimited.com/crystaldreams*

LOCATION	Eighteen miles south of Highway 133 from Carbondale, 50 miles from Aspen, and 28 miles from Glenwood Springs.
OPEN	All year
DESCRIPTION	A 1997 three-story Victorian country inn with cozy, romantic interior, located along the Crystal River.
NO. OF ROOMS	Three rooms with private bathrooms.
RATES	Year-round rates are $90-100 for a single or double with a private bathroom. There is no minimum stay and cancellation requires seven days' notice.
CREDIT CARDS	No
BREAKFAST	Full gourmet breakfast is served in the dining room by candlelight. Lunch is available upon request.
AMENITIES	Clawfoot tubs, terry robes, turndown service, chocolates, bath salts.
RESTRICTIONS	No smoking, no pets, no children. The twin tuxedo cats are Ele Ihu and Akala Ihu. They're the "local boys" from Hawaii.
MEMBER	Bed & Breakfast Innkeepers of Colorado
AWARDS	Best New B&B, 1997, by the Bed & Breakfast Innkeepers of Colorado

GAMEKEEPERS COTTAGE

18679 Highway 133, Redstone, CO 81623   970-963-2701

The Redstone Ccastle Health & Wellness Resort, Redstone

McClure House

22995 Highway 133, Redstone, CO 81623
Judy Melby, Resident Owner
EMAIL *mcclure@sopris.net*

970-963-1020
800-303-3929

LOCATION	Five miles from Redstone, across from the Crystal River.
OPEN	All year
DESCRIPTION	A chalet-style host home.
NO. OF ROOMS	Four bedrooms with private bathrooms.
RATES	Year-round rates are $75-125.
CREDIT CARDS	MasterCard, Visa
BREAKFAST	Full breakfast is served in the dining room.
AMENITIES	Great Room and game room. Lots of decks with views.
RESTRICTIONS	No smoking, no pets, children are welcome.
KUDOS/COMMENTS	"Judy is outstanding." (1997)

THE REDSTONE CASTLE
HEALTH & WELLNESS RESORT

0058 Redstone Boulevard
Redstone, CO 81623
EMAIL *castle@sopris.net*

970-963-3463
800-643-4837
FAX *970-704-1834*

LOCATION	Take the southern entrance into Redstone and then an immediate right after the bridge, onto a dirt road. Go one mile, until it ends at the Castle.
OPEN	All year
DESCRIPTION	A 1902 three-story English Tudor manor with original antiques and museum-quality interior; listed on the National Historic Register; located in the Crystal River Valley.
NO. OF ROOMS	Eight rooms with private bathrooms and eight rooms share three bathrooms. Try the Lady Bountiful Suite.
RATES	Year-round rates are $95-150 for a single or double with a private bathroom, $155-175 for a single or double with a shared bathroom, and $155-295 for a suite. There is no minimum stay and a seven-day cancellation policy.
CREDIT CARDS	American Express, MasterCard, Visa
BREAKFAST	Continential plus is served in the sun room with beautiful views of the Redstone cliffs. Dinner is available six days a week.
AMENITIES	Afternoon tea served in the library; wellness day spa services available, including massage, body wraps, facials, chiropractic, and acupuncture; sleigh rides and cross-country skiing right in the front yard; hiking, and fishing; no phones or TV in the rooms; robes in all rooms; game room; complimentary tour with stay; spiced wine and cider in winter, and lemonade and iced tea in summer; full bar available; full wine list; meeting rooms for small groups and weddings.
RESTRICTIONS	No smoking, no pets
REVIEWED	*America's Wonderful Little Hotels & Inns, Recommended Country Inns Rocky Mountain Region*
MEMBER	Distinctive Inns of Colorado, American Bed & Breakfast Association, National Bed & Breakfast Association
KUDOS/COMMENTS	"Fantastic turn-of-the-century atmosphere. Exquisite service. Gourmet dinner a must-experience." "A totally delightful experience. A chance not only to live like royalty, but also to be treated that way." "Wonderful setting and history." (1994) "A national treasure! We enjoyed sitting next to a crackling fire as snow fell outside; one of a kind." "The setting is beautiful. The property is well maintained. A great wedding site." (1996)

RIDGWAY

A very real, very "western" ranching community in the San Juan Mountains that boasts major film credits, such as *True Grit* and *How the West Was Won*. Ridgway State Park offers good fishing, boating, camping, cross-country skiing, and ice skating. Only 10 miles north of Ouray and 25 miles south of Montrose at the junction of Scenic Highways 62 and 550.

THE ADOBE INN

251 Liddell Drive, Ridgway, CO 81432   970-626-5939
Joyce & Terre Bucknam, Resident Owners

LOCATION	From Highway 550, take Highway 62 for 0.25 mile, then take the first dirt street to the left after crossing river; the B&B is one block off the highway.
OPEN	All year except Thanksgiving, Christmas Eve, and Christmas
DESCRIPTION	A 1984 southwestern adobe country inn and Mexican restaurant with southwestern furnishings, a small patio, and a wonderful view of the mountains. The inn is at the edge of town on 1.5 acres with nice grounds.
NO. OF ROOMS	Three rooms share two baths. The best room in the house is 1.
RATES	Year-round rates are $35-45 for a single or double. There is no minimum stay. Cancellation requires 48 hours' notice except for holidays, when five days are required.
CREDIT CARDS	American Express, MasterCard, Visa
BREAKFAST	Continental breakfast includes coffee, homemade muffins, and juice. Dinner is available in the Mexican restaurant.
AMENITIES	Patio, lounge with fireplace, TV in rooms, telephone in hallway.
RESTRICTIONS	No smoking. There is a resident Himalayan cat called Annie.
REVIEWED	*The Colorado Guide, Recommended Country Inns of the Rocky Montain Region*
AWARDS	1990 Business of the Year, awarded by the Ouray County Chamber of Commerce

CHIPETA SUN LODGE

304 South Lena, Ridgway, CO 81432   970-626-3737
Lyle & Shari Braund, Innkeepers   800-633-5868

KUDOS/COMMENTS "Beams with uniqueness." "Lyle and Shari are terrific hosts." (1997)

Gazebo Country Inn Bed & Breakfast, Salida

SALIDA

On the banks of the Arkansas River at the mouth of the Arkansas Headwaters Recreation Area, Salida is the jumping-off place for major white-water rafting. In mid-June, when the spring thaw swells the Arkansas to flood stage, the town goes bonkers for the prestigious championship FIBARK (First in Boating on the Arkansas) River Boat Race. Less turbulent adventures can be had at the Salida Hot Springs Pool, and the downtown Historic District is worth a leisurely stroll. Rock hounds take notice: The surrounding area offers up a richness of gems. From Pueblo, 97 miles west via Highway 50.

THE CENTURY HOUSE BED & BREAKFAST

401 East First Street, Salida, CO 81201   719-539-7064
Ruth Fisher, Resident Owner   800-922-0460
WEBSITE *www.vtinet.com/centuryhouse*

LOCATION	Highway 291, across from the hospital.
OPEN	All year
DESCRIPTION	An 1890 two-story Second Empire "Painted Lady" with mansard roof, transoms, high ceilings, brass lighting, and antique furnishings.
NO. OF ROOMS	Two rooms have a private bathroom and two rooms share one bathroom. The Woodland is the best room.
RATES	Year-round rates are $75-85 for a single or double with a private bathroom and $60-70 for a single or double with a shared

bathroom. Cancellation requires seven days' notice.

CREDIT CARDS	MasterCard, Visa
BREAKFAST	Full breakfast, served in the dining room, includes quiche, Canadian bacon, homemade cinnamon rolls, and beverages.
AMENITIES	Robes, early morning coffee, and afternoon snack.
RESTRICTIONS	No smoking, no pets, children over eight are welcome.
MEMBER	Bed & Breakfast Innkeepers of Colorado
KUDOS/COMMENTS	"Charming turn-of-the-century atmosphere; very homey and clean." "Ruth is a gracious host." (1997)

GAZEBO COUNTRY INN BED & BREAKFAST

507 East Third Street, Salida, CO 81201
Sharon & Jeff Rowe, Innkeepers
EMAIL srowe1023@aol.com
WEBSITE www.gazebocountryinn.com

719-539-7806
800-565-7806
FAX 719-539-6971

LOCATION	Located in downtown Salida at the corner of 3rd and B Streets, which is five blocks east of F Street (Salida's main street) and two blocks south of Highway 291 (1st Street).
OPEN	All year
DESCRIPTION	A 1901 two-story Victorian inn with light country decor.
NO. OF ROOMS	Three rooms with private bathrooms. Sharon and Jeff recommend the Monarch Rose Room.
RATES	Year-round rates are $75-85 for a single or double and $240 for the entire B&B. There is no minimum stay and cancellation requires seven days' notice.
CREDIT CARDS	American Express, MasterCard, Visa
BREAKFAST	Full breakfast is served in the dining room and begins with early riser coffee and tea, followed by homemade breakfast breads, seasonal fruit dishes, savory egg casseroles or breakfast puddings, and perhaps a side of bacon or sausage. Special meals are available with advance notice.
AMENITIES	Mary Kay bath and personal care products in each room; hot tub on the patio; beach towels; garden gazebo with white wicker furniture; garage storage for bicycles, skis, motorcycles, and other toys; extensive book and video libraries; located within walking distance of the Historic District; shady porch and sunny deck; modem connections in each room; accommodations for small conferences (8-10 people); and, of course, homemade cookies each afternoon.

River Run Inn, Salida

RESTRICTIONS	No smoking, no pets, children over 14 are welcome. Mandy and Art are the resident cats.
REVIEWED	*Recommended Country Inns Rocky Mountain Region*
MEMBER	Bed & Breakfast Innkeepers of Colorado, Professional Association of Innkeepers International

Piñon and Sage Bed & Breakfast Inn

803 F Street, Salida, CO 81201   719-539-3227
Jocelyn Mullen, Resident Owner   800-840-3156
Some French and "decent" Spanish spoken   FAX 719-539-3227 *(call first)*

LOCATION	On the corner of 8th and F Streets.
OPEN	All year
DESCRIPTION	A 1901 two-story Victorian with casual southwestern decor.
NO. OF ROOMS	One room with a private bathroom, three rooms share two bathrooms. Jocelyn recommends the Old West Room.
RATES	High-season (includes the summer months, Thanksgiving, Christmas, New Year's, and March) rates are $55-70 for a double with a shared bathroom and $75 for a double with a private bathroom. Off-season rates are $45-60 for a double with a shared bathroom and $65 for a double with a private bathroom. There is no minimum stay and cancellation requires two weeks' notice.

CREDIT CARDS	MasterCard, Visa
BREAKFAST	Full breakfast is served in the dining room, in guestrooms, or on the balconies and is "cooked to order."
AMENITIES	Robes, hot tub on patio, business services and meeting space available, large-screen TV, walking distance to downtown restaurants and Arkansas River.
RESTRICTIONS	No smoking, pets and children on a case-by-case basis. The dog is called Sweet Pea and the potbellied pig goes by the name of Tar Baby.

RIVER RUN INN

8495 County Road 160, Salida, CO 81201
Virginia Nemmers, Resident Owner
EMAIL *riverrun@amigo.net*
WEBSITE *www.riverruninn.com*

719-539-3818
800-385-6925
FAX 719-539-3818 (call first)

LOCATION	Three miles east of Highway 285, just north of Highway 50. Look for the B&B sign on the highway.
OPEN	All year
DESCRIPTION	An 1895 three-story brick Victorian country inn set on 5 acres on the Arkansas River with gracious porches, 12-foot ceilings, spacious interiors, and comfortable period furnishings. Listed on the National and State Historic Registers.
NO. OF ROOMS	Four rooms with private bathrooms and four rooms share two bathrooms. Virginia recommends the Lobelia Room.

The Thomas House Bed & Breakfast, Salida

RATES	Year-round rates are $70 for a room with a private bathroom, $60 for a room with shared bathroom. The dorm is $25 per bed and the entire B&B may be rented for $775 plus tax. There is no minimum stay and a 14-day cancellation policy.
CREDIT CARDS	American Express, MasterCard, Visa
BREAKFAST	Full breakfast, served in the dining room, includes beverages, fresh fruits, yogurt, egg or pancake/French-toast specialties, bacon, sausage, ham, homemade breads, and coffeecakes. Lunch, dinner, and special meals are available as part of a package deal.
AMENITIES	Homemade cookies, brandy, and sherry in the evenings; riverfront park; fishing on the premises; partial handicapped access.
RESTRICTIONS	No smoking indoors, no pets, children over 12 are welcome. Coon is the resident blue heeler. He won't beg, but he loves a little petting.
REVIEWED	*Fodor's Rockies; The Complete Guide to Bed & Breakfasts, Inns and Guesthouses; The Offical Guide to American Historic Inns; Colorado Cabins, Lodges, and Country B&Bs; Recommended Country Inns Rocky Mountain Region; Travel Smart*
MEMBER	Bed & Breakfast Innkeepers of Colorado, Professional Association of Innkeepers International, Chaffee County Lodging Association

THE THOMAS HOUSE BED & BREAKFAST

307 East First Street, Salida, CO 81201
Tammy & Steve Office, Resident Owners
EMAIL *office@thomashouse.com*
WEBSITE *www.thomashouse.com*

719-539-7104
888-228-1410
FAX 719-530-0491

LOCATION	From historic downtown Salida, the inn is two blocks east of F Street on the corner of 1st and D Streets.
OPEN	All year
DESCRIPTION	An 1888 two-story railroad boarding house with an eclectic mix of American antiques, family heirlooms, and collectables.
NO. OF ROOMS	Six rooms with private bathrooms. Tammy and Steve suggest the Buffalo Peaks Cottage.
RATES	Year-round rates are $55-75 for a single or double, $90 for a one-bedroom suite, and $165 for a two-bedroom suite. The guesthouse goes for $100, and the entire B&B rents for $460. There is no minimum stay and a 14-day cancellation policy, 30 days for holidays and special events.
CREDIT CARDS	American Express, MasterCard, Visa
BREAKFAST	Continental breakfast, served in the dining room, includes

The Tudor Rose B&B, Salida

	homebaked muffins and sweet breads, breads for toasting, yogurt, granola, cheese, fruit, and beverages.
AMENITIES	Outdoor hot tub holds 14; robes; evening refreshments; reading room stocked with current newspapers and magazines as well as an assortment of fiction and nonfiction books; TV in the suite; shady deck; kitchenettes for light cooking; full kitchen and TV in cottage; sodas, coffee, and tea available at all times.
RESTRICTIONS	No smoking, no pets. The resident pooch, Spud, and cats, BB and Stinky, are confined to private quarters.
MEMBER	Bed & Breakfast Innkeepers of Colorado, Chaffee County Lodging Association

THE TUDOR ROSE B&B

6720 Paradise Road, Salida, CO 81201
Jon & Terre Terrell, Resident Owners
EMAIL tudorose@amigo.net
WEBSITE www.bbonline.com/co/tudorose

719-539-2002
800-379-0889
FAX 719-530-0345

LOCATION	One-and-a-half miles southeast of Salida and 0.5 mile south of Highway 50 on County Road 104 at the top of the hill.
OPEN	All year
DESCRIPTION	A 1979 three-story Tudor inn: a country manor of stately elegance and homelike comfort nestled into piñon pines on 37 hilltop acres.

NO. OF ROOMS	Four rooms with private bathrooms and two rooms share two bathrooms. The Terrells recommend the Henry Tudor Suite.
RATES	Year-round rates for a single or double with a private bathroom are $65-120, rates for a single or double with a shared bathroom are $50-85, and a suite is $85-120. The entire B&B rents for $500. There is a minimum stay during holidays and some weekends, and cancellation requires 72 hours' notice with "100% refund, no fee."
CREDIT CARDS	American Express, Discover, MasterCard, Visa
BREAKFAST	Full breakfast is served in the dining room or on the deck and may include seasoned eggs over puff pastry with béarnaise sauce, potato crepes with béarnaise sauce, sausage, cherry crepes, breads, juice, coffee and tea.
AMENITIES	Sunken hot tub on deck, exercise room, robes, overnight horse boarding, outdoor dog pens, Jacuzzi suite, feather beds, and sweetheart package with champagne, dinner, and chocolate-covered strawberries.
RESTRICTIONS	No smoking inside, pets outside only, children over eight are welcome. The resident Keeshonds are Keesha and Chivas, and the Lab is Zeus.
REVIEWED	*America's Wonderful Little Hotels & Inns, The Colorado Guide, Horse Travel Guide, Inns of the Rocky Mountain Region*
MEMBER	Bed & Breakfast Innkeepers of Colorado, Professional Association of Innkeepers International
RATED	AAA 2 Diamonds, Mobil 2 Stars
AWARDS	"Best B&B to bring your own horse." — *Denver Post*, June 1998
KUDOS/COMMENTS	"Perfect for a romantic getaway; Jon and Terre pay a lot of attention to detail." (1995) "The inn backs up to a national forest." "A welcome change of pace for those needing a weekend away from noise and traffic." (1997)

SAN ACACIO

A sleepy little village located in the San Luis Valley, 35 minutes from Dunes National Park, and only eight miles from the Cumbres Toltec Narrow-Gauge Railroad. Head south 35 minutes to Ski Rio in New Mexico. From Alamosa, 22 miles south on Highway 285, then east on Highway 142 for 25 miles.

THE DEPOT B&B

Route 1, Box 186, San Acacio, CO 81150
Neil Fletcher, Resident Owner
Some Spanish spoken

719-672-3943
800-949-3949

LOCATION	Eight miles west of San Luis on Highway 142 — the largest building on the east end of town.
OPEN	All year
DESCRIPTION	A 1910 two-and-a-half-story historic train depot with stucco frame construction, Victorian furnishings, and a large freightroom that has been converted into a private dining room for guests.
NO. OF ROOMS	Two rooms with private bathrooms and two rooms share two bathrooms. Neil suggests the master, or downstairs, suite.
RATES	Year-round rates are $44-59 for a single or double with a shared or private bathroom. There is no minimum stay.
CREDIT CARDS	No
BREAKFAST	Full buffet-style breakfast is served in the dining room or outside on the deck. "As much food as possible is served straight from our gardens," says Neil. Special meals are delivered from the local buffalo ranch and special-request dinners are served by the owners.
AMENITIES	Terrific view, large lawns, flower and vegetable gardens in a country setting, retreat packages.
RESTRICTIONS	No smoking. The resident critters include chickens, goats, cats, and canaries. The backpacking goats are for mountain treks.

SAN LUIS

The oldest town in Colorado, San Luis is built around its adobe plaza. In south-central Colorado, halfway between Fort Garland and the New Mexico border on Highway 159.

CASA DE SALAZAR

603 Main Street, San Luis, CO 81152   719-672-3608

KUDOS/COMMENTS "Gracious innkeeper."

EL CONVENTO BED & BREAKFAST

512 Church Place, San Luis, CO 81152   719-672-4223
Connie Morrell, Resident Manager

LOCATION	Two blocks west of Main Street.
OPEN	All year

DESCRIPTION	A 1905 two-story adobe convent with southwestern furnishings.
NO. OF ROOMS	Four rooms with private bathrooms.
RATES	Year-round rate is $60 for a single plus $10 more for each additional adult and $5 for each additional child under 12.
CREDIT CARDS	MasterCard, Visa
BREAKFAST	Full breakfast is served in the dining room.
AMENITIES	Library, house with fireplace and kitchen available for families (inquire about rates), skiing at Ski Rio in New Mexico (about 20 miles away), small meeting room.
RESTRICTIONS	No smoking in rooms, children of all ages are welcome.
REVIEWED	*The Colorado Guide*

SILVER PLUME

BREWERY INN BED & BREAKFAST

238 Main Street, Silver Plume, CO 80476
Greg Hein, Resident Manager

303-569-2284
800-500-0209

SILVERTHORNE
(SUMMIT COUNTY)

Tucked beside the base of Buffalo Peak in the Lake Dillon Area, Silverthorne is a hub to no fewer than seven major ski areas. Try hiking to Cataract Lake and Falls, or brave the crowds at one of dozens of factory outlet stores. Seventy miles west of Denver via I-70.

HOME AND HEARTH

1518 Rainbow Drive, Silverthorne, CO 80498
Trudy & Bruce Robinson, Innkeepers
EMAIL *brobin@csn.net*
WEBSITE *www.colorado-bnb.com/hhearth*

970-468-5541
800-753-4386
FAX 970-262-6242

LOCATION	From I-70 west, take exit 205 (Dillon-Silverthorne). Bear right one block to Wendy's (Rainbow Drive) and turn right. Go straight one

Mountain Vista Bed & Breakfast, Silverthorne

mile to the gate. Punch in #1254 on the keypad and go another 0.5 mile. The B&B is on the right, the second home from the end.

OPEN	All year
DESCRIPTION	A 1973 three-story alpine host home decorated with antiques in a quiet, private neighborhood.
NO. OF ROOMS	Five bedrooms with three shared bathrooms. Trudy and Bruce suggest the Raggedy Ann Room.
RATES	November through April, rates are $30-75 for a single or double. May through October, rates are $25-65 for a single or double. There is no minimum stay and cancellation requires 10 days' notice.
CREDIT CARDS	No
BREAKFAST	Full breakfast is served in the dining room and includes meat and egg dishes, homemade breads, muffins, scones, jams, fresh fruit, and juice.
AMENITIES	Outdoor hot tub, wine and hors d'oeuvres, large room for summer retreats.
RESTRICTIONS	Smoking is restricted. Pets are OK with prior arrangements. Charlie is the resident chocolate Lab. "He's an old dog."
MEMBER	Summit County Bed & Breakfast Association, Colorado Travel and Tourism Association

MOUNTAIN VISTA BED & BREAKFAST

358 Lagoon Lane, Silverthorne, CO 80498 970-468-7700
Sandy Ruggaber, Resident Owner 800-333-5165
Very limited Spanish and German spoken
EMAIL *mtnvistabnb@juno.com* WEBSITE *www.colorado-mtnvista.com*

LOCATION	From I-70, take exit 205. At Wendy's in Silverthorne turn right and then take another right at the next stop sign. Pass the Village Inn and turn left on Lagoon Lane; drive to the sixth house on the right, with a flagpole in the driveway.
OPEN	All year
DESCRIPTION	A 1976 two-story contemporary mountain-style host home with contemporary interior and a private entrance to the guest area.
NO. OF ROOMS	One room with a private bathroom and two rooms share one full bathroom and a powder room. The best room is Bedroom C with the private bath.
RATES	Winter rates, December through April, are $90-100 for a single or double with private or shared bathroom. Summer rates, May through November, are $70 for a single or double with a private or shared bathroom. The entire B&B rents for $55 per room for a minimum of two nights. There is a minimum stay during holidays and there is a nonrefundable deposit.
CREDIT CARDS	American Express, Discover, MasterCard, Visa
BREAKFAST	Full breakfast, served in the dining room, includes fruit, a hot entrée, and a breakfast dessert.
AMENITIES	Robes in each room, guest kitchen with snacks and drinks, fireplace and TV on each level, VCR, ski and bike storage in heated garage, and discount tickets to community recreation center.
RESTRICTIONS	Smoking outside only. Dogs OK, but no other pets allowed. Children over six preferred.
REVIEWED	*Bed & Breakfast USA, West and Midwest; Pets Welcome Southwest*
MEMBER	Summit County B&B Association, Tourist House Association of America
KUDOS/COMMENTS	"Nice, clean, contemporary B&B, close to bus route, in town location, good arrangement of space." (1996)

SILVERTON

This National Historic Landmark in the San Juan Skyway features ornate Victorian architecture at its grandest. Evidence of Silverton's opulent past is reflected in the gold-domed courthouse. Fun events include the Jubilee Folk Music Festival in late June and the Great Western Rocky Mountain Brass Band Festival in mid-August. The Durango & Silverton Narrow Gauge Railroad, operating since 1882, terminates here. Forty-five miles north of Durango via awesome Highway 550.

TELLER HOUSE HOTEL

1250 Greene, Silverton, CO 81433   *970-387-5423*

VILLA DALLAVALE

1257 Empire, Silverton, CO 81433   *970-387-5555*

WINGATE HOUSE BED & BREAKFAST

1045 Snowden Street, Silverton, CO 81433   *970-387-5520*
Judy Graham, Resident Owner

Snowmass and Snowmass Village

Part of the Aspen complex, but just far enough away from the glitz to offer a more tranquil experience—though there are still multitudes of restaurants and spendy shops. Summer activities are on the rise and center around the Village Music Series and the Anderson Ranch Arts Center. Twenty-three miles southeast of Glenwood Springs.

Connables' Guest Home

3747 Brush Creek Road, Snowmass Village, CO 81615   970-923-5034
Ce Ce & Bruce Connable, Resident Owners   FAX 970-923-5034
French and Spanish spoken

LOCATION	From Highway 82, take Brush Creek Road 3.6 miles. The B&B is on the right. Look for the sign at the bottom of the driveway.
OPEN	Winter: Thanksgiving to mid-April; summer: June 15 to September 30
DESCRIPTION	A 1991 contemporary two-story wood- and log-accented home with eclectic furnishings and southwestern flavor.
NO. OF ROOMS	One room with a private bathroom and two rooms share one bathroom. The best room has a fireplace and panoramic view.
RATES	Winter rates are $100-125, except at Christmas when they are $150-175. Summer rates are $50-75. Cancellation requires 30 days' notice.
CREDIT CARDS	No
BREAKFAST	Full breakfast is served in the winter, continental plus in the summer.
AMENITIES	Terry robes; outdoor hot tub; afternoon wine, juices, and daily goodies; game table; three fireplaces; Great Room.
RESTRICTIONS	No smoking, no pets. The resident Persian cat is named Noni.

Pokolodi Lodge Bed & Breakfast

25 Daly Lane, Snowmass Village, CO 81615   970-923-4310
Vanessa Adams, Innkeeper   800-666-4556
EMAIL *lodging@pokolodi.com*   FAX 970-923-2819
WEBSITE *www.pokolodi.com*

LOCATION	From Aspen, take Highway 82 north to the Snowmass Village turnoff (Brush Creek Road). Go three miles, turn left at the Conoco, and take an immediate right when the road forks. Follow Snowmelt Road for 0.25 mile to Daly Lane and turn left.
OPEN	All year
DESCRIPTION	A 1967 four-story mountain lodge adjacent to Snowmass ski area.
NO. OF ROOMS	Forty-five rooms with private bathrooms.
RATES	Low and summer-season rates are $89-99 for a single or double. Regular, value, preholiday, and holiday season rates range from $137 to $198 for a single or double. There is a minimum stay. Ask about a cancellation policy.
CREDIT CARDS	American Express, Diners Club, MasterCard, Visa
BREAKFAST	Continental breakfast is served in the lobby and includes cold cereals, fruit, Danish, juice, coffee, and tea.
AMENITIES	Mini-refrigerators, coffee-makers, hair dryers, irons, ironing boards, shampoo, and lotion in rooms; heated outdoor swimming pool and therapy pool; "welcome" wine and cheese (December through April only); complimentary transportation to and from Aspen airport; meeting space; some rooms handicapped accessible.
RESTRICTIONS	No pets
RATED	AAA 2 Diamonds

STARRY PINES

2262 Snowmass Creek Road, Snowmass, CO 81654   *970-927-4202*
Shelley Burke, Resident Owner   *800-527-4202*
    FAX 970-927-9134

LOCATION	Turn off Highway 82 at Snowmass, go 1.5 miles to a stop sign, then bear left on Snowmass Creek Road and look for the first mailbox on the left (horses on the mailbox).
OPEN	All year
DESCRIPTION	A 1982 two-story contemporary ranch home with whiteash wood, high ceilings, and a fieldstone interior, situated on 70 acres with a trout stream.
NO. OF ROOMS	Three rooms with private bathrooms, two of which share a shower/tub. Shelley recommends the Mount Sopris Room.
RATES	Thanksgiving through April 15, rates are $90-95 for a single or double with a private bathroom and $120 for a suite. Mid-April until Thanksgiving, rates are $80-85 for a single or double with a private bathroom and $100 for a suite. There is a two-night minimum stay and cancellation requires 30 days' notice.

CREDIT CARDS	No
BREAKFAST	Continental plus is served in the dining room and includes fresh fruits, juices, teas, and coffee, fresh-baked muffins and breads, cereals, granola, and yogurt. Special meals can be catered on request.
AMENITIES	Flowers and robes, outdoor hot tub, swing and benches, fireplace, TV/VCR, trout fishing in pond or stream, picnic area with hammock, horses boarded.
RESTRICTIONS	No smoking, no pets, children over six are welcome. Crystal is the resident cat.
MEMBER	Bed & Breakfast Innkeepers of Colorado

SPRINGFIELD

This tiny town is hidden away on the plains in the southeastern corner of Colorado on the northern fringes of Comanche National Grassland. Springfield celebrates the spring and fall equinox with festivals.

PLUM BEAR RANCH B&B

29461 County Road 21, Springfield, CO 81073   719-523-4344
Jim & Juanita Zachary, Innkeepers   FAX 719-523-4324

LOCATION	From Main Street heading south, turn right on 2nd Avenue (which turns into a gravel road). Go four miles to Colorado Road 21 and turn right. Travel to the end of the lane and turn left into the ranch's driveway.
OPEN	All year except five days during Thanksgiving and five days during Christmas
DESCRIPTION	A 1995 two-story ranch house with country and ranch-style furnishings, listed on the State Historic Register.
NO. OF ROOMS	Three rooms with private bathrooms and four rooms share two bathrooms. Try the Minnick Room.
RATES	Year-round rates are $45 for a single or double with a private bathroom and $40 for a single or double with a shared bathroom. There is no minimum stay or cancellation policy.
CREDIT CARDS	MasterCard, Visa
BREAKFAST	Full country breakfast is served in the dining room and includes eggs, ham, sausage, bacon, fresh fruit, toast or biscuits, specialty breads (banana, zucchini), juice, milk, coffee. Special meals are also available.
AMENITIES	Robes for shared baths, air conditioning, handicapped access, large meeting/conference room, TV room with satellite/Direct TV, open

snack bar, bottled water, individual soaps and shampoo, pond with birds and ducks.

RESTRICTIONS   No smoking, no alcohol. The resident poodles are Lady Di and Sir Henry. Mares and colts will be in the corrals at various times.

STEAMBOAT SPRINGS

"Ski Town USA" is a world-class resort and cowboy-populated ranching area with two major hot springs. Standout events include the Cowboy Downhill in January, the week-long Winter Carnival in February, the month-long Strings in the Mountains Festival, and the hot-air balloon Rainbow Weekend in July. In the Yampa Valley, 166 miles northwest of Denver via I-70 and Highway 40.

ALPINE ROSE BED & BREAKFAST

724 Grand Street, Steamboat Springs, CO 80487   970-879-1528
WEBSITE www.stonerose.com

CAROLINE'S BED & BREAKFAST

838 Merritt, Steamboat Springs, CO 80487   970-870-1696
                                                     800-856-4029

THE HOME RANCH

54880 RCR 129, Clark, CO 80428   970-879-1780
Ken & Cile Jones, Resident Owners   FAX 970-879-1795
Swiss, German, and French spoken
EMAIL hrclark@cmn.net   *WEBSITE www.homeranch.com*

LOCATION   Take Highway 40 from Steamboat Springs, exit onto County Road 129, and go 18 miles to Clark. Ranch entrance is 0.25 mile past the Clark General Store on the right.

OPEN   December 20 through March, and June to October

DESCRIPTION   A traditional western-style ranch with main lodge and cabins with eclectic furnishings, situated on a 1500-acre working cattle ranch bordering the Routt National Forest.

NO. OF ROOMS   Six rooms with private bathrooms in the main lodge and eight cabins.

The Inn at Steamboat, Steamboat Springs

RATES	Seasonal rates start at $500 for lodge rooms and $600 for cabins. There is a minimum stay of seven nights in the summer and three nights in the winter, and a 90-day cancellation policy.
CREDIT CARDS	American Express, Discover, MasterCard, Visa
BREAKFAST	Full breakfast, served in the dining room, includes hot and cold buffet and à la carte items. Lunch and dinner are also included in the rates.
AMENITIES	Horseback riding, fly-fishing, hiking, cross-country skiing, shuttle for downhill skiing, hayrides, barbecues, barn dances, gourmet cuisine; each cabin has a hot tub, down comforters, and a wood-burning stove; there is a hot tub, heated pool, and sauna near the main lodge.
RESTRICTIONS	No pets, no cellular phones. Children over six are welcome. The resident dogs are Dancer, Bronco, and Sugar Bear.
REVIEWED	*The Colorado Guide*
RATED	Mobil 4 Stars, Relais & Châteaux Green Rating

HOTEL BRISTOL

917 Lincoln Avenue, Steamboat Springs, CO 80477   970-879-3083
Tonya Dean, Manager   800-851-0872
EMAIL *hotelbristol@compuserve.com*   FAX 970-879-8645
WEBSITE *www.toski.com/bristol*

LOCATION   Center of town, between 9th and 10th Streets.

OPEN	All year
DESCRIPTION	A 1948 Victorian motor inn.
NO. OF ROOMS	Twenty-two rooms with private bathrooms and shared tubs and showers.
RATES	Holiday rates are $134-189 for a single or double with a private bathroom; winter rates are $64-80; spring rates are $64-89; and summer rates are $49-79. There is a reservation/cancellation policy. Please call for details.
CREDIT CARDS	American Express, Diners Club, Discover, MasterCard, Visa
BREAKFAST	Full breakfast is served in the on-site, full-service restaurant called Mazzola's. Lunch and dinner are also available.
AMENITIES	Hot tub in game room, fireplace in library, cable TV and phones in rooms, ski lockers, city bus service with bus stop on the corner, meeting facilities, full-service restaurant and bar, pizza served until midnight, handicapped access, off-street parking.
RESTRICTIONS	No pets, some rooms are nonsmoking. Children are welcome.
REVIEWED	*The Colorado Guide*

THE INN AT STEAMBOAT

3070 Columbine Drive, Steamboat Springs, CO 80477   970-879-2600
Tom & Roxane Miller-Freutel, Innkeepers   800-872-2601
EMAIL *inn@inn-at-steamboat.com*   FAX 970-879-9270
WEBSITE *www.inn-at-steamboat.com*

LOCATION	Take Highway 40 into Steamboat Springs. Turn east on Walton Creek Road and drive 0.75 mile to Columbine Drive. Turn south on Columbine Drive. The inn is 100 yards down on the left.
OPEN	All year
DESCRIPTION	A 1973 three-story European-style inn overlooking the Yampa Valley and the Park Range Mountains, decorated with a country theme.
NO. OF ROOMS	All rooms have private bathrooms. Tom and Roxane recommend the Crawford Room.
RATES	December through March, rates are $69-164 for a single or double. April through November, rates are $49-120 for a single or double. There is a minimum stay and cancellation requires 30 days' notice.
CREDIT CARDS	American Express, Diners Club, Discover, MasterCard, Visa
BREAKFAST	Continental plus is served in the dining room and includes homemade muffins, pastries and breads; hot and cold cereals, juices, coffee, tea, hot chocolate, fresh fruit, and berries.

AMENITIES	Après-ski wine and cheese and homemade soups, outdoor heated pool, sauna, game room, winter shuttle service, meeting facilities, phones, TVs, full concierge service, robes and flowers in the Lincoln and Crawford Rooms.
RESTRICTIONS	No smoking, no pets, children are welcome. Honey is the resident Labrador retriever.
RATED	AAA 2 Diamonds, ABBA 2 Crowns, Mobil 2 Stars

MARIPOSA BED & BREAKFAST

855 North Grand Street, Steamboat Springs, CO 80477   *970-879-1467*
Paul Greco, Resident Owner   *800-578-1467*
WEBSITES *www.steamboatweb.com:80/stlodging/mariposa.htm/*
www.travelassist.com

LOCATION	Take a right on Sixth Street and go through three stop signs. Sixth becomes Laurel at the elementary school. Grand Street is the first left past the big white house.
OPEN	All year
DESCRIPTION	A 1992 southwestern inn located on the banks of Soda Creek. The inn features log-beam ceilings and Santa Fe-style handcrafted doors.
NO. OF ROOMS	Three rooms with private bathrooms. Paul Greco's favorite room is the Pine Room.
RATES	Seasonal rates are $75-95 for a single or double. There is no minimum stay and cancellation requires 21 days' notice and a $25 fee.
CREDIT CARDS	MasterCard, Visa
BREAKFAST	Full breakfast is served in the dining room and changes every day.
AMENITIES	Greenhouse/sunroom overlooking the pond.
RESTRICTIONS	No smoking, no pets, children of any age are welcome with notification.
REVIEWED	*Recommended Country Inns Rocky Mountain Region*
KUDOS/COMMENTS	"Open, low-key southwestern feel. Ask for the Pine Room; you will sleep in a handmade (by the owner) pine bed about three feet off the floor. Sit in the sunroom and overlook a field of horses and a pond." (1995)

SKY VALLEY LODGE

PO Box 3132, Steamboat Springs, CO 80477   970-879-7749
Jon Hardman, Resident Owner   WEBSITE *www.steamboat-lodging.com*

LOCATION	Nestled in the mountains, seven miles from Steamboat Springs, on Highway 40.
OPEN	All year except May
DESCRIPTION	Two mountain lodges built in 1973.
NO. OF ROOMS	Twenty-four rooms with private bathrooms.
RATES	Summer and fall rates are $69-109; winter rates are $99-173.
CREDIT CARDS	American Express, Diners Club, Discover, MasterCard, Visa
BREAKFAST	In summer, deluxe continental breakfast is served, full breakfast in winter.
AMENITIES	Two hot tubs, two saunas.
RESTRICTIONS	No smoking, no pets, children OK

STEAMBOAT BED & BREAKFAST

442 Pine Street, Steamboat Springs, CO 80477   970-879-5724
Gordon Hattersley, Resident Owner   FAX 970-879-5724 *(call first)*

LOCATION	Two blocks north of Main Street.
OPEN	All year
DESCRIPTION	A renovated 1889 three-story Victorian with Victorian furnishings.
NO. OF ROOMS	Seven rooms with private bathrooms.
RATES	Winter rates are $95-135 for a single or double, and summer rates are $75-85 for a single or double. Prices are about $10 higher on weekends. There is no minimum stay. Cancellation requires two weeks' notice for full refund.
CREDIT CARDS	Discover, MasterCard, Visa
BREAKFAST	Full breakfast, served in the dining room, includes a hot entrée, home-baked breads, fresh fruit, cereals, and beverages.
AMENITIES	Hot tub and deck, complimentary fruit and beverages, music conservatory with piano, TV and movies, large yard for weddings and family reunions, walking distance to restaurants and shops in downtown Steamboat Springs.
RESTRICTIONS	No smoking, no pets, no children. The resident golden retriever is Josh—he loves to play fetch. Jazz is the resident cat.

STEAMBOAT VALLEY GUEST HOUSE

1245 Crawford Avenue, Steamboat Springs, CO 80477   970-870-9017
George & Alice Lund, Innkeepers   800-530-3866
EMAIL george@steamboatvalley   FAX 970-879-0361
WEBSITE steamboatvalley.com

LOCATION	From Denver, take I-70 west to Dillon/Silverthorn (exit 205). Head north on Highway 9 to Kremmling, then west on Highway 40 to Steamboat Springs. Go through downtown and turn north on 12th Street. Go two short blocks to Crawford. Look for the sign.
OPEN	All year
DESCRIPTION	A remodeled 1957 three-story log guesthouse with English and Scandinavian decor, built with logs from the town mill and bricks from the old flour mill.
NO. OF ROOMS	Four rooms with private bathrooms.
RATES	High-season (January, February, March, June, July, August, and September) rates are $93-148 for a single or double. Low-season (April, May, October, November, and early December) rates are $80-108 for a single or double. Rates are higher during the Christmas holiday. There is a minimum stay on most weekends and holidays and a reservation/cancellation policy.
CREDIT CARDS	American Express, Diners Club, Discover, MasterCard, Visa
BREAKFAST	Full breakfast is served in the dining room and includes "always something hot," such as Swedish pancakes with lingonberries, green-chile and cheese soufflé, or a steaming bowl of Irish oatmeal topped with cinnamon, brown sugar, and walnuts.
AMENITIES	Outdoor hot tub, covered parking, fireplace and grand piano in Great Room, wildflower garden, free town bus.
RESTRICTIONS	No smoking, children over 10 are welcome. The official greeter is Bergen the Newfoundland landseer, a year-round outdoor dog.
REVIEWED	*The Colorado Guide*
MEMBER	Bed & Breakfast Innkeepers of Colorado, Professional Association of Innkeepers International
KUDOS/COMMENTS	"George and Alice run a lovely business!" (1997)

STONEHAM

Southeast of the Pawnee National Grasslands and Pawnee Buttes on the route of the Texas-Montana Trail, Stoneham features the New Raymer Fair and Rodeo at the end of July and Stoneham Days during the last Saturday in September.

ELK ECHO RANCH COUNTRY B&B

47490 WCR 155, Stoneham, CO 80754   970-735-2426
Craig & Noreen McConnell, Resident Owners   FAX 970-735-2427
EMAIL elkecho@henge.com   *WEBSITE www.elkecho.com*

LOCATION	Twenty miles west of Sterling, then five miles north on Country Road 155.
OPEN	All year
DESCRIPTION	A 1994 three-story contemporary log home with lodge-style interior, including trophy heads and log beds, on a 2,000-acre elk ranch.
NO. OF ROOMS	Four rooms with private bathrooms. The owners suggest the Pheasant Landing Room.
RATES	Friday and Saturday rate is $99 for a single or double. There is a two-night minimum stay at Thanksgiving.
CREDIT CARDS	MasterCard, Visa, American Express
BREAKFAST	Full breakfast, served in the dining room, includes French toast with homemade syrup or strawberries and whipped cream, ham, light kielbasa sausage, grape clusters, and beverages. Dinner and a special Thanksgiving Day meal are available.
AMENITIES	Homemade pie and coffee or tea in the evening, soap and shampoo, fresh ice-water carafe, mints, guest journal in rooms, elk and bison tour, elk boarding, air conditioning, stone fireplace in Great Room, meeting facility, gift shop, handicapped access on main floor.
RESTRICTIONS	No pets; smoking limited to wraparound deck, balcony, and patio areas; well-behaved children are welcome. KJ is the tame elk cow "you can pet" and Remington is the bull elk "you can see close-up." In addition, there are 300 elk and 20 bison on the property.
MEMBER	Bed & Breakfast Innkeepers of Colorado, Professional Association of Innkeepers
KUDOS/COMMENTS	"Beautiful lodge and interesting tours of the elk they raise." (1996)

TELLURIDE

This tiny Victorian gem, set in a box canyon high in the San Juan Mountains, was once a brawling mining supply camp—and the site of Butch Cassidy's first bank robbery. Now it's a major ski area, and THE festival capitol of the universe. Its most famous events include the Film Festival and Hang Gliding Festival (the largest in the world) in September, the Bluegrass Festival in June, and the acclaimed Chamber Music Festival and Jazz Celebration in August. Getting to this National Historic Landmark on the scenic San Juan Skyway is half the fun: 66 miles south of Montrose via Highways 550, 62, and 145.

ALPINE INN BED & BREAKFAST

440 West Colorado Avenue, Telluride, CO 81435   970-728-6282
Denise & John Weaver, Innkeepers   800-707-3344
EMAIL *dhw@alpineinn.com*   FAX 970-728-3424
WEBSITE *www.alpineinn.com/telluride*

LOCATION	As you enter town on Colorado Avenue, the inn is about three blocks east on the right and about one-and-a-half blocks from the center of town.
OPEN	All year
DESCRIPTION	A historic 1903 two-story Victorian inn furnished with antiques and handmade quilts, with breathtaking views from the sun room. Listed on the National Historic Register.
NO. OF ROOMS	Seven bedrooms with private bathrooms and two rooms with one shared bathroom. Denise and John suggest the Palmyra Room.
RATES	December through March, rates are $140-170 for a single or double with a private bathroom, $130-145 for a single or double with a shared bathroom, $200-230 for a suite with a fireplace, and $1200 for the entire inn. April through November, rates are $97-165 for a single or double with a private bathroom, $90-165 for a single or double with a shared bathroom, $135-230 for a suite with a fireplace, and $920 for the entire inn. There is a minimum stay during winter and during some festivals.
CREDIT CARDS	Discover, MasterCard, Visa
BREAKFAST	Full breakfast is served in the dining room or the sun room and starts with a fruit appetizer. The main course includes a hot entrée such as artichoke egg casserole, with fresh breads, homemade granola, and beverages.
AMENITIES	Large deck with hot tub; parlor; fireplace; après-ski daily in winter with hot cider, wine, and appetizers; one-and-a-half blocks to central downtown and gondola.
RESTRICTIONS	No smoking, no pets, children over 10 are welcome. Just is the resident Border collie.

Bed & Breakfast Innkeepers of Colorado, Professional Association of Innkeepers International

RATED

Mobil 3 Stars

BEAR CREEK BED & BREAKFAST

---

221 East Colorado Avenue, Telluride, CO 81435   *970-728-6681*
Colleen Whiteman, Innkeeper   *800-338-7064*
EMAIL colleenw@bobcat.sni.net   *FAX 970-728-3636*
WEBSITE www.telluridemm.co/bearcreek.html

LOCATION	On historic Colorado Avenue in downtown Telluride.
OPEN	All year
DESCRIPTION	A 1984 three-story brick Victorian inn that couples European ambiance with Old West hospitality.
NO. OF ROOMS	Nine rooms with private bathrooms. Colleen suggests the Observatory.
RATES	November 24 through April 11, rates are $117-187 for a single or double, and the entire B&B goes for $1363 (maximum of 18) or $1500 (maximum of 24). April 12 through November 23, rates are $65-147 for a single or double, and the entire B&B rents for between $815 and $1161. Call about a minimum stay requirement and cancellation policy.
CREDIT CARDS	American Express, Discover, MasterCard, Visa
BREAKFAST	Full breakfast is served in the gathering room before a fireplace with a raised hearth. Breakfast may be pineapple-ham-stuffed French toast, potato or corn quiche, zesty southwestern-style scrambled eggs, or banana-pecan pancakes, served with fruit, multigrain breads, yogurt, granola, and dry cereals.
AMENITIES	Afternoon refreshments, including homemade cookies, coffee, and tea; phone, cable TV/HBO in the rooms; fireplace in the common areas; steam room; sauna; garden terrace with hot tub and panoramic views of Telluride and mountains; ski lockers; complimentary après-ski; parking and ski shuttle.
RESTRICTIONS	No smoking, no pets, children over 12 are welcome.
REVIEWED	*The Colorado Guide, Colorado Handbook, Journey to the Southwest, Hidden Colorado*
MEMBER	Bed & Breakfast Innkeepers of Colorado, Colorado Hotel and Lodging Association, Professional Association of Innkeepers International, Inns of the San Juan Sky Way
RATED	AAA 2 Diamonds, Mobil 2 Stars
AWARDS	Bed & Breakfast Innkeepers of Colorado Award of Excellence

---

THE JOHNSTONE INN

403 West Colorado, Telluride, CO 81435
Bill Schiffbauer, Resident Owner
EMAIL *bschiff@rmii.com*
WEBSITE *www.johnstoneinn.com*

970-728-3316
800-752-1901
FAX 970-728-0724

LOCATION	Near the center of town on the main (Colorado) street.
OPEN	All year except for mud season (mid-April to mid-May) and mid-October to Thanksgiving.
DESCRIPTION	A restored 1891 two-story Victorian boarding house decorated with Victorian furnishings and listed on the National and State Historic Registers.
NO. OF ROOMS	Eight rooms with private bathrooms. Bill recommends the Columbine Room.
RATES	Winter rates are $110 for a double, $125-170 during holidays. Summer rates are $80 for a double, $70-160 during festivals. There is a four-day minimum stay during festivals and a reservation/cancellation policy.
CREDIT CARDS	American Express, MasterCard, Visa
BREAKFAST	Full breakfast is served in the dining room.
AMENITIES	Après-ski refreshments during winter, sitting room with fireplace, outdoor hot tub, fresh flowers, TVs, and telephones in each room.
RESTRICTIONS	No smoking, no pets, children over 10 are welcome.
MEMBER	Bed & Breakfast Innkeepers of Colorado

MANITOU BED & BREAKFAST HOTEL

333 South Fir, Telluride, CO 81435
Steve Hilliard, Resident Manager

970-728-4011
800-538-7754
FAX 970-728-6160

PENNINGTON'S MOUNTAIN VILLAGE INN

100 Pennington Court, Telluride, CO 81435
Michael & Judy MacLean, Resident Managers

970-728-5337
800-543-1437
FAX 970-728-5338

LOCATION	Just outside Telluride, stay on Highway 145 toward Ophir, turn right and go two miles west of town, then continue another two to three miles. Turn left at our sign.
OPEN	Closed May 1 to May 23 and November 1 through November 23
DESCRIPTION	Contemporary French country inn with Victorian furnishings on the 12th fairway of the Telluride Golf Course.
NO. OF ROOMS	Twelve rooms with private bathrooms, three suites.
RATES	Winter rates are $160-185 for a single or double, and summer rates are $180-210 for a single or double. Off-season rates are $140-165. Suites are $210. Christmas and festival rates are higher. There is a reservation/cancellation policy.
CREDIT CARDS	American Express, MasterCard, Visa
BREAKFAST	Full breakfast is served in the dining room.
AMENITIES	Complimentary happy hour, library lounge, indoor Jacuzzi and steam room, game room with TV, entry-level lockers, laundry facilities, small meeting facilities, handicapped access.
RESTRICTIONS	No smoking, no pets. Children of all ages are welcome.
MEMBER	Distinctive Inns of Colorado
KUDOS/COMMENTS	"The most beautiful mountain setting I have ever seen! This is a first-class, high-end inn in every way!" "Luxurious rooms with bountiful amenities. Lovely, peaceful; great food." (1996)

THE SAN SOPHIA INN

330 West Pacific Avenue, Telluride, CO 81435
Keith Hampton & Alicia Bixby, Innkeepers
EMAIL *san_sophia@infozone.org*
WEBSITE *www.sansophia.com*

970-728-3001
800-537-4781
FAX *970-728-6226*

LOCATION	Half a block from the Oak Street ski lift.
OPEN	Closed October 21 through November 26 and early April to mid-May.
DESCRIPTION	A 1988 contemporary Victorian with country furnishings.
NO. OF ROOMS	Sixteen rooms with private bathrooms.
RATES	Winter rates are $190-245 and summer rates are $114-159. Christmas and festival rates are higher, so call for details. Bargain rates during the winter and summer; call for details. There is a five-night minimum stay during Christmas and two- to three-night minimum stay during festivals. There is a $25 charge per person over a double occupancy. Ask about a reservation/cancellation policy.

CREDIT CARDS	American Express, MasterCard, Visa
BREAKFAST	Full gourmet breakfast is served in the dining room or on the deck.
AMENITIES	Complimentary cocktail hour in the evening, in-room beverage service, extensive après-ski, cable TV/VCR and phones in the room, tubs for two, robes, covered parking, gazebo with sunken Jacuzzi, observatory, library with fireplace, concierge services, English garden.
RESTRICTIONS	No smoking, no pets, and children over 10 are welcome.
REVIEWED	*Recommended Country Inns Rocky Mountain Region*
MEMBER	Distinctive Inns of Colorado, American Bed & Breakfast Association
RATED	AAA 4 Diamonds, ABBA 5 Crowns, Mobil 4 Stars

TRINIDAD

This busy railroad and coal-mining district is a straight shot south on I-25 from Denver, just 19 miles from the New Mexico border. The Corazon de Trinidad National Historic District is a charmer and there are some good museums too, including Mitchell Memorial Museum and Gallery, Baca House, and Bloom Mansion.

CHICOSA CANYON BED & BREAKFAST

32391 County Road 40, Trinidad, CO 80182   719-846-6199
Keena Unruh, Innkeeper   *FAX 719-846-6199 (call first)*
EMAIL *chicosa@ruralnet.net*   WEBSITE *www.bbonline.com/co/chicosa*

LOCATION	Twelve miles northwest of Trinidad.
OPEN	All year
DESCRIPTION	A 1904 one-story native-stone ranch-style inn situated on 64 acres of peaceful canyon land.
NO. OF ROOMS	Three bedrooms with private bathrooms and one room shares a bathroom. Keena recommends the cabin.
RATES	Year-round rates are $75-95 for a single or double with a private bathroom and $65-85 for a single or double with a shared bathroom. There is a minimum stay and cancellation requires 24 hours' notice.
CREDIT CARDS	MasterCard, Visa
BREAKFAST	Full or continental breakfast is served in the Great Room. Breakfast is "homemade and memorably delicious."

AMENITIES	Hot tub in the sunny solarium; terrycloth robes in each room; horse boarding; wine, soft drinks, tea, and coffee.
RESTRICTIONS	No smoking, children over five are welcome. Gretchen and Cimarron are the resident pointers. Horse boarding is available.
REVIEWED	*The Colorado Guide, Canine Colorado*

INN ON THE SANTA FE TRAIL

402 West Main Street, Trinidad, CO 81082   *719-846-4636*
Evelyn Keys, Resident Owner

LOCATION	On the historic Santa Fe Trail, take the Main Street exit off I-25, and follow Main Street for three blocks; house sits on the southwest corner of Main and Animas.
OPEN	All year
DESCRIPTION	A 1900 two-story brick Victorian with eclectic and southwestern furnishings; several verandas have gardens.
NO. OF ROOMS	Five rooms with private bathrooms and two rooms share one bathroom. Try room 3 or 2.
RATES	High-season rates are $45 for a single with bathroom, $70 for a double with bathroom, and $85 for a group of four. Off-season rates are $10 less. Reservations are requested but not required. There is a cancellation policy.
CREDIT CARDS	American Express, Diners Club, Discover, MasterCard, Visa
BREAKFAST	Three-course breakfast is served in the dining room.
AMENITIES	The inn has fresh flowers in season, two rooms with fireplaces, air conditioning downstairs and ceiling fans upstairs, two TVs in common areas, a glass of wine or hot chocolate upon check-in, candies and cookies for children, fresh fruit in season.
RESTRICTIONS	Mostly nonsmoking. Housebroken, well-behaved pets are allowed. Children are welcome.

Twin Lakes

In the shadow of towering Mount Elbert, Colorado's highest point, Twin Lakes celebrates the Ice Carnival in mid-February with a Victorian ball and a snowshoe race up Elbert. In August, drop in with your burro for the Mosquito Pass Marathon or trash yourself in the Leadville 100, an ultra-marathon for the insane that never drops below 9000 feet and tops out at a lung-exploding 12,000 feet on Hope Pass to the south. From Leadville, go south on Highway 24 for 14 miles and turn right onto Highway 82.

Mount Elbert Lodge

10764 Highway 82, Twin Lakes, CO 81251
Scott Boyd & Laura Downing, Innkeepers
EMAIL *mtelbert@amigo.net*
WEBSITE *www.colorado-bnb.com/mtelbert*

719-486-0594
800-381-4433
FAX 719-486-2236

LOCATION	Four-and-a-half miles west of Twin Lakes Village on Highway 82.
OPEN	All year
DESCRIPTION	A 1918 two-story half-log lodge located 9700 feet up in the beautiful Colorado Rockies and surrounded by National Forest, with simple country decor, quilts, and comfortable antiques.
NO. OF ROOMS	Three bedrooms with private bathrooms and two rooms with one-and-a-half shared bathrooms.
RATES	Year-round rates are $69-84 for a double with a private bathroom and $59 for a double with a shared bathroom. Cabins rent for $78-144, and the entire lodge rents for $355. There is a two-night minimum stay in the cabins and cancellation requires seven days' notice.
CREDIT CARDS	American Express, Discover, MasterCard, Visa
BREAKFAST	Full breakfast is served in the dining room or on the lawn. Breakfast is ample and varied, and includes a fresh-baked bread item such as scones or muffins; an egg dish of the day; a fresh fruit dish; toast, bagels, and cream cheese; oatmeal, dry cereal, and yogurt; plus coffee, teas, milk, orange juice, and cocoa. Dinner packages are available from November through April.
AMENITIES	Quiet and peaceful; views in every direction; pond for fishing or ice skating; back door access to the Black Cloud Trail up Mount Elbert; advice regarding area trails, fishing, mountain biking, snowshoeing, shopping, and dining options.
RESTRICTIONS	No smoking, no pets in the B&B rooms. Pets are OK in the cabins, but there is an $8 charge per pet per day. Fargo is the resident canary and there are also ducks on the property. Fargo serenades guests each morning from November through May.

Black Bear Inn of Vail, Vail

MEMBER	Bed & Breakfast Innkeepers of Colorado, Professional Association of Innkeepers International

Twin Lakes Mountain Retreat

95 Lang Road, Twin Lakes, CO 81251
Larry & Barbara Marcum, Innkeepers

719-486-9761
877-486-9761

LOCATION	From I-70, take the Copper Mountain exit (91) south through Leadville on Highway 24 for 17 miles to Highway 82. Go west seven miles to Twin Lakes Village. Turn right at the general store and go one block, turning right on Lang Road.
OPEN	All year except three weeks in winter
DESCRIPTION	An 1880 two-story Victorian farmhouse decorated with antiques and floor-to-ceiling windows, surrounded by spectacular views of mountains and lakes. Listed on the National Historic Register.
NO. OF ROOMS	One room with a private bathroom and two rooms share one bathroom.
RATES	Year-round rate for a single or double with a private bathroom is $63 and a single or double with a shared bathroom is $73. There is a minimum stay during weekends.
CREDIT CARDS	MasterCard, Visa

BREAKFAST	Full breakfast is served in the dining room. Picnic lunches and dinner are available upon request.
AMENITIES	Fresh wildflowers in each room; soaps, lotions, and shampoo; robes; hors d'oeuvres; home-baked goods; lounge chairs for bird-watching; complimentary glass of wine.
RESTRICTIONS	No smoking, no pets, and children over seven are welcome. Amber is the resident yellow Lab and Charlie is the cat.
REVIEWED	*Distinguished Country Inns, Country Inns and Bed & Breakfasts*
MEMBER	Bed & Breakfast Innkeepers of Colorado
KUDOS/COMMENTS	"A lovely B&B in one of the original miner's homes in Twin Lakes. Charmingly decorated; breathtaking views from the front porch." (1996)

TWIN LAKES NORDIC INN

6435 Highway 82, Twin Lakes, CO 81251   *719-486-1830*

VAIL AND AVON

In the Gore Creek Valley, surrounded by three wilderness areas, this world-class resort is the largest ski complex in the nation, famous for its back bowls and its serious glitz. Summers are filled with celebrations, cultural and sporting events, and concerts. Not to miss are performances of the Bolshoi Ballet Academy and the Colorado Music Festival. From Denver, 100 miles west on I-70.

BLACK BEAR INN OF VAIL

2405 Elliott Road, Vail, CO 81657   *970-476-1304*
Jessie & David Edeen, Resident Owners   *FAX 970-476-0433*
German spoken   *WEBSITE www.vail.net/blackbear*

LOCATION	Take the West Vail exit 173 to South Frontage Road and then go west 0.1 mile to Elliott Road.
OPEN	All year except during mud season (mid-April through May)
DESCRIPTION	A 1991 two-story handcrafted log inn with contemporary furnishings on Gore Creek.
NO. OF ROOMS	Twelve rooms with private bathrooms.
RATES	Mid-November through mid-April, rates are $120-245 for a single or double. Memorial Day through mid-November, rates are $105-

115. There is a minimum stay during the winter season and cancellation requires 21 days' notice, or 30 days for groups and during the Christmas holiday, plus a $50 fee.

CREDIT CARDS	Discover, MasterCard, Visa
BREAKFAST	Full breakfast, served in the dining room, includes fresh fruit, a "chef's gourmet creation," fresh-baked breads, rolls, and muffins.
AMENITIES	Outdoor hot tub; handcrafted log or brass beds; down comforters; afternoon hors d'oeuvres; ski and boot storage; game room with pool table, game table, TV, and pinball; and an executive conference room.
RESTRICTIONS	No smoking, no pets
REVIEWED	*The Colorado Guide, America's Wonderful Little Hotels & Inns, Recommended Country Inns Rocky Mountain Region*
MEMBER	Distinctive Inns of Colorado
KUDOS/COMMENTS	"Beautiful, handcrafted log inn, rustic with elegance. The happy hour appetizers and food are superb." "Relaxing atmosphere, close to the slopes yet out of the way of the hustle and bustle of Vail, David and Jessie are exceptional innkeepers." "Best log structure as a B&B in Colorado, rustic with elegance." "Happy hour and food are great." (1996)

JUST RELAX INN, COLORADO'S ELEGANT BED & BREAKFAST

5756 Wildridge Road, Avon, CO 81620   970-845-8885
Patty & Marvin Simon, Innkeepers   888-257-8245
Some German spoken   FAX 970-845-8886
EMAIL VailVacation@hotmail.com
WEBSITE www.eeguide.com/travel/relax.html

LOCATION	At exit 167, 109 miles west of Denver on I-70. Turn north at the roundabout, continue west on Nottingham Road less than a mile to the stop sign. Turn right on Metcalf Road and go 3.5 miles on the main road (which becomes Wildridge Road).
OPEN	All year
DESCRIPTION	An elegant 1996 two-story Andalusian inn overlooking the slopes at Beaver Creek.
NO. OF ROOMS	Three rooms with private bathrooms. The Country Room is totally handicapped accesssible.
RATES	High season rates are $182 for a single or double. Regular season rates are $79 for a single or double. There is no minimum stay and cancellation requires 30 days' notice for a full refund (a gift certificate is issued if cancellation is made within 30 days).

CREDIT CARDS	Discover, MasterCard, Visa

BREAKFAST Full breakfast is served in the dining room and may include freshly baked bread, juice, eggs, hot and cold cereal, pancakes, waffles, bacon and sausages, crepes, coffee, tea, and milk. Special requests can be accommodated.

AMENITIES Big fluffy robes in each room; large indoor hot tub; entertainment room with big-screen cable TV/VCR with hundreds of videos; refrigerator in the entertainment room, stocked with complimentary soft drinks and juices; popcorn machine in the entertainment room; snacks served each afternoon; covered parking for each guest room; large viewing deck outside the guest-rooms provides a magnificent panorama of the Vail Valley; the Country Room is totally handicapped accessible, and the other two rooms are partially accessible.

RESTRICTIONS No smoking, no pets, no charge for children under two ($10 per day for children under 12 and $15 per day for others in the same room with parents). Prince, Tammy, and Paddy are the resident Pomeranians. The dogs are not permitted in the guest wing.

MEMBER Professional Association of Innkeepers International

THE LAZY RANCH

0057 Lake Creek Road, Edwards, CO 81632   970-926-3876
Buddy & Linda Calhoun, Resident Owners
WEBSITE *www.vail.net/lazyranch*   FAX 970-926-3876 *(call first)*

LOCATION	Ten miles west of Vail, on a secluded ranch.
OPEN	All year
DESCRIPTION	A clapboard Victorian farmhouse on 60 acres.
NO. OF ROOMS	One bedroom with private bathroom and three with shared baths.
RATES	Summer rtes are $70-100; high-season rates range from $90-150.
CREDIT CARDS	Discover, MasterCard, Visa
BREAKFAST	Full country-style breakfast is served in the dining room or outside in the summer.
AMENITIES	Horseback riding, a private trout stream, farm animals, hiking trail, and snowshoeing.
RESTRICTIONS	No smoking inside, pets OK, children are welcome.
KUDOS/COMMENTS	"A wonderful little place with great hosts. Working ranch that's been in the same family for over 100 years." (1996) "Unique experience. A great place and great owners. Even though it's close to town, it still seems extremely rural." (1999)

VICTOR

This 1890s gold-mining boomtown at the base of Battle Mountain is part of the Cripple Creek-Victor National Historic District. The Lowell Thomas Museum tells all about Victor's famous resident. Take a ride on the Cripple Creek-Victor narrow Gauge Railroad. Some local events include Gold Rush Days, the Cripple Creek Donkey Derby Days, aspen and antique car tours, and the Chili Cook-Off. From Colorado Springs, 50 miles southwest via Highway 24.

MIDNIGHT INN

305 South 4th Street, Victor, CO 80860   719-689-3711
David McCormick, Resident Owner
Some Spanish spoken

LOCATION	Six miles from Cripple Creek on Highway 67.
OPEN	All year
DESCRIPTION	A restored 1894 two-story Victorian with classic Victorian interior decor.
NO. OF ROOMS	Four rooms share two bathrooms. David recommends the back apartment (full kitchen and loft).
RATES	Year-round rates are $35-50 for a single or double with a shared bathroom. There is no minimum stay and a 24-hour cancellation policy.
CREDIT CARDS	No
BREAKFAST	Full American or Mexican breakfast is served in the dining room. Lunch, dinner, and special meals, including vegetarian, are available.
AMENITIES	Private fishing club, mountain bike tours, secluded hiking.
RESTRICTIONS	None. The resident dog is called Barney.

WALDEN

WINDING RIVER GUEST RANCH
BED & BREAKFAST

PO Box 37, Walden, CO 80480   970-723-4587
Debbie Holsinger, Resident Owner   FAX 970-723-4771

WALSENBURG

THE GRAPE GARDEN

24857 US Highway 160, Walsenburg, CO 81089   719-738-1136

PLAZA INN

118 West 6th Street, Walsenburg, CO 81089   719-738-5700

WINDSOR

Once a center for sugar beet processing, Windsor remains a farming community. Over Labor Day weekend, Windsor celebrates the annual Harvest Days festival with a parade and bazaar. Windsor is also home to numerous antique shops and old-fashioned ice cream and confectionery parlors.

PORTER HOUSE BED & BREAKFAST INN

530 Main Street, Windsor, CO 80550   970-686-5793
Tom & Marni Schmittling, Resident Owners   888-686-5793
EMAIL phbbinn@aol.com   FAX 970-686-7046

LOCATION	Located 55 miles north of Denver and 10 miles southeast of Fort Collins. Take I-25 to exit 262, then head east for 4.5 miles to 6th and Main Street. The inn is on the northeast corner.
OPEN	All year
DESCRIPTION	A restored 1898 two-story Queen Ann Victorian inn with turret, gabled roof, and period antique furnishings.
NO. OF ROOMS	Four rooms with private bathrooms. The owners' favorite is the Hobbit Room.
RATES	Year-round rates are $79-115 for a single or double. There are no minimum stay requirements. Ask about a cancellation policy.
CREDIT CARDS	American Express, Discover, MasterCard, Visa
BREAKFAST	Full breakfast is served in the dining room and includes homemade muffins and bread, freshly squeezed juice, stuffed French toast, omelets, eggs Durango, fresh fruit, and coffee. Lunch, dinner, and

special meals (heart-healthy and box lunches) are available with 24 hours' notice.

AMENITIES   Fresh flowers, robes, homemade truffles, bottomless cookie jar, afternoon wine and tea served in parlor, down comforters, hammock, antique store on site, air conditioning, fax, copier.

RESTRICTIONS   No smoking, no pets. Children over 12 are welcome.

REVIEWED   *Recommended Country Inns Rocky Mountain Region*

MEMBER   Bed & Breakfast Innkeepers of Colorado, Professional Association of Innkeepers International

KUDOS/COMMENTS   "This charming, dollhouse-like inn is one of the best-kept secrets in northern Colorado." (1996)

WINTER PARK AND FRASER

Three interconnected ski mountains and the world's largest mountain bike trail system—covering 600 miles—ensure that Winter Park and Fraser bustle with activity year-round. Competitive events fill the seasons, but summer is special for its festivals and fairs: the Jazz and Music Festivals in July; the Alpine ArtFair and the Rocky Mountain Wine and Food Festival in August. The Fall ColorFest, the Spring Splash, and the Christmas Torchlight Ski Down round out this partial list. There are weekend rodeos all summer long. Try the Denver & Rio Grande Ski Train on winter weekends. From Denver, 67 miles northwest via I-70 and Highway 40.

ALPEN ROSE

244 Forest Trail, Winter Park, CO 80482　　　970-726-5039
Robin & Rupert Sommerauer, Resident Owners　　800-531-1373
German spoken　　　　　　　　　　　　　FAX 970-726-0993

LOCATION   In Winter Park, turn west on Vasquez Road, cross the railroad tracks, take the first right onto Forest Trail, and go to the second house on the left, 0.5 mile from Highway 40.

OPEN   All year

DESCRIPTION   A 1965 mountain lodge with Austrian-American furnishings and a spectacular view of the Continental Divide. Just two miles from the ski area.

NO. OF ROOMS   Five rooms with private bathrooms. Check out the Alpen Rose Room with the tub for two or the Sunflower Room with a Jacuzzi.

RATES   December 1 through April 15, rates are $95-125 for a single or double. The off-season rates are $65-105 for a single or double. There is a minimum stay during Christmas and March.

Bear Paw Inn, Winter Park

CREDIT CARDS	Discover, MasterCard, Visa
BREAKFAST	Full breakfast, served in the dining room, includes an egg and meat dish, fresh fruit, homemade yogurt, granola, bread, and coffeecake.
AMENITIES	Robes; one room has a fireplace and one room has a tub for two; outdoor hot tub with a view of the Continental Divide; afternoon snack.
RESTRICTIONS	No smoking, no pets (there is a resident chow mix called Teddy), children over 10 are welcome.
REVIEWED	*Non-Smokers Guide to Bed & Breakfasts*
MEMBER	Bed & Breakfast Innkeepers of Colorado, Bed & Breakfast Winter Park, Colorado Hotel and Lodging Association

ANNA LEAH BED & BREAKFAST

1001 County Road 8, Fraser, CO 80442   970-726-4414
Patricia Handel, Resident Owner   800-237-9913

KUDOS/COMMENTS "Pat does an excellent job of providing a beautiful, comfortable atmosphere for her guests. Each detail is attended to! A gorgeous home filled with antiques." "Large property with spectacular views." (1996) "Charming Victorian, comfy rooms, antiques, and a wonderful hostess." "I send all my overflow to Pat Handel. A great innkeeper with a beautiful place." (1999)

BEAR PAW INN

871 Bear Paw Drive, Winter Park, CO 80482   970-887-1351
Susan & Rick Callahan, Resident Owners   FAX 970-887-1351 *(call first)*
EMAIL *bearpaw@rkymtnhi.com*
WEBSITE *www.bestinns.net/usa/bearpaw.html*

LOCATION	Take Highway 40 through Winter Park and Fraser. Look for the town sign of Tabernash. Approximately 1.8 miles after the Tabernash sign turn right on County Road 858, drive approximately 0.4 mile to the crossroads, and turn left. Go about 1.2 miles to Bear Paw Drive ön° turn right. At the crossroads with Conifer Lane, continue left on Bear Paw Drive for 0.2 mile.
OPEN	All year
DESCRIPTION	A luxurious 1990 two-story log lodge decorated with suede and leather furniture and antiques, with spectacular views of Rocky Mountain NntloPar ank ahd toetCnnniae tiliDev
dO. NF.ROO SOTMo	bwd oemr oishwpti arevbtt raohso
mA.ER	*ToSe*Nbvrm1e h5otgr uphiA r4l 2a,er trs a1e0$155-f6r aos n li gredou lo.bAer lp2i h5otgr uoheNbvrm1e, r4t saaee $r4 -150 1o5 f riagsenel$ orbdeu lo.iHal dayer trs a1e0$165- 7h.rT eseait o nwo-night minimum stay during weekends. Ask about a reservation/cancellation policy.
CREDIT CARDS	Discover, MasterCard, Visa
BREAKFAST	Three-course gourmet breakfast is served in the dining room and includes a choice of juice, seasoned fruit plate, homemade granola, and an entrée such as huevos rancheros, eggs Blackstone (Benedict with crab), or Belgian waffles with fresh blackberries, potatoes, and meats. Catered breakfast is available for groups by request. Early coffee is delivered to rooms one hour before breakfast.
AMENITIES	Flowers; robes and slippers; Caswell Massey amenities (shampoo, rinse, body wash, vanity packs); feather beds; Jacuzzis; private decks; home-baked cobblers or cookies; cheese and crackers; fridges in rooms; chocolate-chip cookies in rooms upon arrival; complimentary balloon bouquet for birthdays, anniversaries, etc.; assistance with booking activities and planning itineraries; maps; summer dining al fresco.
RESTRICTIONS	No smoking, no pets, no children. Ernie Banks is the resident weimaraner, Budley Bonkers is the Gordon setter, and there are deer, bear, moose, and other wild animals wandering the woods.
REVIEWED	*American Historic Inns*
MEMBER	Bed & Breakfast Inns of Colorado
AWARDS	A 1998 travel writers' poll recognized the Callahans for Outstanding Hospitality.

"Very friendly hosts, very comfortable and beautifully decorated rooms." "Somewhat remote location with spectacular views." (1996) "Great breakfast, spectacular view of the Continental Divide, most gracious hosts." (1999)

BEAU WEST BED & BREAKFAST

148 Fir Drive, Winter Park, CO 80482   970-726-5145
Bobby Goins, Resident Owner   800-473-5145
EMAIL *beauwest@crkymtnbi.com*   FAX 970-726-8607
WEBSITE *www.beauwest.com*

LOCATION	By the base of Winter Park resort. From Highway 40, turn left at Old Town Drive and go to the bottom of the hill. Turn right onto Winter Park Drive, then left onto Fir Drive.
OPEN	All year
DESCRIPTION	A 1968 three-story contemporary mountain inn decorated with western eclectic furnishings, at the base of Winter Park ski area.
NO. OF ROOMS	Five rooms with private bathrooms. Bobby suggests the Coos Bay Suite.
RATES	Winter rates are $115 for a single or double, $135-145 for a suite, and $645 for the entire B&B (up to 10 guests). May through October, rates are $100 for a single or double, $120-130 for a suite, and $570 for the entire B&B. Rates are slightly higher during the holidays and festival weekends. There is a three-night minimum stay during the holidays and cancellation requires 14 days' notice.
CREDIT CARDS	MasterCard, Visa
BREAKFAST	Full buffet-style breakfast is served in the dining room or out on the deck.
AMENITIES	Queen-size beds; TVs; phones; private Jacuzzis in three minisuites and fireplaces in two; robes; walk to the base of Winter Park resort; feather beds; down comforters; handicapped access; lift ticket packages.
RESTRICTIONS	No smoking, no pets, no children. The three gray-striped tabbies are Beau Beau, Iggy, and Pywacket. They are sisters and brother.
REVIEWED	*The Complete Guide to Bed & Breakfasts, Inns & Guesthouses*
MEMBER	Professional Association of Innkeepers International

BROTHER MOOSE BED & BREAKFAST

1221 County Road 5, Fraser, CO 80442   970-726-8255
Jo & John Tweed, Innkeepers   888-999-1616
EMAIL *jtweedmoose@yahoo.com*   WEBSITE *www.bbhost.com/brothermoose*

LOCATION	Take I-70 west from Denver about 30 miles to Highway 40, turn right, and go about 26 miles over Berthoud Pass. Continue through Winter Park and Fraser and turn left on County Road 5.
OPEN	All year
DESCRIPTION	A 1990 three-story mountain lodge nestled among six acres of serene pine forest, with a lodge-style interior, cedar siding, antiques, wooden floors, and Berber carpet.
NO. OF ROOMS	Five bedrooms with private bathrooms. The Tweeds suggest the Iron Horse Room.
RATES	December through March, rates are $130-170 for a single or double. April through November, rates are $100-130 for a single or double. There is a two-night minimum stay on weekends during high season and three nights during Christmas season. Cancellation requires 30 days' notice less a $20 charge.
CREDIT CARDS	American Express, MasterCard, Visa
BREAKFAST	Full breakfast is served in the dining room or on the deck and includes a chef's choice of entrée such as macadamia nut waffles with rum-raisin syrup; fresh fruit; side of breakfast meat; juices; coffee; and muffins or coffeecake.

Grand Victorian at Winter Park, Fraser

AMENITIES	Jacuzzi for two in every room, gas log stoves in every room, three rooms have TV/VCR, video collection, fresh flowers and chocolates in rooms, complimentary drinks and hors d'oeuvres in the afternoon, wood-burning stove in living room, large deck, garden pavilion and fire pit, lodge is minutes from Winter Park ski area.
RESTRICTIONS	No smoking, no pets
MEMBER	Grand County Bed & Breakfast and Historic Lodge Association

ENGELMANN PINES BED & BREAKFAST

1035 Cranmer Avenue, Winter Park, CO 80482
Margaret & Heinz Engel, Resident Owners
German spoken

970-726-4632
800-992-9512
FAX 970-726-5458

LOCATION	From Winter Park, go north two miles on Highway 40 toward Fraser. Turn right at the traffic light at Safeway, follow to the top of the hill, turn right on Cranmer, and go 0.5 mile.
OPEN	April 15 through December 15
DESCRIPTION	A 1985 tri-level contemporary mountain inn nestled among the pines, decorated to be "elegant but comfortable" with European and American antiques.
NO. OF ROOMS	Five rooms with private bathrooms and two rooms share one bathroom. Pick the King/Queen room.
RATES	Rates are $75-95 for a single or double with a private bathroom, and a single or double with a shared bathroom is $55-65. The entire B&B rents for $545 per night. There is no minimum stay and cancellation requires 20 days' notice.
CREDIT CARDS	American Express, Discover, MasterCard, Visa
BREAKFAST	Full breakfast, served in the dining room, is "hearty and healthy" and includes fresh fruit, fresh-baked goodies, and a gourmet entrée.
AMENITIES	Jacuzzi tubs in bathrooms, full kitchen for guest use, TV room and videos, sitting room with a piano and library, most rooms have private decks.
RESTRICTIONS	No smoking, no pets, the black Lab mix is called Bear.
REVIEWED	*Recommended Country Inns Rocky Mountain Region, The Colorado Guide, Frommer's Colorado*
MEMBER	Bed & Breakfast Innkeepers of Colorado, Bed & Breakfasts of Winter Park

GRAND VICTORIAN AT WINTER PARK

78542 Fraser Valley Parkway, Fraser, CO 80442
Whitney & Bonnie Warren, Innkeepers

970-726-5881
800-204-1170
FAX 970-725-5602

WEBSITE www.bbchannel.com/bbc/p601001.asp

LOCATION	In downtown Winter Park at the intersection of Lions Gate Drive and Fraser Valley Parkway behind the Post Office and 0.25 mile northwest of the visitors center.
OPEN	Closed during May
DESCRIPTION	A 1995 three-story neo-Victorian "gingerbread" country inn, set in a lodgepole pine forest, with luxurious period decor.
NO. OF ROOMS	Ten bedrooms with private bathrooms. Try the Peter the Great Suite.
RATES	December 20 through March 31, rates are $155-220 for a single or double, $235-440 for a suite, and $2500-2700 for the entire B&B. November 24 to December 19 (early bird season), rates are $145-395. April and June through November 23, rates are $100-260. There is a minimum stay and cancellation requires 30 days' notice with a $50 charge.
CREDIT CARDS	American Express, Diners Club, Discover, MasterCard, Visa
BREAKFAST	Multicourse gourmet breakfast is served in the dining room or the Turret Room and includes custom-blended coffees and a rotating menu that features entrées prepared by the resident chef, such as apple pecan pancakes, Grand Marnier crepes, quiche, etc. Special dietary needs are accommodated. Dinner and private Golden Service are also available.
AMENITIES	Robes, slippers, hair dryers, fresh flowers, complimentary Colorado wines and microbrewed beers, champagne for newlyweds and anniversary celebrants, digital multichannel sound systems, cable TV/VCRs, digital satellite TV, grand après-ski fondues with complimentary alcoholic beverages, accommodations for up to 50 for weddings, private parties, and corporate retreats.
RESTRICTIONS	No smoking, no pets, children over 15 are welcome.
MEMBER	Professional Association of Innkeepers International, InnPoints Worldwide

Mountain Home Bed & Breakfast, Winter Park

HIGH MOUNTAIN LODGE

425 County Road 5001, Fraser, CO 80482   970-726-5958
Katie Bogle & Blaine Gulbranson, Innkeepers   800-772-9987
Spanish spoken
EMAIL *info@himtnlodge.com*   WEBSITE *www.himtnlodge.com*

LOCATION	From Winter Park go north to the Safeway and take a left. Take the right fork under the railroad tracks and follow the signs to the lodge.
OPEN	Closed May
DESCRIPTION	A 1982 three-story Swiss chalet-style lodge built on a bluff overlooking a meadow, decorated with pine furnishings, and featuring wainscoting, brick fireplaces, and wood-beamed ceilings.
NO. OF ROOMS	Thirteen rooms with private bathrooms. Katie and Blaine recommend the Moose Suite.
RATES	Mid-November through April, rates are $90-120 per person for a double ($15-30 per extra person). June through mid-November, rates are $40 per person for a double ($15 per extra person). There is a minimum stay during Christmas, spring break, Thanksgiving, and Presidents' Weekend. Cancellation requires seven days' notice, 30 days during holidays.
CREDIT CARDS	American Express, MasterCard, Visa

BREAKFAST	Full breakfast is served in the dining room and may include blueberry French toast cobbler served with bacon or a baked egg soufflé served with muffins and sausage. During high season, a four-course dinner is included in the room price.
AMENITIES	Ceiling fans in all rooms, fireplaces in all but two rooms; free shuttle to ski resorts and discount lift tickets available in season; indoor heated swimming pool, hot tub, and sauna; game room with pool table, video games, and big-screen TV with over 400 videos; reading room with computer hookups; full bar.
RESTRICTIONS	No smoking, pets allowed in certain rooms, children welcome. Pepper is the resident Lab and Cody is the spaniel. Pepper loves to play catch, tug of war, fetch, or whatever else you can dream up.

KAREN'S BED & BREAKFAST

54 County Road 507, Fraser, CO 80442   970-726-9398

MOUNTAIN HOME BED & BREAKFAST

92 East Viking Drive, Winter Park, CO 80482   970-726-6954
Donna Truitt, Allan Bronstein,   FAX 970-726-6954 *(call first)*
Marvin Bronstein, Innkeepers
Spanish spoken

LOCATION	Roughly 75 miles northwest of Denver in Winter Park. Take I-70 west from Denver for 40 miles to exit 232 (Winter Park/US 40) and drive 30 miles to Winter Park.
OPEN	All year
DESCRIPTION	A 1995 three-story hewn log and river-rock home secluded among the aspen and pine, with modern mountain decor.
NO. OF ROOMS	Two bedrooms with private bathrooms.
RATES	November through April, rates are $100-115 for a single or double. May through October, rates are $90-105 for a single or double. There is a two-night minimum stay during weekends (three nights preferred during holidays) and cancellation requires 30 days' notice.
CREDIT CARDS	MasterCard, Visa
BREAKFAST	Full breakfast is served in the dining room and includes crabcake Benedict, stuffed French toast, salmon hash, fresh juice, fresh-baked scones, muffins, house-made syrups, preserves, and gourmet coffee.

AMENITIES	Huge rooms with ample dressers, large private baths, separate access to deck, large closets, common room with entertainment center, telephone, turndown with special treat, close to shopping and restaurants, located on free shuttle route to town and ski areas.
RESTRICTIONS	No smoking, no pets, children over 11 are welcome. Calle is the golden retriever and Spice is the calico.
MEMBER	Professional Association of Innkeepers International

OUTPOST BED & BREAKFAST INN

657 County Road 517, Winter Park, CO 80482   970-726-5346
Barbara & Ken Parker, Innkeepers   800-430-4538
Czech and German spoken   FAX 970-726-0126
EMAIL *outpost@coweblink.net*   WEBSITE *www.bbhost.com/outpost*

LOCATION	Eighty miles northwest of Denver and five miles northwest of the town of Winter Park.
OPEN	All year
DESCRIPTION	A 1967 two-story ranch-style guest house with elegant furnishings and antiques in ranch country, miles from the highway and train traffic.
NO. OF ROOMS	Seven bedrooms with private bathrooms. Try room 7.
RATES	High season rates are $108-115 for a single or double. Regular season rates are $90 for a single or double. There is a minimum stay during weekends.
CREDIT CARDS	American Express, Discover, MasterCard, Visa
BREAKFAST	Full four-course breakfast is served in the dining room on antique china with silver and linens. Breakfast includes home-baked bread, fruit, juices, and a wide variety of entrées.
AMENITIES	Soup for supper during the week in ski season; atrium hot tub; video lounge; loft for meetings for up to 12.
RESTRICTIONS	No smoking, no pets. Schicki is the resident English springer.
MEMBER	Bed & Breakfast Innkeepers of Colorado

THE PINES INN OF WINTER PARK

115 County Road 716, Winter Park, CO 80482   970-726-5416
Jan & Lee Reynolds, Resident Owners   800-824-9127
EMAIL lee.reynolds@internetmci.com   FAX 970-726-1062
WEBSITE best/inns.net/usa/co/pine.html

LOCATION	Quarter of a mile off Highway 40, just north of the Winter Park ski area in Old Town Winter Park.
OPEN	All year
DESCRIPTION	A 1958 alpine country inn with knotty pine and rustic furnishings.
NO. OF ROOMS	Six rooms with private bathrooms and two rooms share one bathroom. The Reynolds suggest room 8.
RATES	November through April, rates are $70-120 for a single or double with a private bathroom and $60-110 for a single or double with a shared bathroom. Summer rates are $60-80 for a single or double with a private bathroom, $40-70 for a single or double with a shared bathroom. There is a two-night minimum stay on the weekends, three nights during holidays. Inquire about a reservation/cancellation policy.
CREDIT CARDS	American Express, Discover, MasterCard, Visa
BREAKFAST	Full breakfast, served in the dining room, includes a hot entrée, breads, cereals, yogurt, and fruit.
AMENITIES	Outdoor Jacuzzi, robes for shared bathroom, transportation to and from ski area, telephone and TV in common area, afternoon refreshments, meeting facilities, game room.
RESTRICTIONS	No smoking, no pets. Children of all ages are welcome. Shadow is the resident black Lab.
MEMBER	Professional Association of Innkeepers International, Bed & Breakfast Innkeepers of Colorado, B&Bs of Grand County
KUDOS/COMMENTS	"Close to skiing, great hearty breakfast, shuttle to skiing, outdoor hot tub in great setting, affordable too!"

WHISTLE STOP BED & BREAKFAST

Fraser Avenue, Fraser, CO 80442 970-726-8767
Warren Watson & Susan Stone, Innkeepers 888-829-2632
Russian and Spanish spoken
EMAIL *whistle@rkymtnhi.com*
WEBSITE *www.bestinns.net/usa/co/whistlestop.html*

LOCATION	Approximately 30 miles west of Denver, take exit 232 off I-70 onto Highway 40 and travel northwest for approximately 40 miles. Continue through Winter Park to Fraser (two miles north of Winter Park) and turn left (west) at the Conoco station onto Eisenhower Avenue. Cross the railroad tracks, turn left (north) onto Leonard Lane, then left (west) onto Fraser Avenue.
OPEN	All year
DESCRIPTION	A 1987 three-story contemporary host home with stucco and redwood interior—bright, clean, and simple, yet welcoming.
NO. OF ROOMS	Three bedrooms with private bathrooms.
RATES	November through May, rates are $65-100 for a single or double. June through October, rates are $45-85 for a single or double. There is a minimum stay during weekends and peak season. Deposits are secured with credit cards. Cancellation requires written 14 days' notice, less a $15 fee per room.
CREDIT CARDS	MasterCard, Visa
BREAKFAST	Full breakfast is served in the dining room and includes coffee; tea; juice; fresh fruit; homemade breads, muffins, or biscuits; and egg and meat dishes. Special breakfasts include a downhome Southern breakfast with hashbrowns and grits, Warren's waffles, and Susan's dreamsicle French toast casserole. Dietary restrictions are accommodated.
AMENITIES	Bedtime candy, bottomless cookie jar, cookie care package for the day, robes and oversized towels for the hot tub on the deck, sun room, romantic video collection, afternoon refreshments, secure storage of bike or ski equipment, free shuttle bus within short walk, only 12 minutes to the ski resort, "Insiders Tips to Skiing Winter Park Resort" and information sheet available with reservation, on-site parking.
RESTRICTIONS	No smoking, no pets, no children

WOLCOTT

WOLCOTT INN

27190 US Highway 6, Wolcott, CO 81655   *970-926-5463*

WOODLAND PARK
(COLORADO SPRINGS)

The largest of a chain of mountain communities west of Colorado Springs, Woodland Park offers access to Pikes Peak, Garden of the Gods, gaming in historic Cripple Creek, and all manner of recreational opportunities. Check out the Ute Trail Stampede, the Old-Fashioned Fourth of July, and December's month-long Magic of Lights celebration.

THE LION & THE ROSE CASTLE

547 Douglas Fir Drive, Woodland Park, CO 80863   719-687-9745
Eric & Nancy Glanzer, Innkeepers   888-536-4564
Limited German spoken   FAX 719-687-1944
EMAIL LRCastle@ix.netcom.com   WEBSITE *www.lionrosecastle.com*

LOCATION	Take exit 141 off I-25 in Colorado Springs and go 18 miles west to Woodland Park. Veer north on Route 67 toward Deckers for 8.1 miles and turn right onto Spruce Road. Follow this road for about 3.5 miles and turn left onto Douglas Fir Drive. Go about 0.3 mile to the locked gate and turn right up the driveway.
OPEN	All year
DESCRIPTION	A 1996 three-story stone castle on 20 mountaintop acres with elegant period furnishings, fountains, and an entry waterfall.
NO. OF ROOMS	Three bedrooms with private bathrooms.
RATES	High-season rates are $225-450 for a single or double. Regular rates are $200-425 for a single or double. There is no minimum stay and cancellation requires one weeks' notice.
CREDIT CARDS	American Express, Discover, MasterCard, Visa
BREAKFAST	Full gourmet or continental breakfast is served in the dining room. Gourmet breakfast includes beverages, fruit, an egg dish, pork sirloin, and multiple pastries. Continental includes beverages, fruit, and multiple pastries.
AMENITIES	Wine or other beverages and a light refreshment upon arrival;

robes, TV/VCR in rooms; a limited movie selection; ambiance, views, and solitude.

RESTRICTIONS No smoking, no pets, no children. "My wife and I are very involved in feline rescue work," Eric says. There are several resident cats that are not permitted in the guest bedrooms or common areas.

MEMBER Bed & Breakfast Innkeepers of Colorado

AWARDS Best Bed & Breakfast in the Colorado Springs area in 1998 awarded by *Go* magazine on June 18th 1998.

PIKES PEAK PARADISE

236 Pinecrest Road, Woodland Park, CO 80866   *719-687-6656*
Tim Stoddard, Martin Meier, &   *800-728-8282*
Priscilla Arthur, Resident Owners   *FAX 719-687-9008*
WEBSITE *www.cyber-bbs.com/ppp*

LOCATION Take Highway 24 from I-25 to Woodland Park. From the signal light at Highway 67, travel 0.9 mile to Trout Creek Road. Right on Trout Creek Road 1.9 miles to the Aspen Hills and Coyote Trail sign. Right on Coyote Trail 0.9 mile to 236 Pinecrest Road (follow signs).

OPEN All year

DESCRIPTION A 1988 three-story Georgian-Greek Revival overlooking Pikes Peak, with spacious rooms.

NO. OF ROOMS Six rooms with private bathrooms. The owners suggest the Sage Room.

RATES Year-round rates are $95 for a single or double, and suites are $135-220. There is no minimum stay. Cancellation policy: "Refunded if cancelled within seven days of making reservation. Otherwise, gift certificates."

CREDIT CARDS American Express, Discover, MasterCard, Visa

BREAKFAST Continental plus is served in the dining room or guestrooms and includes cheese soufflé, blueberry croissants, fresh fruit, juice, and coffee. Breakfast in bed costs an additional $15.

AMENITIES In-room hot tubs, fireplaces, snacks, mountain views, handicapped accessible.

RESTRICTIONS No smoking, pets are OK, children over 12 are welcome. There are three Pomeranians in residence: Bear, Tiffany, and Scarlett.

WOODLAND INN BED & BREAKFAST

159 Trull Road, Woodland Park, CO 80863
Frank & Nancy O'Neil, Innkeepers
EMAIL woodlandbb@aol.com
WEBSITE www.bbonline.com/co/woodland/

719-687-8209
800-226-9565
FAX 719-687-3112

LOCATION	From Highway 24, turn onto Trull Road (beside the Swiss Chalet Restaurant) and drive 0.2 mile to the second house on the left.
OPEN	All year
DESCRIPTION	A 1965 two-story brick-and-cedar contemporary guest house with comfortable country decor, on 12 secluded, wooded acres with spectacular views of Pikes Peak.
NO. OF ROOMS	Seven bedrooms with private bathrooms. Try the Blue Lilac Room.
RATES	Year-round rates are $70-90 for a single or double and $550 for the entire B&B. There is a minimum stay during weekends from May through September and cancellation requires one weeks' notice.
CREDIT CARDS	American Express, Discover, MasterCard, Visa
BREAKFAST	Full breakfast is served in the dining room or on the patio and includes fresh-squeezed orange juice, fresh seasonal fruit, Nancy's fancy French toast, Frank's seafood omelet, quiches, crepes, pancakes, waffles, muffins, and breads. Box lunches for day trips are also available.
AMENITIES	Fresh flowers, soft terry robes, cookies, beverages, evening wine, meeting facilities, hot-air ballooning with hosts, ice skating rink in the winter.
RESTRICTIONS	No smoking, no pets. Sam is the resident Siamese cat; Cinnamon is the llama; Nutmeg is the Sicilian miniature donkey. "Sam loves laps, but is not allowed in the guest rooms. The llama and donkey are curious and friendly."
REVIEWED	*America's Favorite Inns, Bed & Breakfasts and Small Hotels*
MEMBER	Bed & Breakfast Innkeepers of Colorado, Authentic Inns of the Pikes Peak Region, Bed & Breakfasts of the Pikes Peak Area
KUDOS/COMMENTS	"Lovely, quiet setting." "Wooded acreage, deer grazing nearby. Helpful hosts." (1997)

INDEX